PIVOT

From Military Service to Public Purpose
Insights from a Former Federal Hiring Manager

Dr. Jason Piccolo

Veteran | Federal Hiring Expert | Lean Six Sigma Champion

PIVOT: From Military Service to Public Purpose Insights from a Former Federal Hiring Manager

Copyright © 2024 by Nexus Resolve, LLC All rights reserved.

No part of this publication may be reproduced, distributed, or transmitted in any form or by any means, including photocopying, recording, or other electronic or mechanical methods, without the prior written permission of the publisher, except in the case of brief quotations embodied in critical reviews and certain other noncommercial uses permitted by copyright law.

First Edition: 2024

Published by Nexus Resolve, LLC

Printed in the United States of America

For information about permission to reproduce selections from this book, write to: Nexus Resolve, LLC, PO Box 265, Dunn Loring, VA 22027

Author: Dr. Jason Piccolo

Dedicated to every veteran facing the challenges of transition. Your service shaped you into someone extraordinary - may this book help you show the civilian world exactly what you're capable of.

"There are no secrets to success. It is the result of preparation, hard work, and learning from failure."

- GENERAL COLIN POWELL

CONTENTS

Introduction..1

PART ONE
WARNO: Prepare To Pivot

Chapter 1:
Taking the First Steps..5

Chapter 2:
Finding Your Next Mission..13

Chapter 3
FRAGO...37

Chapter 4:
Veterans: Time to Execute Your Career Change.........................51

Chapter 5:
Let's Talk About SkillBridge..63

PART 2:
OPORD: Planning For Mission Success

Chapter 6:
Know Yourself, Know Your Value..75

Chapter 7:
Building Your Resume - Making the Civilian Switch................83

Chapter 8:
The Federal Resume - Your Ticket to Federal Service...............109

Chapter 9:
What Do You Want To Do?...143

Chapter 10:
Where to Find Civilian Jobs...177

Chapter 11:
Navigating USAJOBS Like a Pro 227

Chapter 12
The Resume: Back To Basics 247

Chapter 13:
Federal Veteran Hiring Authorities: Your Secret Weapon for
Government Jobs 271

PART THREE:
Execute! Execute! Execute! Make It Happen

Chapter 14:
Making Your Military Story Work for You: A Guide to Cover Letters .. 301

Chapter 15:
The Network Effect 321

Chapter 16:
Crushing Your Interview: Making the Leap from Military to
Civilian Life 345

Chapter 17:
What Happens After the Interview: The Next Steps 377

Chapter 18:
Post-Mission Analysis: You're Hired or Back to Base 403

About The Author: 431

Introduction

Take a deep breath. Whether you're in your barracks during your final months of service, in your on-base housing after deciding to leave mid-career, or in your office planning for retirement, you've made a momentous decision. After years of wearing the uniform, you're preparing to transition back to civilian life.

The military has been more than just a job – it's been your identity, community, and way of life. Every morning, you knew exactly what to wear, spoke a language of acronyms that civilians couldn't grasp, and operated within a clear chain of command. Now, you're facing a world that can seem chaotic and uncertain in comparison.

But here's the truth: you're not alone. Every year, 200,000 service members make this same transition. That's the population of a small city annually. Since World War II, millions of veterans have successfully navigated this exact path you're about to walk.

This guide is different. Consider it a conversation with a battle buddy who's made it to the other side. We'll break down your transition like any other military operation, whether you're aiming for federal service, the private sector, or the growing world of defense contracting. You'll learn how to:

- Convert your military experience into civilian success
- Navigate complex hiring systems and preferences
- Build powerful professional networks
- Choose between federal service, contracting, and corporate careers
- Continue your mission of service in new ways

The skills that made you successful in uniform – discipline, adaptability, leadership, attention to detail, and performing under pressure – are incredibly valuable in civilian life. Your desire to serve doesn't end when you take off the uniform. Whether you choose federal service, find your calling supporting veterans in the private sector, or discover a new way to give back to your community, there's a path forward that allows you to continue your mission.

So, gear up. You're about to embark on one of the most significant operations of your career. But you've got millions of veterans who've gone before you, a strong support network, and a practical guide to help you navigate this transition into a role where you can continue to serve.

Let's begin this new mission together.

PART ONE

WARNO: Prepare To Pivot

Dr. Jason Piccolo

Chapter 1: Taking the First Steps

Remember that deep breath I asked you to take in the prologue? Take another one because now we're getting into the actual work. You've decided to leave the military, and like any good military operation, success depends on proper planning and preparation.

The Time Factor: When to Start Planning

Here's something I learned the hard way: you can never start planning too early. The military's official Transition Assistance Program (TAP) typically begins 18 months before separation, but the most successful transitions often start even earlier. This isn't just a job change; it's a life change.

Let's break this down into a timeline that makes sense:

24-18 Months Out

- Start honest self-assessment
- Begin researching career fields that interest you
- Start saving money
- Begin networking with veterans who've transitioned
- Start gathering information about your benefits
- Consider your geographic preferences

18-12 Months Out

- Schedule and attend TAP

- Get your medical records in order
- Document every training, certification, and award
- Start drafting your resume
- Research education options if needed
- Begin looking at job markets

12-6 Months Out

- Finalize your transition timeline
- Complete remaining military schools/certifications
- Start serious job hunting
- Begin interview preparation
- Get VA benefits paperwork in order
- Build your civilian wardrobe

6 Months to Separation

- Intensify job search
- Complete final medical examinations
- Ensure all paperwork is in order
- Begin terminal leave planning
- Finalize housing arrangements
- Complete final out-processing

The Mental Game: More Than Just Changing Clothes

One of the most profound challenges isn't finding a job or navigating benefits – it's figuring out who you are without your uniform. For years, your identity has been crystal clear. Your rank and uniform told everyone exactly who you were and what you'd accomplished. That instant recognition is about to disappear.

You're moving from a world of clear structures to one where success and status are more fluid. The direct, efficient military communication style that served you so well might need softening. That command presence might need occasional dialing back. Even your decision-making approach needs adjustment – you're entering a world where authority is often unclear, and procedures vary widely.

The cultural shift is significant. The military's "mission first" mentality might seem out of place in organizations that emphasize work-life balance. The unit cohesion you're used to might be replaced by more individualistic approaches. Don't let this discourage you – your military experience has given you incredible strengths. The key is learning to translate these strengths while developing new skills to complement them.

The Paperwork Game: Getting Your Documentation in Order

Getting this right early will save you major headaches later. Here's what you need to gather:

1. **Service Records**
    - DD Form 214 (you'll need this for everything)
    - Performance evaluations
    - Awards and decorations
    - Training certificates
    - Security clearance documentation

2. **Medical Records**
    - Complete medical history
    - Dental records
    - Mental health records (if applicable)
    - Copies of any profiles or restrictions
    - Documentation of service-connected conditions

3. **Personal Documents**
   - Birth certificate
   - Social Security card
   - Marriage certificate (if applicable)
   - Dependent documentation
   - Driver's license and passport
   - Educational transcripts

Professional Wardrobe: Looking Sharp Without Breaking the Bank

You don't need to drop a month's pay on professional attire. Start with the basics:

- 1-2 good interview suits or professional outfits
- A few dress shirts or blouses
- Professional shoes
- Basic accessories

Smart shopping strategies:

- Shop at TJ Maxx, Marshalls, and Ross for name-brand wear at 50-70% off
- Check consignment shops in upscale areas
- Visit outlet malls during sales
- Use military aid society vouchers when available
- Consider borrowing an interview outfit if needed

The Family Factor

This isn't just your transition. Your spouse and kids are going through their own profound changes. The military life they've known is ending, too. Your spouse has probably weathered multiple PCS moves, put their career on hold, and built a life around your service. Now, they're facing their own uncertainties about career, community, and identity.

The kids? They're military kids through and through. They know how to be the new kid at school and make friends quickly. Now, they're facing a transition to civilian schools where teachers might not understand their unique experiences.

Financial pressures can be intense. You're losing BAH and other allowances, facing new healthcare costs, and possibly moving to an area with a higher cost of living. Finding the right location becomes a complex puzzle of job opportunities, school quality, cost of living, and family needs.

The Reality Check: When Debt is Part of Your Reality

Not everyone transitions with a healthy savings account. For many service members, the reality includes:

- Credit card debt
- Car payments that seemed manageable with BAH
- Student loans
- Medical bills not covered by TRICARE
- Family obligations back home

Smart Compromises vs. Settling:

- Smart Compromise: Taking a job that pays less but offers training

- Smart Compromise: Working outside your desired field but with transferable skills
- Settling: Accepting unsafe working conditions
- Settling: Taking pay that can't support basic needs

Action Items for Success

1. **Financial Preparation**
    - Get a free credit report
    - Meet with military and financial counselors
    - Create a bare-minimum budget
    - Research cost of living in target areas

2. **Job Search Strategy**
    - Cast a wider net in your search
    - Consider multiple industries
    - Look for jobs with training programs
    - Focus on positions with health benefits

3. **Resource Management**
    - Use military aid societies if needed
    - Connect with veteran service organizations
    - Research veteran housing assistance
    - Use American Job Center resources

The Bottom Line

Your military career taught you to be methodical, thorough, and dedicated. Apply those same qualities to your transition. Every successful military operation starts with proper planning and preparation. Your transition is no different.

Remember: This isn't a race. Some family members might adapt quickly, while others struggle longer. Use available resources like Military OneSource counseling, school liaison officers, and veterans service organizations. You don't have to figure everything out alone.

Take these steps one at a time, and remember: this is just the beginning of your new mission. In the next chapter, we'll dive deeper into translating your military skills into civilian terms – a crucial skill for both federal and private-sector employment.

Chapter 2: Finding Your Next Mission

Finding Your Next Career: A Military Transition Guide

You've decided to leave the military – now comes the crucial question: "What's next?" Whether you're two years out or counting down your final months, the time to start planning is now. Just like any military mission, your transition requires proper preparation, intelligence gathering, and a solid plan of action.

Understanding Your Skills: Beyond Your MOS

Don't limit yourself to just your Military Occupational Specialty. Consider the broader skills you've developed:

Leadership and Management

- Team leadership experience
- Project planning and execution
- Resource management
- Crisis handling and decision-making

Soft Skills

- Clear communication
- Adaptability under pressure
- Strong work ethic
- Problem-solving
- Training and mentoring others

Technical Abilities

- Specific systems expertise
- Equipment maintenance
- Technical documentation
- Process implementation

Finding Your Career Sweet Spot

Success comes from finding the intersection of three key elements:

1. Skills: What you're genuinely good at
2. Interests: What you find satisfying
3. Market Reality: What employers need and will pay for

Self-Assessment Questions

- What parts of your military role did you enjoy most?
- Which tasks energized rather than drained you?
- What do others consistently praise you for?
- What problems do people often ask you to solve?

Practical Steps for Career Planning

1. **Document Your Achievements**
    - List major projects and responsibilities
    - Gather performance evaluations

- Note any awards or recognition
- Record training and certifications

2. **Research Potential Paths**
    - Federal service
    - Defense contracting
    - Private sector roles
    - Education or training positions
    - Security and law enforcement
    - Operations and logistics

3. **Reality Check**
    - Your first civilian job probably won't be your forever job
    - Focus on positions that build experience and skills
    - Consider roles that maintain your clearance if applicable
    - Look for opportunities with growth potential

Remember: Your military experience has given you valuable skills that civilian employers need. The key is learning to translate these skills effectively and finding the right opportunity to apply them.

Your next mission is finding where your abilities can make the biggest impact – both for your career and your future employer.

What Does the Market Need?

When planning your civilian career, understanding market needs helps align your skills with real opportunities. Your goals need to meet real-world demands to find something realistic, sustainable, and well-matched to your life.

1. **Location and Job Availability**
    - Research job markets in your preferred locations

- Consider remote work opportunities, especially in tech
- Use job boards, company career pages, and LinkedIn to assess demand
- Remember: Different regions have different dominant industries
- Some fields, like healthcare and education, offer opportunities everywhere
- Tech hubs like Seattle or Austin may offer more specialized roles

2. **Salary Considerations**
   - Research average salaries for target roles
   - Factor in cost of living for different areas
   - Use resources like Glassdoor or PayScale
   - Calculate what you need to maintain your lifestyle
   - Remember: A $60,000 salary means different things in different places
   - Filter out roles that won't meet your financial needs early

3. **Industry Growth and Stability**
   - Focus on growing fields like:
     - Technology
     - Healthcare
     - Renewable energy
     - Cybersecurity
   - Research industry trends and future projections
   - Look for sectors with advancement opportunities
   - Growing industries often mean more job security and room for promotion
   - Consider which sectors align with your military experience

4. **Job Requirements**
   - Review qualifications for target roles
   - Identify common certifications (CompTIA, CISSP, PMP)
   - Note required degrees or licenses

- Assess which requirements you already meet
- Plan for additional training needs
- Look for overlap between military experience and civilian requirements
- Consider whether your security clearance provides advantages

5. **Training Investment**
   - Calculate time and cost for needed certifications
   - Research GI Bill coverage for training
   - Consider program length and commitment
   - Balance training investment against career potential
   - Some certifications take weeks, others take years
   - Evaluate return on investment for different training paths
   - Look for programs specifically designed for veterans

6. **Lifestyle Fit**
   - Evaluate work-life balance requirements
   - Consider travel expectations
   - Assess schedule flexibility needs
   - Match job demands with family commitments
   - Some roles require night shifts or extensive travel
   - Others offer remote work or flexible scheduling
   - Consider the impact on family time and personal goals

Remember: Multiple paths often lead to the same career goal. For example, if you're interested in technology, you could pursue IT support, project management, cybersecurity, or technical writing. Each path uses similar skills but requires different qualifications. Focus on finding roles that match your skills, meet market needs, and fit your lifestyle requirements.

The key is finding a career that's not just available and well-paying, but also aligns with your personal life and values. Take time to research thoroughly - this investment in understanding the market will pay off in finding the right fit for your next career chapter.

Making the Connection

Example 1: Meet Alex, an Air Force mechanic.

Alex was great at fixing things, but what he really enjoyed was figuring out why things went wrong in the first place. He often took on the role of troubleshooting and figuring out the root causes of mechanical failures. Beyond his mechanical skills, he had a talent for problem-solving and analyzing data to improve maintenance processes. When he looked at his skills (mechanical knowledge, problem-solving, data analysis), his interests (improving processes, troubleshooting), and the job market (high demand in quality assurance and process improvement), he found a fit as a quality assurance analyst for a manufacturing company.

Example 2: Meet Sarah, a Navy communications officer.

Sarah had spent her time in the Navy coordinating communication lines and managing information flow, but she realized she got the most satisfaction from organizing complex systems and helping her team stay on track. She also had a natural knack for bringing different departments together and making sure everyone was on the same page. When Sarah assessed her skills (organization, communication management, team coordination), her interests (keeping projects running smoothly, working with different groups), and the market demand (high need for project managers in tech), she decided to transition into a project management role in a technology company.

Example 3: Meet Jesse, an Army medic.

Jesse's medical skills were strong, but what he valued most was the personal connection he built with the soldiers he cared for. He was a natural when it came to building trust, explaining health concepts in simple terms, and putting people at ease. After considering his skills (medical knowledge, empathy, communication), his interests (working one-on-one with people, healthcare), and the market needs (a growing demand for patient-centered care in healthcare), Jesse found his ideal role as a patient care coordinator in a healthcare facility.

Example 4: Meet Ben, a Coast Guard electronics technician.

Ben was always the go-to guy when the equipment needed fixing, but he realized he especially enjoyed simplifying technical problems for others and showing them how things worked. With skills in electronics, troubleshooting, and explaining technical concepts to non-tech folks, he knew he'd enjoy working with both tech and people. Taking a look at his skills (technical expertise, troubleshooting, teaching), his interests (helping others, working in tech), and the job market (demand for customer support roles in tech), he found his ideal match as a technical support specialist for a telecommunications company.

Example 5: Meet Rachel, a Marine Corps supply chain specialist.

Rachel was responsible for managing supplies and ensuring everything was where it needed to be, but she also had a talent for identifying ways to streamline supply processes. She loved creating efficiency and making things run smoother. Looking at her skills (logistics, process optimization, planning), her interests (efficiency, logistics, solving logistical puzzles), and the job market (high demand in supply chain management due to e-commerce growth), Rachel found a great fit as an inventory and logistics coordinator for an online retail company.

These examples show that when veterans align their unique skills and interests with market needs, they can find fulfilling careers that not only match their background but also allow them to pursue what they genuinely enjoy. Whether it's in healthcare, logistics, tech, or consulting, the civilian workforce offers many paths to leverage military experience in ways that are meaningful and in demand.

What Does the Market Need?

When planning your civilian career, understanding market needs helps align your skills with real opportunities. Your goals need to meet real-world demands to find something realistic, sustainable, and well-matched to your life.

1. **Location and Job Availability**
   - Research job markets in your preferred locations
   - Consider remote work opportunities, especially in tech
   - Use job boards, company career pages, and LinkedIn to assess demand
   - Remember: Different regions have different dominant industries
   - Some fields, like healthcare and education, offer opportunities everywhere
   - Tech hubs like Seattle or Austin may offer more specialized roles

2. **Salary Considerations**
   - Research average salaries for target roles
   - Factor in cost of living for different areas
   - Use resources like Glassdoor or PayScale
   - Calculate what you need to maintain your lifestyle
   - Remember: A $60,000 salary means different things in different places
   - Filter out roles that won't meet your financial needs early

3. **Industry Growth and Stability**
   - Focus on growing fields like:
     - Technology
     - Healthcare
     - Renewable energy
     - Cybersecurity

- Research industry trends and future projections
- Look for sectors with advancement opportunities
- Growing industries often mean more job security and room for promotion
- Consider which sectors align with your military experience

4. **Job Requirements**
    - Review qualifications for target roles
    - Identify common certifications (CompTIA, CISSP, PMP)
    - Note required degrees or licenses
    - Assess which requirements you already meet
    - Plan for additional training needs
    - Look for overlap between military experience and civilian requirements
    - Consider whether your security clearance provides advantages

5. **Training Investment**
    - Calculate time and cost for needed certifications
    - Research GI Bill coverage for training
    - Consider program length and commitment
    - Balance training investment against career potential
    - Some certifications take weeks, others take years
    - Evaluate return on investment for different training paths
    - Look for programs specifically designed for veterans

6. **Lifestyle Fit**
    - Evaluate work-life balance requirements
    - Consider travel expectations
    - Assess schedule flexibility needs
    - Match job demands with family commitments
    - Some roles require night shifts or extensive travel
    - Others offer remote work or flexible scheduling
    - Consider the impact on family time and personal goals

Remember: Multiple paths often lead to the same career goal. For example, if you're interested in technology, you could pursue IT support, project management, cybersecurity, or technical writing. Each path uses similar skills but requires different qualifications. Focus on finding roles that match your skills, meet market needs, and fit your lifestyle requirements.

The key is finding a career that's not just available and well-paying, but also aligns with your personal life and values. Take time to research thoroughly - this investment in understanding the market will pay off in finding the right fit for your next career chapter.

Let me share a few real examples:

- A Marine Corps infantryman who became a successful software developer
- An Army medic who opened a restaurant
- A Navy nuclear technician who went into real estate
- An Air Force security forces member who became a teacher
- A Coast Guard operations specialist who started a marketing firm

None of these paths were "obvious" transitions from their military roles, but they all worked because these veterans permitted themselves to explore what they really wanted to do.

You also have permission to:

- Take some time to figure things out (no, you don't have to have it all planned the day you separate)
- Change your mind (that first civilian job? It can be a stepping stone, not a life sentence)
- Combine different interests (maybe you want to use your technical skills AND your love of teaching)
- Start something completely new (yes, even if you've never done it before)
- Say no to "obvious" opportunities that don't excite you
- Take calculated risks (you've handled bigger challenges before)

- Learn from trial and error (remember your first few weeks in the military?)
- Create a career path that doesn't fit in a neat box

Here's another important permission slip: You can take time to explore options before committing. This might mean:

- Informational interviews in different industries
- Shadowing professionals in fields that interest you
- Taking classes or certifications to test your interest in a field
- Starting a side hustle while working a steady job
- Volunteering in different roles to gain exposure
- Attending industry events to learn more about different fields
- Connecting with veterans who've made unusual career transitions

And remember: Your first civilian career choice isn't a lifelong commitment. Many successful professionals change careers multiple times before finding their sweet spot. The military gave you a foundation of skills – now it's time to build on it in whatever direction calls to you.

Every skill you learned – leadership, adaptability, problem-solving, team building, crisis management – translates to ANY career field. You're not starting from zero; you're starting with a foundation you can build on in any direction.

So give yourself permission to dream bigger and explore paths that might not be obvious. The only limits that really matter are the ones you put on yourself. You've earned the right to choose your own path.

The Practical Approach

Start your exploration with these steps:

1. **Skills Inventory**
   - List everything you're good at, military and civilian
   - Include soft skills and personal traits
   - Get input from others who know you well
   - Look at your evaluations for forgotten accomplishments

2. **Interest Exploration**
   - What parts of your job did you enjoy most?
   - What do you do in your free time?
   - What topics do you like learning about?
   - What problems do you enjoy solving?

3. **Market Research**
   - Research growing industries
   - Look at job requirements in different fields
   - Network with veterans in different industries
   - Investigate salary ranges and job availability
   - Consider geographic factors

4. **Reality Testing**
   - Informational interviews with people in target careers
   - Volunteer work or part-time jobs in areas of interest
   - Professional association meetings
   - Online courses or certifications to test interests
   - Job shadowing opportunities

Remember, finding the right path is often an iterative process. Your first civilian job might help you discover what you really want to do – or don't want to do. That's valuable information. Each step teaches you something about yourself and your preferences, helping you refine your direction.

Taking Stock: What Do You Actually Have to Offer?

Let's start with something that might surprise you – you probably have more marketable skills than you realize. Military service develops abilities that civilian employers crave, but you've probably been taking them for granted. Leadership, adaptability, problem-solving under pressure, project management, and team coordination – these aren't just military skills; they're highly valued business skills.

Take a moment to think about your military experience differently. At that time, did you manage a maintenance schedule for a fleet of vehicles? That's logistics and asset management. Led a team through a difficult training evolution? That's project management and leadership. Coordinated with multiple units for a mission? That's cross-functional team collaboration. The key is learning to translate your military experiences into civilian terms.

But here's the real talk – you need to be honest about your skills, not just optimistic. Make three lists:

1. Skills you can prove with certifications or documented experience
2. Skills you have but need to translate into civilian terms
3. Skills you need to develop for your target career

This isn't just about what you did in the military. Think about your off-duty education, volunteer work, and personal projects. Maybe you've been taking college classes, managing your unit's volunteer programs, or working on vehicles in your free time. It all counts.

Understanding the Playing Field: Civilian Career Paths

The civilian job market might seem chaotic compared to the military's structured career progression, but there are patterns you can understand. Let's break down some common paths:

Federal Service

- Easiest transition culturally
- Veterans' preference in hiring
- Similar benefits structure
- Clear career progression
- Military time counts toward retirement
- BUT... often slower hiring process
- May start at a lower grade than expected

Contracting

- Familiar environment
- Values security clearance
- Often higher initial pay
- Utilizes military knowledge
- BUT... contract stability varies
- May require frequent moves
- Benefits might not match military

Private Sector

- Most career flexibility
- Often faster advancement
- Potentially higher salary ceiling
- More negotiating power
- BUT... bigger culture shock
- Less structured progression

- May need additional education/certification

Entrepreneurship

- Complete autonomy
- Unlimited earning potential
- Use the GI Bill for business programs
- BUT... highest risk
- Inconsistent initial income
- Need business skills
- Requires significant planning

Matching Timeline to Goals

Your preparation strategy depends heavily on your remaining time in service. Let's break it down:

Two Years or More Out:

- Perfect time for degree completion
- Get advanced certifications
- Build a civilian network
- Research thoroughly
- Consider internships
- Shadow civilians in target careers
- Test different options

One Year Out:

- Focus on specific certifications
- Network aggressively
- Start job searching
- Prepare application materials
- Plan financially

- Research target companies

Six Months or Less:

- Focus on immediate qualifications
- Leverage existing network
- Target specific positions
- Prepare for a quick transition
- Consider bridge employment
- Use veteran hiring programs

Building Your Qualifications While Still in Service

Here's something many separating service members miss – your current command can be an incredible resource for building civilian qualifications. While you're still in uniform, you have access to:

Training and Education

- Tuition Assistance
- Credentialing programs
- Military schools
- Certification programs
- Skills training

Experience Building

- Additional duties
- Special projects
- Cross-training opportunities
- Leadership roles
- Training responsibilities

Networking

- Military-civilian events
- Professional organizations
- LinkedIn building
- Industry conferences
- Veteran organizations

The Reality Check: Setting Realistic Expectations

Let's have a frank conversation about expectations – the kind of conversation you might not get in TAP class or from well-meaning transition counselors. If you're coming off a successful military career, especially if you've held leadership positions, this part might be tough to hear. But it's crucial for your long-term success.

The Initial Step Back

Picture this: You're a senior NCO or officer who's led hundreds of troops, managed million-dollar budgets, and been responsible for life-or-death decisions. Now you're looking at civilian job postings asking for "5 years of industry experience" for what seems like a junior position. It's frustrating. It might even feel insulting. But here's the reality – you might need to take a step back to move forward.

Think of it like a tactical retreat. In military operations, sometimes you need to give up advantageous terrain temporarily to achieve a better long-term position. Your civilian career might require the same strategy. That first job isn't your final objective – it's your initial foothold in the civilian world.

Why The Step Back Happens

Let's break down why this initial adjustment is often necessary:

1. **Industry-Specific Experience Matters**
    - Civilian employers value industry experience heavily
    - Your military skills are valuable, but sector-specific knowledge is crucial
    - Technical terms, industry standards, and business practices vary widely
    - You need to learn the "language" of your new industry

2. **Different Leadership Styles**
    - Military leadership is direct and authority-based
    - Civilian leadership often relies more on influence and consensus
    - The chain of command is less clear
    - You need to learn new ways to motivate and direct teams
    - Your team might include people older than you or with more industry experience

3. **Business Context**
    - Military missions focus on operational success
    - Civilian businesses focus on profitability
    - You need to learn about budgets in terms of profit and loss
    - Understanding business politics is crucial
    - Customer service might be a new priority

Salary Realities

Let's talk money – another area where expectations often need adjustment. You might be looking at civilian salaries and thinking they look good, but remember:

- BAH isn't added on top
- Healthcare will likely cost more
- Taxes might be higher
- Civilian retirement contributions come from your salary
- Cost of living varies widely by location

A civilian job offering $75,000 might actually provide less disposable income than your military pay. This is why many veterans take bridge jobs while building their civilian careers or work multiple jobs initially.

The Good News

Now, here's the encouraging part – this step back is usually temporary and often shorter than you might expect. Veterans tend to advance quickly once they prove themselves because:

- Your leadership experience does matter
- Your work ethic stands out
- You're used to learning and adapting
- You handle pressure well
- You bring a fresh perspective
- You're typically more mission-focused than your civilian peers

Many veterans find themselves advancing faster than their civilian counterparts after that initial adjustment period. Your military experience becomes a significant advantage once you learn to apply it in civilian contexts.

Making the Adjustment Work

Here's how to handle this transition period effectively:

1. **Set Realistic Short-term Goals**
   - Focus on learning the industry
   - Build your civilian network
   - Master your new role, even if it seems "beneath" you
   - Document your achievements
   - Start planning your next move

2. **Maintain Perspective**
   - Remember this is temporary
   - Focus on learning, not status
   - Build relationships at all levels
   - Keep your long-term goals in mind
   - Stay humble but confident

3. **Use Your Advantages**
   - Military work ethic
   - Ability to handle stress
   - Leadership experience
   - Problem-solving skills
   - Adaptability
   - Professionalism

4. **Watch for Opportunities**
   - Internal job postings
   - Special projects
   - Cross-training
   - Leadership roles in civilian organizations
   - Industry certifications

Making Peace with the Process

This adjustment period isn't a reflection of your military service or capabilities. It's a necessary part of transitioning to a new environment. Think of it like being a highly experienced NCO returning to a specialty school – you might know more than most students about leadership and military operations, but you still need to learn the specific skills being taught.

Remember – you're not starting over, you're starting different. Your military experience isn't being erased; it's being translated and adapted. The skills that made you successful in the military – adaptability, determination, leadership, work ethic – these will make you successful in the civilian world too. You just need to learn to apply them in new ways.

The key is to approach this transition period with the right mindset. You're not taking a step back; you're repositioning for future success. Stay focused, stay humble, keep learning, and trust that your proven ability to excel will serve you well in this new environment.

Creating Your Action Plan

Time for practical steps. Grab a notebook or open a new document. You need to map out:

1. Timeline Assessment
    - Exactly how long until separation?
    - What are your financial needs?
    - Family considerations?
    - Geographic restrictions?

2. Career Research
    - Target industries
    - Required qualifications

- Salary ranges
- Growth potential
- Location factors

3. Gap Analysis
   - Current qualifications
   - Needed qualifications
   - Time to acquire them
   - Resources available
   - Potential obstacles

4. Resource Identification
   - GI Bill options
   - Certification programs
   - Training opportunities
   - Networking events
   - Veteran programs

5. Milestone Planning
   - Education goals
   - Certification deadlines
   - Network building
   - Application timing
   - Interview preparation

Moving Forward

Remember, this process isn't just about finding a job – it's about starting a new career. Take time to do it right, but don't get paralyzed by endless planning. Set clear goals, make a realistic plan, and start taking action now, even if they're small steps.

In the next chapter, we'll dive into the nuts and bolts of the actual job search – resumes, interviews, and networking. But for now, focus on honest self-assessment and thorough career research. The better you understand yourself and your options, the more effective your job search will be.

Your next mission is out there. Time to start planning for it.

Debrief: Chapter 2 - Finding Your Next Mission

1. **Define Your Target Objective:**
   Identify the overlap between your skills, interests, and market demand—the "Career Triangle"—to guide your career path. This approach ensures a balance of passion, practicality, and opportunity.

2. **Identify Transferable Skills:**
   Translate military experience into civilian terms by focusing on leadership, adaptability, problem-solving, and teamwork. Highlight these qualities in ways that resonate with civilian employers.

3. **Recon the Job Market:**
   Research industries and roles that align with your skills and interests. Consider factors like job availability, salary expectations, and required qualifications in your target location.

4. **Stay Mission-Focused:**
   Your first civilian job might not be your dream position, but it's a stepping stone. Focus on roles that provide income, experience, and a pathway to your long-term career goals.

5. **Permission to Pivot:**
   Don't box yourself into familiar roles or "obvious" career choices. Explore new industries and opportunities, leveraging your ability to learn, adapt, and grow in uncharted territory.

6. **Test the Waters:**
   Use informational interviews, job shadowing, and volunteer opportunities to explore potential careers before committing. These experiences provide valuable insights into civilian workplaces.

7. **Leverage Veteran Resources:**
   Take advantage of programs like SkillBridge, TAP, and veterans' networks to gain training, mentorship, and connections in your desired field.

Chapter 3
FRAGO

FRAGO: When Plans Change - From College to Job Hunt

Let's talk about something that happens more often than you might think – the sudden need to pivot from your original transition plan. Maybe you planned to use your GI Bill for college, but family obligations are pushing you toward immediate employment. Or perhaps you're realizing that sitting in classrooms isn't what you want right now. Whatever the reason, changing plans mid-transition is completely normal, and more importantly, it's manageable.

Think of this like receiving a FRAGO (Fragmentary Order) in the military. Your original mission plan has changed, and now you need to adapt quickly while still accomplishing your objectives. The good news? The military taught you how to be flexible and adjust to changing situations.

Immediate Actions

First, don't panic. This might feel like a major disruption to your plans, but remember: the military trained you to adapt and overcome. You already have valuable skills employers want – now it's time to put them to work.

Step 1: Skills Inventory Take immediate stock of your marketable assets:

- Security Clearance: If you have one, this is gold. Defense contractors

and federal agencies are always seeking cleared personnel, often with salaries matching or exceeding what you'd earn after college.
- Technical Certifications: Those military schools weren't just check-the-box exercises. Your Army Defense Information School certification might qualify you for civilian IT roles. Your maintenance credentials could translate to aerospace jobs.
- Leadership Experience: Did you manage troops? Lead missions? Train personnel? These experiences translate directly to supervisory and management positions in the civilian sector.
- Specialized Training: Whether it's logistics, healthcare, cybersecurity, or maintenance, your military operational experience has civilian equivalents.

Step 2: Quick-Win Opportunities Focus on immediate openings where veterans have a natural advantage:

- Federal Employment: Your veteran's preference points make you competitive right now
- Defense Contractors: They understand military experience and often value it over education
- Law Enforcement: Many agencies offer veteran preference and accept military experience in lieu of college
- Transportation & Logistics: Your military experience often directly translates
- Emergency Services: Skills in crisis management and quick decision-making are highly valued

Step 3: Bridge Employment Strategies Think of this as a tactical repositioning, not a retreat from your education goals:

- Seek Companies with Education Benefits:
    - Many defense contractors offer tuition assistance up to $10,000 annually

- Large corporations like Amazon, Walmart, and Starbucks have college programs
- Federal agencies often provide education reimbursement
- Some companies partner directly with universities for employee education

• Consider Hybrid Positions:

- Weekend shift work that leaves weekdays free for classes
- Remote or flexible positions that accommodate study time
- Seasonal or project-based work that allows for school during off-periods
- Part-time positions with full benefits

• Look for Growth Potential:

- Companies with clear career progression paths
- Organizations that promote from within
- Employers who value continuous learning
- Positions that offer mentorship programs

Step 4: Getting Paid Now - The Bridge Job Strategy

Let's be honest: Sometimes you just need a paycheck, and that's okay. While others might consider this controversial, here's the truth: Not every job needs to be your dream career or even related to your long-term goals. A bridge job is exactly what it sounds like – it bridges the gap between where you are and where you want to be.

Here's something many transition guides won't tell you: Bridge jobs aren't just entry-level positions. They can range from basic roles to senior management – any job can be temporary if you treat it that way.

Bridge Jobs at Different Levels:

Entry Level Bridges

- Security guard positions
- Warehouse workers
- Delivery drivers
- Customer service representatives
- Retail associates
- Administrative assistants

Mid-Level Bridges

- Security supervisors (especially with clearance)
- Warehouse managers
- Project coordinators
- Technical support leads
- Sales managers
- Office managers
- Training coordinators
- Operations supervisors

Senior-Level Bridges

- Program managers (especially in the defense sector)
- Operations directors
- Regional managers
- Security directors
- Consulting roles
- Technical project managers
- Quality assurance managers
- Facilities directors

Remember: Your rank and experience don't mean you have to start at the top. Sometimes, taking a mid-level position with less responsibility can give you breathing room to plan your next move while maintaining a solid income.

Why Bridge Jobs Work at Any Level:

- Immediate income matching your experience
- Less emotional investment than a "career" position
- Opportunity to learn civilian workplace dynamics
- Time to plan your next move without financial stress
- Benefits and stability while networking
- Chance to build civilian credentials

Strategic Approaches by Level:

Entry Level Strategy:

- Focus on jobs with flexible schedules
- Look for positions with room for quick advancement
- Consider jobs with tips or overtime opportunities
- Use the simplicity of the role to focus on your next move

Mid-Level Strategy:

- Leverage military leadership experience
- Take roles with good benefits but manageable stress
- Use the position to learn civilian business practices
- Network with other professionals at your level

Senior Level Strategy:

- Consider contract or interim management positions
- Look for roles in transition (helping companies through changes)
- Take positions below your max capability for better work-life balance
- Use the role to understand civilian executive dynamics

Pro Tips for Any Level:

- Don't undersell yourself – bridge jobs can still pay well
- Be selective about responsibilities – it's okay to take a step back
- Keep your long-term goals in mind
- Network at whatever level you're working
- Save money while in the bridge position
- Keep applying for roles that better align with your goals
- Stay professionally engaged in your desired field

Remember: Whether you're a former E-4 or O-6, there's no shame in taking a job that's just a stepping stone. Your military experience might qualify you for senior roles, but it's perfectly acceptable to choose a lower-stress position while planning your next move. The key is finding a role that provides the stability you need without preventing you from pursuing your ultimate goals.

A bridge job's primary purpose is to provide stability and space – regardless of its level. Use this time wisely, but don't feel trapped by the role or the level. Your career goals are still valid, but they don't have to happen immediately. Focus on getting paid now, and work on building your ideal future while maintaining financial security.

Pro Tips for Success:

- Keep your security clearance active if possible – it's a valuable asset
- Join professional associations in your field – many offer free or discounted memberships to veterans
- Consider taking a few certification courses while job hunting to show civilian equivalency
- Network with veteran employee resource groups at target companies

- Use military transition programs like SkillBridge or Career Skills Program if still on active duty

Remember: Your military career taught you to achieve objectives through multiple approaches. This is just a tactical adjustment to your transition strategy. Many successful veterans started their civilian careers without degrees and built their education over time. Some employers even prefer to hire veterans who can bring immediate real-world experience to the table.

The key is to position this change not as a setback but as a strategic decision to build your civilian career through a different sequence of events. You're not abandoning your education goals; you're creating a more sustainable path to achieve them while maintaining financial stability and gaining valuable civilian experience.

Quick-Response Job Search Strategy

1. **Update Your Documentation**
   - Convert your military records (ERB/ORB/ESR) into a civilian resume
   - Gather your evaluation reports for achievement examples
   - Get your security clearance documentation in order
   - Request copies of all military certificates and training records

2. **Tap Into Veteran Resources**
   - Register with your local Veterans Job Center
   - Connect with Veteran Service Organizations (VSOs)
   - Join veteran job boards like HireVets and VetJobs
   - Reach out to veteran-friendly companies in your area

3. **Federal Employment Fast Track**
   - Apply for Veterans' Preference
   - Use the Military Spouse Preference if applicable

- Learn about Direct Hiring Authorities
- Consider contracting positions that value clearances

Building Your Support Network

- Connect with veterans who've already made the transition
- Join professional organizations in your target industry
- Attend job fairs specifically for veterans
- Find a mentor through veteran networking groups

Real-World Examples: Bridge Jobs That Work

Entry-Level Bridge Jobs

Carlos - Infantry to Corporate Security Carlos needed immediate income when his first child arrived. He took a security supervisor position at a corporate office complex starting at $22/hour. Though below his military leadership experience, the job offered immediate health insurance and predictable hours. The steady schedule allowed him to attend the police academy on weekends. After 18 months, he transitioned to law enforcement but kept the security position for weekend overtime. The bridge job provided stability during his training and extra income after landing his target career.

Ashley - Military Tech to Help Desk With depleting savings, Ashley needed quick employment. She accepted a help desk position at $25/hour, well below her military technical experience. The role provided immediate benefits and straightforward work. The low-stress environment allowed her to focus on obtaining advanced cybersecurity certifications during off-hours. Within eight months, she moved into a cybersecurity position that better matched her skills and doubled her salary.

Mid-Level Bridge Jobs

Maria - Personnel to Office Management Unexpected housing issues forced Maria to seek immediate civilian employment. She took an office manager position at $55K annually. While not her target HR role, the position let her use her military organizational skills while learning civilian HR practices. The company's tuition assistance funded her HR certifications. Within a year, she secured an HR coordinator position at $75K with a defense contractor.

Miguel - Aviation Electronics to Casino Tech The early arrival of twins pushed Miguel to find stable income and insurance quickly. He became a slot machine technician, earning $28/hour plus a night differential. The technical work was straightforward compared to military aviation, and the night shift schedule allowed him to take morning engineering classes. He leveraged this civilian tech experience to land an automation technician role at a semiconductor plant 14 months later.

Senior-Level Bridge Jobs

Jennifer - Signal Officer to Sales Engineer Family medical expenses required Jennifer to find stable income quickly. She accepted a sales engineer position offering $85K base salary plus commission. Though below her military leadership level, the role provided immediate income with flexible hours. This allowed her to develop her business plan during off hours. Two years later, she launched her tech company while maintaining part-time sales work for financial stability.

David - Senior NCO to Retail Management When his spouse lost their job, David needed quick income. His leadership experience helped him secure a retail store manager position at $65K. The role had less responsibility than his military position but offered immediate start and straightforward duties. The reduced stress level gave him time to network effectively. He found his target position as an operations director within four months.

Unexpected Bridge Jobs

Samantha - Ordnance to Quality Control Needing proof of income for a mortgage approval, Samantha took a quality control inspector role at $24/hour in food processing. She applied her precision skills from ordnance work to the new position. The first shift schedule allowed her to complete teaching certification classes in the evening. She now teaches high school and maintains the QC position during summer breaks for additional income.

Tony - Aircraft Maintenance to Manufacturing Tony's daughter's early college acceptance created an immediate need for a steady income. He started as a maintenance supervisor at $58K in a manufacturing plant. Though not aviation-related, his mechanical skills transferred effectively. The position allowed significant overtime for college savings while he completed his A&P license. He moved to commercial aviation six months later with valuable civilian leadership experience.

Keys to Successful Bridge Jobs:

1. **Quick-Start Priorities**
   - Immediate income
   - Health insurance coverage
   - Predictable schedules
   - Manageable stress levels
   - Flexible hours when needed
   - Overtime possibilities
   - Fast hiring process

2. **Strategic Benefits**
   - Time for career planning
   - Civilian work experience
   - Networking opportunities

- Education/training flexibility
- Certification pursuit
- Benefits during job search

3. **Best Practices**
   - Accept positions below experience level if needed
   - Focus on schedule flexibility
   - Prioritize benefits over prestige
   - Look for quick-hire opportunities
   - Keep building skills while working
   - Maintain networking efforts
   - Save aggressively when possible

Remember: A bridge job serves as temporary stability while positioning yourself for your target career. The key is finding a role that meets immediate needs without compromising long-term goals. A bridge job is a tactical pause providing stability while you maneuver toward your ultimate objective - not a career compromise.

The Bottom Line

Plans change – that's a fact of life we learned well in the military. Just like receiving a FRAGO in combat operations, your transition plan might need rapid adjustment. That's not failure; it's tactical adaptation.

Think of a bridge job as establishing a hasty fighting position:

- It provides immediate security (financial stability)
- Gives you time to gather intel (explore opportunities)
- Lets you maintain contact (networking)
- Allows you to maneuver toward your objective (dream job)

The key is maintaining your strategic objective (building a successful civilian career) while adjusting your tactical approach. Your military experience has given you valuable skills that employers need right now. By leveraging these skills while keeping your education goals on the horizon, you can create a successful transition that works for your current situation.

Remember:

- This is just a tactical pause after receiving your FRAGO
- You're not settling; you're establishing a base of operations
- Your "dream job" or career is still the objective
- You're maintaining momentum while repositioning
- Bridge jobs are temporary fighting positions, not permanent duty stations
- Keep developing your plan of attack while maintaining security
- Mission accomplishment often requires flexibility in execution
- Your transition is no different than adapting to battlefield conditions

The mission hasn't changed – only the route to the objective. Whether your bridge job lasts two months or two years, it's simply a tactical decision point in your overall campaign plan to reach your ultimate civilian career goals.

Debrief: Chapter 3 - Translating Military Skills to Civilian Success

1. **Learn the Language of Civilians:**
   Translate military jargon into terms civilian employers understand. Replace acronyms and MOS codes with skill-based descriptions, such as "team leadership" or "project management."

2. **Focus on Transferable Skills:**
   Highlight core strengths like leadership, adaptability, problem-solving, and mission execution. These traits resonate across industries and make you a valuable candidate.

3. **Build a Civilian-Friendly Resume:**
   Craft a resume tailored to your target industry. Emphasize quantifiable achievements, such as "leading a team of 20 to complete projects ahead of schedule and under budget."

4. **Adapt Your Communication Style:**
   Practice shifting from direct military-style communication to a more collaborative civilian tone. This change helps you connect with diverse teams and workplace cultures.

5. **Align Your Skills with Industry Needs:**
   Research the qualifications and certifications that align with your skills and target career. Consider pursuing credentials like PMP, CompTIA, or Six Sigma to bridge any gaps.

6. **Leverage Networking Opportunities:**
   Use LinkedIn, veteran organizations, and industry events to build connections. Networking helps uncover opportunities and showcases your ability to adapt to civilian environments.

7. **Practice Your Pitch:**
   Develop a concise personal narrative that connects your military experience to civilian roles. Focus on how your background adds value to prospective employers.

Chapter 4: Veterans: Time to Execute Your Career Change

You've been out for a while. Maybe you're in that bridge job we talked about earlier, or perhaps you've been in the same civilian job since transition and feel stuck. Either way, you're ready for a change – a real career move, not just a job. The rest of this book will help you execute that change.

The Timeline Varies

For some of you, this moment comes a year or two after transition. That first civilian job helped you understand the corporate world, but now you see opportunities that better match your goals. Maybe you took that bridge job in logistics because it was familiar, but your real interest is in project management or IT. Or perhaps that security position you took for stability has shown you opportunities in corporate risk management.

Others might be reading this five, ten, or more years after hanging up the uniform. You've built a solid civilian career, but something's missing. Some of you might have climbed the ladder in defense contracting but feel ready to test your skills in commercial industries.

Understanding Where You Are

This isn't like your initial transition from military service. You're not operating from uncertainty anymore. You've learned valuable lessons about the civilian workforce – its culture, expectations, and opportunities. You understand office politics, civilian career progression, and how to translate your military experience. Most importantly, you're making this move from a position of stability rather than necessity.

Signs It's Time for a Change

You might recognize some of these indicators:

- You've mastered your current role and feel unchallenged
- The excitement of learning civilian culture has worn off
- You see opportunities that better align with your long-term goals
- Your skills have grown beyond your current position
- You've developed interests in new fields through civilian exposure
- The salary ceiling in your current path feels too low
- You miss the sense of mission you had in the military
- Your civilian experience has shown you new possibilities

What Makes This Time Different

This career change is fundamentally different from your military transition. You're no longer stepping into the unknown – you're making a strategic move with experience and knowledge behind you. The civilian workplace is familiar territory; you understand its culture, expectations, and unwritten rules.

You've mastered corporate communication, knowing when to be direct and when to be diplomatic. Your professional network has grown significantly, with colleagues and mentors who understand your capabilities and can vouch for your civilian experience. Plus, you have a proven track record of civilian success, giving you credibility and negotiating power you didn't have before.

Most importantly, your current position provides stability, allowing you to approach this change strategically rather than reactively. You can take time to find the right opportunity rather than accepting the first offer.

Key advantages you now possess:

- Understanding of civilian workplace dynamics and culture
- Proven track record of civilian achievement
- Established professional network
- Financial stability for strategic planning
- Knowledge of industry standards and expectations
- Clear understanding of your market value
- Confidence in professional settings
- Time to plan and execute carefully

Your understanding of career paths and opportunities has also expanded significantly. Through exposure to different roles, conversations with colleagues, and professional development experiences, you've gained insight into various career trajectories. You understand the qualifications, experience, and skills needed for different positions, and you can evaluate opportunities more effectively.

Market value awareness is another crucial advantage. You now understand:

- Typical salary ranges in your field
- Value of your experience and skills
- Standard benefits packages
- Negotiation norms and practices
- Career progression timelines
- Industry-specific compensation structures

Remember: This isn't your first major career change. You've already successfully navigated the most challenging transition from military to civilian life. Now you can use that experience, combined with your civilian professional development, to make your next career move even more successful.

Strategic considerations for your move:

- Take time to research thoroughly
- Leverage your professional network
- Update your credentials strategically
- Document your civilian achievements
- Plan your timeline carefully
- Prepare your family for changes
- Maintain current performance
- Build transition contingencies

Whether you're ready to leave that bridge job or make a major career shift after years in the civilian workforce, you're now equipped with advantages you didn't have during your military transition. The principles remain the same: assess, prepare, and execute with purpose. But this time, you have the tools, knowledge, and stability to make your career move strategically rather than reactively.

Why Veterans Make Career Changes

Veterans choose to change careers for many reasons. Some are seeking new challenges, while others are responding to life changes. Here are common scenarios you might recognize:

Career-Driven Changes

The Bridge Job Graduate Sarah took a logistics supervisor position right after leaving the Army. It was familiar, paid well, and offered stability.

Now, three years later, she's ready for more. While the money is good, she realizes her passion lies in project management. She's ready to leverage her leadership skills in a new field that challenges her.

The Federal Service Explorer After five years in federal service, Marcus advanced from GS-11 to GS-13. While grateful for the stability, he feels constrained by federal bureaucracy. Seeing former colleagues thrive in corporate leadership roles, he realizes his federal project management experience could command higher compensation in the private sector.

The Defense Contractor Seeking New Horizons Jennifer excelled as a defense contractor, reaching a senior analyst position with six-figure income. After six years, she's ready to apply her skills beyond the defense industry. She's exploring opportunities in technology and healthcare, where her analytical skills could bring fresh perspective.

Life Changes Driving Transitions

Financial Pressures

Growing Family Needs James loves his federal service job, but with twins on the way and his wife reducing work hours, his GS-11 salary won't cover the new expenses. He's exploring defense contractor positions where his clearance and experience could increase his income by 40%.

Education Costs Maria's logistics management job covered regular bills until her oldest child's college acceptance changed the equation. Now she's pursuing program management positions with defense contractors, specifically targeting those offering dependent education benefits.

Geographical Changes

Spouse's Career Opportunity David's wife received an out-of-state promotion. Rather than rushing to find a similar government contracting role, he's using this change to transition into corporate project management, focusing on positions offering remote work flexibility.

Family Care Requirements Sarah needs to relocate closer to aging parents. Instead of limiting herself to local operations management positions, she's exploring remote work opportunities in technical writing and consulting, leveraging both her military and civilian experience.

Family Status Changes

Post-Divorce Career Shift Jennifer's divorce requires maximizing her income to maintain her children's lifestyle. She's transitioning from administrative work to intelligence analyst positions with defense contractors, leveraging her security clearance for higher compensation.

Single Parent Transition Mike's unexpected transition to single parenthood made his traveling sales position impossible to maintain. He's redirecting his leadership and sales experience toward local operations management, prioritizing stability and predictable hours.

Common Threads in Career Changes

Regardless of the catalyst, most veterans seeking career changes share common experiences:

- Stability in current position
- Better understanding of civilian workplace
- Clearer career goals than during initial transition
- More confidence in civilian abilities
- Established professional network
- Financial foundation to support change
- Better work-life balance perspective

Getting Ready: Documentation Prep

Before executing your career change, get your documentation in order. This time, you're not just proving military experience – you're showcasing both military and civilian achievements.

Essential Documents Checklist

1. **Military Documentation**
   - DD214 (Member Copy 4) - Multiple certified copies
   - Military training records and certifications
   - Performance evaluations and awards
   - Security clearance documentation

2. **Civilian Career Documentation**
   - Current resume with civilian achievements
   - Performance reviews
   - Professional certifications
   - Training certificates
   - Awards and recognition
   - Salary documentation for negotiations

3. **Education Documentation**
   - Military transcripts (JST/CCAF)
   - Civilian education transcripts
   - Professional development certificates
   - Continuing education records

4. **Additional Documentation by Transition Type**

For Federal to Private:

- Last 3-5 performance appraisals
- SF-50s showing promotions
- Special award citations

- Security clearance documentation

For Private to Federal:

- Updated SF-15 for veterans preference
- KSA documentation
- Military awards and decorations
- Specialized questionnaire responses

For Career Field Changes:

- Relevant volunteer work documentation
- Professional association memberships
- Certification program documentation
- Training course completions

Organization Tips

1. **Digital Filing System**
   - Create dedicated folders by category
   - Use clear naming conventions
   - Maintain multiple backups
   - Keep PDF versions ready
   - Create a "quick send" package

2. **Physical Documents**
   - Use a filing system
   - Keep originals secure
   - Have copies ready
   - Create a presentation portfolio

THE BOTTOM LINE

Whether you've been out for one year or ten, whether you're in a bridge job or just ready for change, the principles remain the same: prepare thoroughly, move purposefully, and execute strategically. Think of this as your next mission. You've completed your initial transition (boot camp), gained civilian experience (first duty station), and now you're ready for a real career move (choosing your career path).

Remember these key points about maintaining professional relationships:

- Give proper notice and maintain high performance through your last day
- Document your work and prepare thorough handoffs
- Offer to train your replacement if possible
- Keep relationships professional and positive, regardless of personal feelings
- Connect with colleagues on LinkedIn before leaving
- Express gratitude to mentors and supervisors who helped your development

Never burn bridges – you might need to cross them again. Many veterans end up returning to previous employers with higher positions and better compensation after gaining experience elsewhere. That bridge job you're leaving might be the perfect landing spot years from now when life circumstances change. Your old boss could become your most valuable reference for future opportunities.

Think of professional relationships like your military network – you never know when or where you'll encounter someone again. Just as the military community extends far beyond your last duty station, your civilian professional network will follow you throughout your career. Maintain it with the same integrity and professionalism you learned in the service.

Execute your career move strategically, but always leave doors open behind you. Your next opportunity might come through the very connections you maintain today.

Debrief: Chapter 4 - Navigating the Job Search

1. **Establish a Targeted Job Search Strategy:**
   Focus on roles and industries that align with your skills, interests, and career goals. Tailor your approach to positions that offer both immediate opportunities and long-term growth potential.

2. **Master the Art of Networking:**
   Build and leverage professional connections through LinkedIn, industry events, and veterans' organizations. Personal referrals often open doors that online applications can't.

3. **Craft Customized Applications:**
   Tailor your resume and cover letter for each job. Highlight specific achievements and skills that align with the job description to stand out from other candidates.

4. **Use Veteran-Specific Resources:**
   Take advantage of programs like Hire Heroes USA, American Job Centers, and VA employment resources. Many of these are designed to match veterans with employers who value their experience.

5. **Learn to Navigate Online Job Boards:**
   Use platforms like LinkedIn, Indeed, and USAJOBS effectively. Create keyword-optimized profiles and set alerts for new openings in your target fields.

6. **Prepare for Civilian Interviews:**
   Practice answering behavioral questions that focus on results

and teamwork. Use the STAR method (Situation, Task, Action, Result) to communicate your accomplishments clearly.

7. **Stay Organized and Persistent:**
   Track your applications, follow up on submissions, and be prepared for rejections. The job search process requires resilience and adaptability—qualities you've already honed in service.

Chapter 5: Let's Talk About SkillBridge

Quick Note Before We Dive In

Before we jump into SkillBridge, this chapter is like a snapshot of the program. This is a simple rundown of what SkillBridge is and how it works, but keep in mind that programs like this are always evolving. The companies that participate, the specific rules, and even some of the requirements might change by the time you're reading this.

Who's SkillBridge For? Let's Break It Down

Let's talk about who can benefit from SkillBridge. Whether you're a young enlisted member wrapping up your first contract or a seasoned officer looking at retirement, this program might be your ticket to a smooth transition.

SkillBridge Basics: You need to be within 180 days of separation, have an honorable discharge pending, get command approval, and have served at least 180 days of active duty.

This program is perfect for:

- The "I Need Experience" crowd - bridging the gap between military skills and civilian requirements
- Career switchers looking to test a new field while still getting paid
- "Almost There" folks who need civilian polish and connections
- Strategic planners wanting to build networks and explore locations

It might not be right if you:

- Need to stay at your duty station
- Can't get command approval
- Already have a job lined up
- Plan to start a business or go straight to school

The ideal candidate is open to learning, ready to be a rookie again, manages time well, and has a clear direction. Think of it as reconnaissance for civilian life - a chance to test-drive your next career while still receiving your military paycheck.

Here's a pro tip: if you're not sure if SkillBridge is right for you, visit your base's transition office. These folks have seen hundreds of service members go through this process and can give you the straight scoop on whether it'll help you hit your goals. Think of them as your transition coaches - they've got the playbook and know how to use it.

Remember, even if SkillBridge isn't for you, the fundamentals of preparation, networking, and transition planning are crucial for anyone leaving the military. Use what works for you, and leave what doesn't. Your transition is unique to you, and that's exactly how it should be.

Where This Fits in Your Transition Journey

Transitioning out of the military is a big deal, and SkillBridge is just one of many tools you can use. Whether you're:

- Still in uniform and planning your exit
- Already out and building your civilian career
- Thinking about working for the federal government
- Just trying to figure out your next move

The stories and insights in this chapter can help you out, even if SkillBridge isn't part of your plan.

What We'll Cover (And What We Won't)

Here's what you'll find:

- The basics of what SkillBridge is all about
- How to get started if you're interested
- Stories based on real people who've done it
- Tips on making it work for you
- How it can lead to federal jobs

What you won't find:

- Every single detail about the program
- A complete list of companies that participate
- All the paperwork you'll need
- Specific rules for every military base
- Different requirements for each branch

How This Connects to Everything Else

Think of this chapter as one piece of the puzzle. Later in the book, we'll talk about:

- Making your military resume make sense to civilians
- Crushing your interviews
- Getting that federal job
- Understanding civilian workplace culture
- Using your veteran status to your advantage
- Keeping your security clearance
- Building your professional network
- Growing your career

Remember: SkillBridge is just one option in your toolkit. Throughout this book, we'll explore lots of different ways to make your transition successful. Let's get started.

Who Can Use SkillBridge

Let's cut right to the chase and break down exactly who can participate in SkillBridge. The basic requirements are pretty straightforward, but there are some details you'll want to know about.

First up, you've got to be a service member within 180 days of your separation date. That means any branch - Army, Navy, Air Force, Marines, Coast Guard, or Space Force. Whether you're getting out after your first enlistment or retiring after 20+ years, you're potentially eligible. This includes Active Duty, Guard, and Reserve members who are on active duty orders. Just remember, that 180-day window is crucial - you can't start earlier, and waiting until the last minute might mean missing out on opportunities.

Here's something important: you need to be getting an honorable discharge. If you're looking at anything else - general, other than honorable, or dishonorable - SkillBridge isn't going to be an option. Also, you need to have completed at least 180 days of active duty service before you can participate. Brand new recruits who didn't make it through their first six months aren't eligible.

Now, let's talk about command approval, because this is huge. You can meet every other requirement, but without your command's blessing, it's not happening. Your chain of command needs to sign off that your absence won't hurt the unit's mission. This means if you're in a critical position or your unit's about to deploy, you might have a harder time getting approved. But here's a tip: having a solid plan and showing how you'll handle your responsibilities can help convince your command.

Something people often ask about is clearances and special duties. If you're in a position requiring a security clearance or special access, you can still participate, but there might be extra requirements or restrictions. You'll need to work with your security manager to make sure everything's squared away. Same goes for those with special duty assignments - you'll need to coordinate with your leadership about transitioning those responsibilities.

Education level doesn't matter for eligibility. Whether you've got a GED or a Ph.D., SkillBridge is open to you. Rank doesn't matter either - we've seen everyone from E-3s to O-6s go through the program successfully. What matters is meeting the basic requirements and having a plan.

Medical situations can get tricky. If you're going through a medical board or have a complex medical situation, you can still be eligible, but you'll need to coordinate with your medical team and command. The key is making sure your medical appointments and requirements don't conflict with the program schedule.

Here's something that surprises some folks: if you're on a special contract or have additional service obligations (like from training or education), you need to complete those first or get them waived before you can participate in SkillBridge. This includes things like critical skills retention bonuses or training payback commitments.

One last thing about timing - while you can participate in your last 180 days, you need to start planning way before that. Most people should start looking into programs and getting their paperwork together at least 6-12 months before they want to start. This gives you time to find the right opportunity, get all the approvals, and set yourself up for success.

Remember, meeting the eligibility requirements is just the first step. You'll still need to find a program that works for you, get accepted by the company, and complete all the necessary paperwork. But if you meet these basic requirements and start planning early, you're on your way to making SkillBridge part of your transition plan.

Understanding SkillBridge Programs and Expectations

Types of Programs Available

SkillBridge offers three main types of programs to fit different career paths and learning styles. The first option is internships, which provide traditional workplace learning experiences lasting 3-6 months. These internships focus on helping service members understand organizational culture and industry practices, often including rotations through different departments. Many internships can lead to direct employment opportunities after completion.

For those interested in trades or specific technical skills, apprenticeships offer a more hands-on approach. These programs typically run the full 180-day duration and combine classroom instruction with practical training. Apprenticeships are particularly common in manufacturing, construction, and technical fields, and often include opportunities to earn formal certifications.

The third option consists of focused training programs, which are especially popular with major corporations. These programs emphasize specific industry education and often include formal certifications or credentials. Many are structured as cohort-based learning experiences, combining virtual and in-person instruction to provide comprehensive industry preparation.

Administrative and Financial Considerations

Throughout your SkillBridge participation, you remain on active duty and must maintain military standards and appearance. You'll need to complete separation requirements, respond to military recalls if necessary, and continue regular check-ins with your command. The good news is that your full military pay and benefits continue, including your housing allowance, and program participation itself is cost-free. However, you should plan for potential travel or relocation expenses.

Setting Realistic Expectations

It's important to understand what SkillBridge is and isn't. The program provides valuable training and experience, helps you learn civilian workplace culture, introduces you to industry practices, and offers networking opportunities. However, it's not a guaranteed job offer, a vacation from military duties, an early separation program, or a complete civilian transition solution.

Keys to Success

Success in SkillBridge requires preparation before, during, and after the program. Before starting, thoroughly research your options, network with program alumni, set clear goals, and plan your logistics carefully. During the program, maintain your professionalism, document your experiences, build relationships, and continuously seek feedback and learning opportunities. After completing the program, follow up with your contacts, update your professional materials, apply your new skills, and maintain your network connections. These steps will help maximize your SkillBridge experience and set you up for success in your civilian career.

Debrief: Chapter 5 - Excelling in the Civilian Workplace

1. **Adapt to Civilian Workplace Culture:**
   Learn the norms and expectations of civilian organizations. Embrace a collaborative approach to leadership, where influence and teamwork often replace command structures.

2. **Adjust Your Leadership Style:**
   Transition from directive to participatory leadership. Foster a supportive environment by encouraging input and collaboration from your team.

3. **Develop Emotional Intelligence (EQ):**
   Build skills in empathy, communication, and conflict resolution. These traits help you navigate office dynamics and build strong working relationships.

4. **Embrace a Learning Mindset:**
   View your transition into civilian work as an opportunity to grow. Be open to new processes, technologies, and approaches that may differ from military standards.

5. **Understand Performance Metrics:**
   Civilian success is often measured differently, focusing on outcomes like profitability, customer satisfaction, and team cohesion. Align your efforts with these objectives.

6. **Communicate Effectively:**
   Practice active listening and adapt your communication style to fit your team's needs. Avoid military jargon and use language that resonates with your civilian peers.

7. **Balance Confidence with Humility:**
   While your military background provides valuable skills, approach civilian challenges with humility. Show a willingness to learn and adapt while sharing your expertise when appropriate.

8. **Build Your Civilian Network:**
   Strengthen connections within your workplace and industry. Professional relationships can provide mentorship, collaboration opportunities, and future career advancements.

PART 2:

OPORD: Planning For Mission Success

Chapter 6: Know Yourself, Know Your Value

Translating your military experience into civilian terms can feel like explaining TikTok to your grandparents. You know exactly what you did in service, but putting it into words that make sense to civilian employers? That's a whole different battle.

Understanding the Translation Challenge

The civilian workforce speaks English, but not quite the military English you know. Instead of saying "I was NCOIC for a platoon of 40 personnel," try "I managed and led a team of 40 professionals, overseeing their training and operations." Your military experience is incredibly valuable when translated correctly. That supply chain reorganization? That's process improvement. Mentoring junior enlisted? That's personnel development. Planning complex missions? That's project management gold.

Unpacking Your Military Experience

Combat Arms Roles

Even seemingly combat-focused roles pack serious civilian value:

- Strategic planning capabilities

- Risk assessment and management
- Resource allocation expertise
- Crisis management skills

Technical Roles

Combat Medics

- Managing complex medical supply inventories
- Documenting detailed patient care
- Coordinating emergency operations
- Making critical decisions under pressure

Civilian translations:

- Hospital emergency departments value your crisis management
- Medical supply companies need your inventory expertise
- Healthcare administrators appreciate your documentation skills
- Emergency response teams want your decision-making abilities

Logistics Specialists You're basically Amazon Prime with body armor:

- Coordinating complex shipments
- Managing extensive inventories
- Maintaining challenging supply chains
- Handling multiple transportation modes

Translates to:

- Supply chain management
- Distribution center operations
- Inventory control systems
- Transportation logistics

Intelligence Analysts Your skills are premium in civilian sectors:

- Data analysis that tech companies value
- Pattern recognition expertise
- Critical thinking under pressure
- Clear communication of complex findings

Leadership Experience Breakdown

Fire Team Leader (E-4)

- Managing 3-4 people with life-or-death responsibility
- Making split-second tactical decisions
- Translates to: Team lead positions, project coordinators
- More responsibility than most first-time civilian supervisors

Squad Leader (E-5/E-6)

- Managing 9-13 people
- Equipment responsibility worth $500K+
- Budget management
- Daily operations including:
  - Project management (planning operations)
  - Wellness program management (PT)
  - Asset management (equipment maintenance)
  - Staff development (training)
  - Stakeholder relations (unit coordination)
  - Personnel management (counseling)

Platoon Sergeant (E-7)

- Managing 40+ personnel
- Million-dollar equipment responsibility
- Complex operations planning
- Full HR management
- Budget oversight

- Crisis management

Civilian equivalents:

- Operations Director
- Senior Program Manager
- Department Head
- Project Management Lead

First Sergeant (E-8)

- Senior advisor role
- Managing 100+ personnel
- Strategic planning
- Policy implementation
- Professional development programs
- Organizational culture development

Real-World Translation Examples

Scenario 1: Complex Project Management

Weak: "I ran a big training event for about 300 people." Strong: "I managed a complex training initiative involving 300 personnel and $5 million in equipment. This required coordinating across six departments, developing contingency plans, and maintaining operational readiness. We delivered on schedule and 15% under budget."

Scenario 2: Team Development

Weak: "I led a team of nine people in combat operations." Strong: "I led a diverse team of nine professionals, implementing comprehensive development programs that achieved a 40% promotion rate within 18 months and maintained 100% qualification rates on mission-critical certifications."

Translating Common Military Tasks

Combat Operations Planning = Strategic Project Management

"I developed and executed complex operational plans requiring coordination across multiple teams. Each operation required detailed risk assessment, resource allocation, and contingency planning."

Equipment Maintenance = Asset Management

"I implemented preventive maintenance programs for $3 million in equipment, reducing downtime by 30% and extending asset lifecycle by 25%."

Unit Training = Learning and Development

"I designed and delivered comprehensive training programs for groups of 20-100 professionals, reducing certification time by 40% while improving test scores by 25%."

Your Competitive Advantage

By age 25, many veterans have:

- Managed more people than civilian managers will by 40
- Handled larger budgets than many small business owners
- Made higher-stakes decisions than most corporate executives
- Led more diverse teams than many Fortune 500 managers
- Solved complex problems that would make corporate "crises" look simple

Keys to Effective Translation

1. Focus on Quantifiable Results
    - Instead of "managed equipment," say "maintained 100%

accountability for $2.5 million in assets while reducing maintenance costs by 20%."

2. Emphasize Leadership Scope
    - Don't just count people – describe impact: "Developed and led a team of 12 professionals, achieving 100% mission completion rate."

3. Connect Technical Skills
    - Link military systems to civilian equivalents: "Managed complex logistics systems tracking 5,000+ items across multiple locations."

The Bottom Line

Your military experience isn't something to apologize for or minimize – it's your competitive advantage. Stop saying "just a sergeant" when you're describing years of leadership experience most civilians won't acquire until their forties. Don't downplay your supply experience when you've managed complex logistics operations that would impress Amazon executives.

You're not asking for a job – you're offering a solution. You bring tested leadership skills, proven crisis management abilities, and real-world experience handling challenges that would paralyze most civilian organizations. Your new mission is clear: Take pride in your service, own your experience, and communicate your value with the same confidence you brought to your military duties.

Stand tall, speak with confidence, and show them exactly why hiring a veteran is the best decision they'll ever make. You've earned it. Now go prove it.

[Previous content remains the same until the end, then adds:]

DEBRIEF: Chapter 6 - Know Yourself, Know Your Value

1. **Master the Translation**
    - Learn to communicate military experience in civilian terms
    - Focus on transferable skills and universal competencies
    - Remove military jargon while maintaining the substance
    - Use concrete examples and measurable results

2. **Understand Your True Value**
    - Recognize the depth of your leadership experience
    - Acknowledge the scope of your responsibilities
    - Compare your experience level to civilian equivalents
    - Identify unique military advantages (crisis management, high-stakes decision-making)

3. **Break Down Your Experience**
    - Catalog technical skills beyond your primary MOS
    - Document leadership roles and responsibilities
    - List major projects and achievements
    - Identify soft skills developed through service

4. **Quantify Your Impact**
    - Track numbers (people managed, budgets, equipment value)
    - Measure improvements (efficiency gains, cost savings)
    - Document successful outcomes
    - Calculate the scope of responsibilities

5. **Present with Confidence**
    - Stop minimizing military experience
    - Own your accomplishments
    - Present yourself as a solution provider
    - Maintain pride in service while speaking civilian language

6. **Target Your Translation**
    - Research industry-specific terminology
    - Align military experience with job requirements
    - Focus on relevant transferable skills
    - Adapt examples to match employer needs

7. **Build Your Success Stories**
    - Develop clear before-and-after scenarios
    - Prepare specific examples of leadership
    - Document problem-solving successes
    - Create civilian-friendly anecdotes

8. **Remember Your Worth**
    - You're not starting over - you're transitioning
    - Your experience is valuable and relevant
    - Military leadership translates to civilian success
    - You bring unique capabilities to civilian employers

Chapter 7: Building Your Resume - Making the Civilian Switch

Let's talk about one of the biggest hurdles when leaving the military - creating a resume that civilian employers actually understand. You're sitting at your desk, staring at a blank screen, wondering how to explain that leading a platoon through complex operations actually means you're great at project management.

You've spent years mastering the military's unique language. Terms like "OIC," "NCO," and "AO" roll off your tongue without a second thought. But most civilian hiring managers have never served. When they see "Battalion S4" on a resume, they're not thinking "logistics expert" - they're just confused.

Next chapter we'll dive into federal resumes, which are a whole different animal. For now, let's focus on catching a civilian employer's attention.

Understanding the Civilian Workplace The civilian work world plays by different rules. In the military, everything is documented in detail, every step is accounted for, and we have standard operating procedures for just about everything. Those lengthy AARs covered everything from initial planning to final execution.

But civilian employers think differently. They're often overwhelmed with applications and looking for quick, clear indicators that you're the right person for the job. While your military report might start with a detailed background and three pages of analysis, civilian hiring managers want to see your value within seconds.

Picture this: A hiring manager has 200 resumes on their desk for one position. They're spending less than 30 seconds on each resume during the first review. In that brief window, they need to understand:

- Who you are
- What you've accomplished
- What value you can bring to their company
- Why they should pick you over the other 199 applicants

This is why your military experience needs to be repackaged. That time you reorganized your unit's supply system? A civilian employer doesn't need to know the 20-step process you use. They want to hear that you "implemented an inventory management system that reduced waste by 30% and saved $100,000 annually."

Remember:

- Military reports focus on process - civilian employers focus on results
- Military values detail - civilian employers value clarity
- Military explains how - civilian employers care about what and why
- Military documents everything - civilian employers want highlights

Your challenge is to take those rich, detailed military experiences and distill them down to their most impressive and relevant points. Think of it like giving a one-minute brief to a General - you keep the important stuff and cut everything else.

What Civilian Employers Really Want to See

Let's dive deep into what makes civilian employers sit up and take notice. These are the golden tickets that can set you apart from other candidates - you just need to know how to present them.

Leadership Skills We're used to saying things like "commanded," "directed operations," or "executed missions." But in the civilian world, these can sound too rigid or aggressive. Instead, think about how you influenced and guided your team:

- Instead of "commanded 30 troops," try "led a team of 30 professionals."
- Rather than "executed training operations," say "developed and implemented training programs."
- Change "directed daily operations" to "managed day-to-day team activities."
- "Supervised" and "coordinated" are great alternatives that show leadership without military intensity

Project Management Every mission you planned was essentially a project. Think about it:

- That field training exercise? A complex training project with multiple moving parts
- Combat operations? High-stakes project management under extreme conditions
- Military ceremonies? Event planning and coordination
- Equipment maintenance schedules? Project scheduling and resource management

Civilian companies love seeing how you:

- Planned and organized resources

- Met deadlines under pressure
- Coordinated multiple teams
- Handled unexpected challenges
- Achieved objectives within constraints

Budget Responsibility Everything in the military has a dollar value, even if you don't think about it that way:

- What equipment did you maintain? Calculate its total value
- Training programs you ran? Add up the resources used
- Personnel you supervised? Include salary responsibilities
- Supplies you managed? Total up the inventory value
- Cost savings from your improvements? Quantify them

For example:

- "Responsible for $3M worth of tactical equipment"
- "Managed annual training budget of $500K"
- "Implemented efficiency measures saving $250K annually"
- "Supervised maintenance operations for $10M vehicle fleet"

Team Development: You didn't just tell people what to do - you helped them grow. Highlight how you:

- Trained new team members
- Mentored junior personnel
- Created development programs
- Improved team performance
- Built high-performing teams
- Helped others earn promotions
- Conducted performance evaluations
- Provided career guidance

Problem-Solving Civilian employers love hearing about how you handle challenges. Think about times you:

- Found creative solutions with limited resources
- Improved existing processes
- Handled unexpected situations
- Resolved conflicts
- Met tight deadlines
- Adapted to changing conditions
- Fixed broken systems
- Turned around underperforming teams

Technical Expertise Your technical skills are valuable, but they need to be explained in civilian terms:

- Instead of "SINCGARS expert," try "Advanced radio communications systems specialist."
- Rather than "BFT operator," say "GPS-based vehicle tracking systems manager"
- Change "GCSS-Army SME" to "Enterprise resource planning systems expert"
- "Proficient in military logistics software" becomes "Experience with supply chain management systems"

Look for civilian equivalents to your military technical skills:

- Weapons systems = Technical equipment
- Combat operations = High-risk operations
- Force protection = Security management
- PMCS = Preventive maintenance
- Supply = Inventory management
- Intel analysis = Data analysis

Remember, civilian employers want to know:

- What you can do for them
- How you've solved problems
- Where you've added value
- When you've improved things

- Why you'd be a good fit

These skills and experiences make you incredibly valuable - you just need to present them in a way that resonates with civilian employers. Think about specific examples from your military career that demonstrate each of these areas, then translate them into civilian terms that show their business value.

Making Your Military Experience Work in the Civilian World

Let me share some real stories and examples that show exactly how to transform your military experience into civilian gold.

Think about a typical day as a Maintenance Platoon Sergeant. You probably started with a morning meeting, checked deadlines, assigned tasks, solved unexpected problems, and kept everything moving. In civilian terms, that's exactly what an Operations Manager does - just without the combat boots.

Let's look at some real-world translations with stories behind them:

Combat Arms Leadership Military Version: "Infantry Squad Leader, led nine soldiers in combat operations."

Civilian Translation: "Team Leader who directed nine professionals in high-stress environments, developed standard operating procedures that increased team efficiency by 40%, and maintained 100% accountability of $1.5M in equipment while meeting aggressive deadlines."

The Story Behind It: As a Squad Leader, you weren't just leading patrols. You were teaching new team members, solving problems on the fly, managing expensive equipment, and keeping everyone safe. That's project management, team development, and risk management all rolled into one.

Logistics and Supply Military Version: "92Y Supply Sergeant is maintaining property books and ordering supplies."

Civilian Translation: "Inventory Control Manager overseeing $3M in assets, implementing digital tracking systems that reduced loss by 75%, and coordinating with 15 departments to maintain optimal stock levels while reducing excess inventory by 30%."

The Story Behind It: Remember those long hours in the supply room? You weren't just counting equipment - you were running a complex inventory management system, forecasting needs, and keeping a whole organization running smoothly.

Vehicle Maintenance Military Version: "Motor Sergeant responsible for company vehicles and maintenance schedules."

Civilian Translation: "Fleet Manager overseeing maintenance operations for 30 vehicles valued at $4.5M, developing preventive maintenance programs that reduced downtime by 50%, and managing a team of 12 technicians while staying under budget."

The Story Behind It: Those endless hours in the motor pool weren't just about fixing vehicles. You were running a full-service maintenance operation, managing people, schedules, and resources.

Communications Military Version: "25U Commo Chief maintaining battalion communications systems"

Civilian Translation: "IT Systems Manager responsible for maintaining critical communications infrastructure supporting 500+ users, implementing new technologies that improved reliability by 85%, and training 50+ personnel on complex technical systems."

Medical Experience Military Version: "68W Combat Medic supporting infantry company"

Civilian Translation: "Emergency Medical Specialist providing healthcare in high-pressure environments, training 100+ personnel in emergency response procedures, and managing $500K of medical equipment with zero loss."

Administrative Leadership Military Version: "Battalion S1 NCOIC processing personnel actions and awards."

Civilian Translation: "Human Resources Manager overseeing personnel operations for the 800-person organization, streamlining administrative processes that reduced processing time by 60%, and managing sensitive data with 100% accuracy."

Here's how to think about your specific roles:

Security Forces: Before: "Conducted force protection operations and access control." After: "Managed comprehensive security operations protecting $50M in assets and 300+ personnel, developing emergency response protocols and leading training programs that improved reaction times by 40%."

Food Service: Before: "Ran DFAC operations serving three meals daily." After: "Restaurant Manager overseeing $500K food service operation, supervising 20 staff members, and serving 1000+ customers daily while maintaining health and safety standards."

Training Instructor: Before: "Drill Sergeant training new recruits" After: "Professional Development Specialist designing and implementing training programs for groups of 60+ new employees, achieving 95% qualification rate and reducing training time by 20%."

The key is thinking about your daily tasks in business terms:

- Those mission briefs? Project planning meetings
- Equipment layouts? Inventory management
- Training sessions? Employee development
- Mission planning? Project management

- Counseling sessions? Performance reviews
- Combat operations? High-risk project execution

Remember that time you:

- Fixed the broken supply system? That was process improvement
- Got your unit through a tough inspection? Quality assurance
- Trained new team members? Staff development
- Planned a complex mission? Project management
- Handled a crisis? Emergency management
- Improved your unit's procedures? Systems optimization

Making Your Military Experience Work in the Civilian World - The Art of Translation

Picture this: You're sitting in a job interview, and the hiring manager asks about your leadership experience. In your mind, you're remembering that time in Afghanistan when your team had to adapt to a sudden change in mission while maintaining security for a critical convoy. That's pure gold in civilian terms - if you know how to tell it right.

Let's break down some real experiences and see how they transform into civilian success stories:

From the Motor Pool to Management: A former Motor Sergeant spent years keeping a fleet of HMWWVs running in harsh conditions. On his first resume, he wrote: "Maintained company vehicles and supervised mechanics." But here's what he really did:

- Managed a team of 15 technicians maintaining 40+ vehicles worth $7M

- Created a preventive maintenance schedule that reduced breakdowns by 65%
- Developed training programs that certified 25 new mechanics
- Implemented a parts inventory system that saved $100K annually

In civilian terms, that's: "Fleet Operations Manager overseeing multi-million dollar vehicle operations, leading maintenance teams, and implementing cost-saving programs that significantly improved efficiency and reduced expenses."

The Supply Room Story: Think about a typical Supply Sergeant's day. Here's how it translates:

Military Reality: "Ran company supply room, maintained property books, conducted inventories."

Civilian Gold: "Inventory Control Manager who:

- Oversaw $5M in assets with 100% accountability
- Supervised warehouse operations and distribution
- Implemented a digital tracking system, reducing processing time by 40%
- Managed vendor relationships and procurement processes
- Developed new storage solutions increasing space efficiency by 30%."

The Communications Expert: A Signal Corps NCO wasn't just "fixing radios." They were:

- Managing critical communications infrastructure
- Training users on complex technical systems
- Maintaining cybersecurity protocols
- Troubleshooting network issues
- Coordinating with multiple departments

This becomes: "IT Infrastructure Manager responsible for:

- Maintaining 99.9% uptime for mission-critical communications systems
- Training 200+ users on new technologies
- Implementing security protocols that prevented any breaches
- Managing $2M in technical assets"

From Combat Leadership to Business Leadership:

Infantry Squad Leader Experience:

- Daily operations planning
- Risk management
- Team training
- Resource allocation
- Crisis response
- Performance evaluation

Becomes: "Operations Manager skilled in:

- Leading high-performance teams in challenging environments
- Developing and executing strategic plans
- Managing risk in high-stakes situations
- Building and mentoring effective teams
- Responding to and resolving critical incidents
- Evaluating and improving team performance"

The Training Transformation:

Military Training NCO:

- Ran qualification ranges
- Conducted physical training
- Taught tactical procedures
- Evaluated performance
- Documented progress

Becomes: "Training and Development Specialist who:

- Designed and implemented comprehensive training programs
- Created performance evaluation metrics
- Developed curriculum for technical skills
- Managed professional development programs
- Tracked and reported on training effectiveness"

Administrative Excellence:

Battalion S1 Experience:

- Processing personnel actions
- Managing service records
- Coordinating with multiple units
- Handling sensitive information
- Processing evaluations and awards

Transforms to: "Human Resources Operations Manager specializing in:

- Managing personnel operations for 800+ employee organization
- Maintaining sensitive personnel records with 100% accuracy
- Coordinating interdepartmental communications
- Processing performance evaluations and recognition programs
- Streamlining administrative procedures, reducing processing time by 50%"

Security Operations:

Military Police Experience:

- Access control procedures
- Threat assessment
- Emergency response
- Personnel searches
- Report writing

Becomes: "Security Operations Manager responsible for:

- Developing comprehensive security protocols
- Conducting risk assessments and implementing mitigation strategies
- Managing emergency response procedures
- Training staff on security measures
- Creating detailed incident reports and analyses."

Crafting Your Professional Summary - Making Those First Lines Count

Think of your professional summary like a movie trailer - you've got to hook them in the first few seconds. Here are key examples of military experience translated for civilian employers:

Logistics/Supply NCO: "Supply chain professional with 10 years of experience managing complex logistics operations. Expert in inventory management and process improvement, consistently reducing costs while maintaining 100% accountability of $10M+ in assets. Led 25-person teams while implementing innovative solutions that improved operational performance."

Combat Arms Leader: "Dynamic operations leader with 12 years of experience directing high-performance teams in challenging environments. Expertise in project management and risk mitigation. Successfully led 50+ professionals, managed $15M in assets, and improved team efficiency by 45%."

Intelligence Specialist: "Data analysis professional with 6 years of experience in intelligence operations. Expert at analyzing complex data sets and producing actionable insights for senior decision-makers. Led teams of 15 analysts while maintaining 100% accuracy in information management."

Maintenance Supervisor: "Technical operations manager with 9 years of experience leading maintenance operations. Expert in fleet management and preventive maintenance programs. Directed $20M in technical equipment while leading 30+ technicians, reducing downtime by 40%."

Medical Personnel: "Healthcare operations manager with 8 years of experience in emergency medicine and team leadership. Expert in crisis management and medical logistics. Managed operations supporting 1,000+ personnel while maintaining 100% readiness."

Each summary focuses on translating military achievements into civilian terms while emphasizing quantifiable results and leadership experience.

Key Elements to Include:

- Years of relevant experience
- Scale of responsibility (team size, budget)
- Key achievements (with numbers)
- Special skills or expertise
- Leadership scope
- Problem-solving abilities

Remember to:

- Lead with your strongest skills
- Include specific numbers
- Focus on transferable skills
- Highlight leadership experience
- Show measurable results
- Keep it concise but impactful

Professional Summaries That Make an Impact

Security Forces/MP: "Security operations professional with 10 years in high-stakes protection and risk management. Expert at developing security protocols and leading multi-agency responses. Managed operations are protecting $100M+ in assets and 2,000+ personnel."

Infantry Platoon Sergeant: "Senior operations manager with 12 years leading high-performance teams. Expertise in strategic planning and risk management. Led teams of 45 professionals, managed $8M in assets, and improved efficiency by 50%."

Cyber Operations: "Information security professional with 8 years protecting critical networks. Expert in cybersecurity protocols and threat detection. Led teams of 20+ technicians while maintaining zero security breaches."

Civil Affairs: "Community relations manager with 7 years coordinating development projects. Expert in stakeholder engagement and cross-cultural communication. Managed $5M in projects while building partnerships with 50+ organizations."

Special Forces: "Strategic operations leader with 15 years directing specialized teams in complex environments. Expert in project management and risk mitigation. Led multi-national teams with a 100% mission success rate. Specialized in developing innovative solutions under pressure."

Each summary emphasizes transferable skills, quantifiable achievements, and leadership experience while avoiding military jargon.

Translating Your Military Experience for Civilian Resumes

One of the biggest challenges facing transitioning service members is effectively communicating their military experience to civilian employers. Your military career has equipped you with valuable skills, but presenting them in a way civilian employers understand requires careful translation.

Let's look at a real transformation in how military experience can be presented. Consider a Marine Corps Staff Sergeant with 12 years of service. Initially, his resume looked basic:

Staff Sergeant, USMC

- Led Marines in combat operations
- Did training and maintenance
- Managed supply room
- Responsible for troop welfare

These bullet points fail to capture the true scope of his responsibilities and achievements. After learning to focus on metrics, achievements, and business impact, his resume transformed into:

Senior Operations Manager Professional Summary: Results-driven operations leader with 12 years of experience directing high-performance teams in challenging environments. Proven track record of improving efficiency, developing future leaders, and managing multi-million dollar resources. Expert in team development, process improvement, and complex project management.

Experience: Senior Operations Manager, U.S. Marine Corps (2018-2024)

- Led a 40-person team across 15 complex projects, achieving a 100% mission completion rate while maintaining zero safety incidents

- Managed $5.5M in technical equipment with perfect accountability through innovative tracking systems
- Developed a new training program, improving team certification rates by 65%
- Streamlined inventory management process, reducing supply delays by 40%
- Mentored 12 junior leaders, with 85% selected for advancement
- Created a new maintenance schedule, decreasing equipment downtime by 50%

This transformation shows how military experience can be translated into civilian terms. The key is highlighting transferable skills and quantifiable achievements. Let's look at more examples:

A Supply Sergeant might think they "just worked in the supply room," but their experience translates to:

Logistics Operations Manager

- Directed $3.5M logistics operation supporting 800+ personnel across 3 locations
- Implemented a new inventory tracking system, reducing loss rates from 5% to zero
- Streamlined ordering process, cutting supply delivery time by 60%
- Managed team of 6 specialists handling 150+ daily transactions
- Developed a new equipment tracking program adopted by the entire organization
- Achieved perfect scores on three consecutive external audits

Even specialized military roles translate well. A Combat Medic's experience becomes:

Healthcare Operations Specialist

- Managed healthcare delivery for the 500-person organization in high-stress environments

- Led an 8-person medical team maintaining a 98% readiness rate
- Created emergency response program reducing reaction time by 45%
- Developed training program certifying 200+ personnel in emergency care
- Managed $1.2M medical supply inventory with zero discrepancies
- Implemented a new patient tracking system, reducing wait times by 50%

Technical roles also translate effectively. An Artillery Section Chief's experience becomes:

Technical Operations Manager

- Led a 15-person technical team, achieving 100% certification rate and zero safety incidents
- Managed $4M equipment set with a perfect accountability record
- Developed a new safety program reducing incidents by 75%
- Created a training system qualifying personnel 30% faster than standard
- Supervised complex operations involving multi-million dollar equipment
- Streamlined maintenance procedures, reducing downtime by 40%

The Key Elements of Effective Translation:

1. Focus on measurable results
2. Highlight leadership and management experience
3. Quantify everything possible (numbers, percentages, dollar values)
4. Emphasize transferable skills
5. Use civilian-friendly language
6. Show progressive responsibility
7. Demonstrate problem-solving abilities

Remember, every military role has valuable civilian applications. That motor pool experience? You were actually managing a complex maintenance operation. Those convoy operations? That's advanced logistics and project management. Your time as a squad leader? That's team leadership and personnel development at its finest.

Let's break down how different military experiences translate to valuable civilian skills:

Leadership Skills Military Experience:

- Leading troops in combat
- Running daily operations
- Managing team readiness
- Conducting training

Civilian Translation:

- Leading teams under pressure
- Managing daily business operations
- Developing employee potential
- Creating training programs

Technical Skills Military Experience:

- Maintaining weapons systems
- Operating communications equipment
- Conducting equipment inspections
- Tracking maintenance schedules

Civilian Translation:

- Managing complex technical systems
- Operating advanced communications platforms
- Performing quality control
- Implementing preventive maintenance programs

Administrative Skills Military Experience:

- Maintaining service records
- Processing evaluations
- Managing training records
- Handling classified information

Civilian Translation:

- Managing personnel documentation
- Conducting performance reviews
- Tracking certification requirements
- Handling sensitive data

Problem-Solving Military Experience:

- Adapting to changing situations
- Working with limited resources
- Meeting tight deadlines
- Managing multiple priorities

Civilian Translation:

- Demonstrating adaptability
- Optimizing resource allocation
- Delivering results under pressure
- Balancing competing demands

Project Management Military Experience:

- Planning operations
- Coordinating support
- Managing timelines
- Ensuring mission success

Civilian Translation:

- Developing project plans

- Coordinating cross-functional teams
- Meeting project deadlines
- Achieving business objectives

Training and Development Military Experience:

- Teaching combat skills
- Conducting readiness training
- Mentoring junior personnel
- Evaluating performance

Civilian Translation:

- Developing technical skills
- Implementing training programs
- Mentoring team members
- Assessing employee performance

The key is understanding that most military duties have direct civilian equivalents. You weren't just "following orders" - you were implementing organizational directives. You weren't just "conducting missions" - you were managing complex operations.

Remember to emphasize:

- Your ability to perform under pressure
- Your experience managing valuable resources
- Your track record of meeting objectives
- Your leadership and team-building skills
- Your adaptability and problem-solving abilities
- Your commitment to continuous improvement
- Your experience with complex systems and processes

These are exactly the qualities civilian employers seek. They may not understand military terminology, but they definitely understand results, leadership, and proven performance.

Think about your military experience in business terms:

- Missions become projects
- Units become teams
- Objectives become goals
- Operations become initiatives
- Training becomes development
- Readiness becomes performance

Think about your daily military tasks. That morning formation wasn't just about counting heads - you were managing teams and establishing daily priorities. When you conducted pre-combat checks, you weren't just going through a checklist - you were implementing quality control processes that ensured mission success. Those endless training sessions weren't just about maintaining readiness - you were developing personnel and improving organizational performance.

Your leadership experience is particularly valuable. In the military, you learned to build and motivate teams, often with people from diverse backgrounds and different skill levels. You developed future leaders through mentorship and training. You achieved challenging goals in high-pressure situations. These are exactly the leadership skills that civilian organizations need.

Think about how you managed risk in the military. You assessed situations, identified potential issues, and developed contingency plans. You ensured safety compliance and mitigated threats. In the business world, these same skills are crucial for protecting assets, ensuring operational continuity, and managing corporate risk.

Your communication skills are another valuable asset. You learned to brief senior leadership clearly and concisely. You wrote detailed reports that had to be accurate and complete. You trained personnel on complex tasks and coordinated across multiple teams. These communication skills are essential in any business environment.

The resource management experience you gained is particularly relevant. Every piece of equipment you maintained, every supply request you processed, every budget you managed demonstrated your ability to optimize resources and improve efficiency. These are skills that directly impact a company's bottom line.

Your military experience isn't just a past career - it's a foundation for future success. Whether you're aiming for management, technical roles, operations, or any other field, your military background has given you the tools to succeed. The key is helping civilian employers understand the full value of your experience and capabilities.

Final Tips

- Use clear, simple language
- Focus on results and achievements
- Quantify everything you can
- Highlight leadership and problem-solving
- Show progression and growth
- Keep it professional but personable
- Proofread multiple times

Remember, your military service has given you incredible skills and experience. Your job now is to help civilian employers understand just how valuable those skills are. Take your time, get feedback, and keep refining your resume until it really showcases what you can bring to the civilian workplace.

The Right Length for Your Civilian Resume

Here's a hard truth that many transitioning service members struggle with while military and federal resumes might run 4-5 pages (or more), civilian resumes need to be much shorter. Let's talk about why and how to make this work.

Most civilian recruiters and hiring managers spend less than 30 seconds on their first review of a resume. That's right - just 30 seconds to make your first impression. This is why length matters so much.

The Standard Rule: For most positions, your civilian resume should be 1-2 pages maximum. Here's how to think about it:

One Page:

- Entry to mid-level positions
- Less than 10 years of experience
- Single career focus
- Recent graduates or junior military ranks

Two Pages:

- Senior positions
- More than 10 years of experience
- Multiple relevant positions
- Senior NCOs and Officers
- Technical specialists with extensive qualifications

But what about all your military experience? Remember, you're not trying to document everything you've done - you're highlighting your most relevant achievements that match the job you want. Think of it like a mission brief: you give the essential information needed for success, not every detail of your career.

Making It Work: Focus on your most recent and relevant positions. For most transitioning service members, this means:

- Last 2-3 positions in detail
- Earlier positions summarized briefly or omitted
- Emphasis on transferable skills and measurable achievements
- Only training and education relevant to the target position

This tight format forces you to be selective and strategic about what you include. Each bullet point needs to earn its place on your resume by demonstrating value to your potential employer.

Think of your resume like a tactical brief: clear, concise, and focused on the mission - which is getting that civilian job. Save the full details of your military career for the interview, where you can expand on your experience in person.

In the next chapter, we'll tackle federal resumes - a whole different challenge that lets you put all those military details to good use. But for now, focus on translating your experience into language that will resonate in the civilian sector.

Debrief: Chapter 7 - Leveraging Veteran Networks and Resources

1. **Harness the Power of Networking:**
   Build a robust professional network through veterans' organizations, LinkedIn, industry events, and alumni groups. Connections often lead to opportunities unavailable through standard job boards.

2. **Engage with Veteran Service Organizations (VSOs):**
   Leverage organizations like the American Legion, VFW, and DAV

for career assistance, mentorship, and community support. Many VSOs provide job boards, training, and financial resources.

3. **Utilize Veteran-Specific Job Platforms:**
Explore platforms such as Hire Heroes USA, RecruitMilitary, and USAJOBS, which cater to transitioning service members and connect them with veteran-friendly employers.

4. **Find Mentors in Your Target Field:**
Seek out veterans who have successfully transitioned into your desired industry. Their insights and advice can help you navigate the challenges of civilian career paths.

5. **Join Professional Networks:**
Participate in industry-specific groups, both online and in-person, to expand your connections and gain insights into your chosen field. Many industries have veteran-focused subgroups.

6. **Tap into Educational Resources:**
Use programs like the GI Bill, Yellow Ribbon Program, and SkillBridge to gain education, certifications, and hands-on experience while building your civilian network.

7. **Give Back to Strengthen Connections:**
Volunteer with veteran organizations or mentor others who are transitioning. Giving back not only supports the community but also expands your network and boosts your reputation.

8. **Stay Engaged Beyond Transition:**
Continue participating in veteran events and organizations even after securing a civilian role. These connections can provide ongoing career opportunities and personal support.

Chapter 8: The Federal Resume - Your Ticket to Federal Service

Let's talk about federal resumes - and prepare to flip everything you know about resume writing on its head. If you've been living in the civilian world of sleek one-page resumes, you're in for a big change.

Think of it like those detailed military operation orders. Federal resumes want the whole story, not just the highlight reel. While your civilian friends are stressing about cutting their resumes down to one page, you'll be writing something that might look more like a short novel. A five-page federal resume isn't just normal; it's often expected.

Here's why: federal hiring managers need all that detail to match specific requirements set by Congress and agencies. If you miss one detail, your application might get kicked back faster than a new private doing push-ups wrong. The federal government wants to know everything because they're investing in you for the long haul.

Don't panic! This isn't about padding your resume - it's about thorough documentation of your experience. That time you managed a team? They want exact numbers, accomplishments, and resources managed. The training program you developed? Break down the hours, people trained, and results.

Finally, you get to detail all those military achievements you've been condensing for civilian resumes. That deployment coordinating logistics across three bases? That massive budget you managed? Your security clearance? It all matters here. Think of your federal resume like the most detailed pass-down log ever - except you're documenting your entire career.

So loosen up that typing hand and get ready to tell your story - your whole story. Because in federal hiring, bigger really is better, as long as every word counts. And trust me, after you've written your first federal resume, those one-page civilian resumes will feel like writing a tweet.

Let's break down exactly how to tackle this beast...

The Two Ways to Get It Done

You've got two options here:

1. Build it right on USAJOBS.gov
2. Create your own and upload it

Both work fine - it's really about what feels more comfortable for you. Let's break down both approaches.

Using USAJOBS.gov (The Built-In Way)

Think of the USAJOBS.gov resume builder as your GPS for this process - except unlike that GPS that got you lost on your last road trip, this one actually works. It's like having a really detail-oriented First Sergeant walking you through your checking account paperwork - it won't let you skip the important stuff.

Getting Started with the Builder

First things first - before you dive in, grab a coffee and get comfortable. You'll want to set aside at least a couple of hours for this. The builder is thorough, and that's a good thing. It's broken down into sections, and you can save as you go (trust me, you'll want to do that often - more on that later).

The Basics (The Stuff You Can't Skip)

Let's break down what you need and why it matters:

Contact Information:

- Full legal name (use the one on your ID, not your nickname)
- Phone number (one you actually answer)
- Email address (keep it professional - "tankcommander420@email.com" might not be your best choice)
- Mailing address (they might send actual mail - yes, people still do that)

Veterans' Status (This Is Huge):

- Veterans' preference points (0, 5, or 10 points)
- Service dates (be exact - they'll verify)
- Campaign badges/medals (relevant ones - they don't need to know about your Good Conduct Medal)
- Disability rating if applicable (this can qualify you for special hiring authorities)

Security Clearance:

- Current clearance level
- Date of investigation
- Whether it's active or when it expired
- Note: Even expired clearances are worth mentioning - reinvestigation is cheaper than starting from scratch

Citizenship Status:

- U.S. Citizen or not
- If naturalized, they'll need that info
- Some jobs have specific citizenship duration requirements

Your Work History (The Meat and Potatoes)

This is where most people either go too big or too small. Here's how to hit it just right:

For Each Position, They Want:

1. **Organization Details:**
   - Full official name (no acronyms - spell out "United States Army" not "USA")
   - Physical location (city, state, base name if military)
   - Organization size and budget (if you know it)

2. **Your Role:**
   - Official title
   - Pay grade/rank
   - Series and grade of previous federal service
   - Dates (MM/YYYY format)
   - Hours per week
   - Salary (yes, really - they use this to determine your pay grade)

3. **Supervisor Information:**
   - Current supervisor's name
   - Their contact info
   - Whether they can be contacted (don't worry, they'll ask permission first)
   - If your supervisor changed, note that

4. **The What and How:** Here's where people usually mess up. Don't just list duties - tell them about:

- Scope of responsibility (people, money, equipment)
- Regular duties AND special projects
- Problems you solved

- Improvements you made
- Results you achieved

How to Write Strong Work Entries

Let's look at some before and after examples:

Before (Too Vague): "Managed supply room and supervised personnel."

After (Just Right): "Supervised supply operation for 150-person infantry company with $3.2M in equipment. Led a team of 5 supply specialists and maintained 100% accountability through 3 deployment rotations. Implemented a new tracking system reducing inventory time by 35%."

Before (Too Military): "Served as BN S3 NCOIC managing training."

After (Civilian-Friendly): "Operations Manager for the 500-person organization. Developed and executed training plans for 20 separate departments. Coordinated 45 major training events annually with a $500K budget. Achieved 98% qualification rate across all required certifications."

Pro Tips for Using the Builder

1. **Save Obsessively**
   - The system times out after 30 minutes
   - Save after completing each position
   - Save after any major section
   - Did I mention you should save?

2. **Use the Preview Function**
   - Check how it looks before submitting
   - Watch for formatting issues

- Make sure everything aligns properly

3. **Dealing with Technical Issues**
    - Use Chrome or Edge browsers (works best)
    - Clear your cache if things get weird
    - Don't use your phone - seriously, don't

4. **Strategic Approaches**
    - Fill out one job completely before moving to the next
    - Keep a Word doc backup of your entries
    - Use spell check before copying text into the builder
    - Have your SF-50s, evaluations, and awards nearby for reference

Remember, the builder might feel restrictive, but that's actually helping you. It's ensuring you don't forget anything crucial. Think of it like a thorough pre-combat inspection - annoying at the time, but you're glad you did it when it matters.

What Your Final Product Should Look Like

After you've filled everything out, each position should tell a clear story about:

- What you were responsible for
- What you actually did
- How well you did it
- What improved because of you
- Who benefited from your work

The builder will format everything consistently, which is what you want. It might not be pretty, but it'll have everything the hiring managers need to see. Think of it like a military uniform - it might not be the most fashionable thing you've ever worn, but it serves its purpose, and everyone knows exactly what they're looking at. The standardized format actually helps hiring managers because they know exactly where to find the information they need.

Just remember - while you can't control the format in the builder, you can control the content. Make every word count, and always ask yourself, "Would a civilian understand what this means?" This is crucial because your resume isn't just going to HR specialists who know military lingo - it's going to various people in the hiring chain who might have never served a day in their lives.

Here's how to make your content shine despite the rigid format:

Use Power Words That Civilians Understand:

- Instead of "commanded," try "led" or "directed."
- Replace "executed" with "carried out" or "implemented"
- Swap "utilized" for "used" or "employed"
- Change "facilitated" to "helped" or "enabled"

Paint Pictures with Numbers:

- "Led 50-person team" is better than "led large team"
- "$1.2M budget" beats "managed resources"
- "99.9% accuracy rate" trumps "high accuracy"
- "Reduced processing time by 45%" is stronger than "improved efficiency."

Tell Success Stories in Bite-Sized Pieces: Think Problem → Action → Result

- Problem: "Faced with outdated inventory system..."
- Action: "Implemented new digital tracking method..."
- Result: "Reduced loss rate by 75% and saved $50K annually"

Make Your Impact Clear:

- Show who benefited: "Trained 200 personnel, improving unit readiness."
- Highlight efficiency: "Streamlined process, saving 20 labor hours weekly."
- Emphasize quality: "Maintained zero safety incidents across 150 operations."
- Demonstrate leadership: "Mentored 12 junior staff, with eight earning promotions."

Avoid These Common Traps:

1. **Alphabet Soup**
   - Bad: "Led QA/QC for PMCS on 50 HMMWVs"
   - Good: "Led quality control inspections for vehicle maintenance on 50 tactical vehicles."

2. **Vague Achievements**
   - Bad: "Improved unit performance"
   - Good: "Raised unit fitness scores by 35% over 6 months"

3. **Passive Voice**
   - Bad: "Training was conducted for new personnel."
   - Good: "Trained 30 new personnel on equipment operations"

4. **Assuming Knowledge**
   - Bad: "Served as BN S4"
   - Good: "Managed logistics operations for the 800-person organization"

Remember, this formatted resume will follow you through your federal career - it's worth taking the time to get it right. Think of it as your "living" career document that you'll update regularly, just like counseling cards or evaluation records. Every new project, achievement, and training course should be added while it's fresh.

Pro tip: Keep a separate "brag sheet" document. Record each project, training, or milestone in civilian terms as they happen. When it's time to update your federal resume, you'll have all your achievements ready to go, already translated into civilian language. This saves you from struggling to remember details of past accomplishments.

The USAJOBS builder might seem restrictive, but these limitations actually simplify your task - focus on making your content clear, impactful, and civilian-friendly. Test your content by reading it to someone who's never served. If they understand what you did and why it mattered, you're on track. If they look confused while nodding, it needs another translation pass.

Remember, this builder is just a tool, and its effectiveness depends on how you use it. Focus on what you can control: clear, impactful content that tells your story in a way anyone can understand.

Your Military Service - Time to Showcase Your Service

This isn't just another section of your resume - this is where you get to lay out the experience that sets you apart from civilian candidates. Remember, federal employers value military service, but they need to understand what that service means. Think of this like translating a foreign language - you know exactly what "I was a squad leader in charge of three fire teams" means, but to a civilian hiring manager, that might as well be written in Sanskrit.

Here's the reality: Your military service is a goldmine of experience, but you need to help civilian hiring managers understand just how valuable that gold really is. They know military service is valuable (that's why veterans' preference exists), but they might not understand why your specific experience matters for their organization.

Let's put this in perspective. When you say you were a Squad Leader, you're not just saying you led some people. You're saying:

- You were directly responsible for the lives and professional development of 9-13 people
- You managed hundreds of thousands of dollars worth of equipment
- You made critical decisions under pressure
- You coordinated complex operations with multiple moving parts
- You developed and executed training programs
- You managed risk in high-stress environments
- You maintained 100% accountability for people and equipment
- You wrote and briefed operations orders
- You evaluated personnel performance and wrote counseling statements

See the difference? One sentence of military experience often equals a page of civilian accomplishments.

Think about it this way: Most civilian managers your age might have led a team of 3-4 people A civilian manager might have led a team in an office - you led 30 people in Afghanistan. They might have handled a $100K project - you managed millions in equipment. They might have taught a few classes - you developed training programs that people's lives depended on.

But here's the catch - if you don't spell it out, they won't know. They won't understand that being a Platoon Sergeant means being a mid-level manager, HR specialist, trainer, and logistics coordinator combined. They won't realize your combat deployment taught you more about leadership and decision-making than most learn in a decade of office work.

This section is your chance to bridge that knowledge gap. Show them you've already proven every skill they want under conditions they can hardly imagine. This isn't bragging - it's an accurate translation. Just like "tactical withdrawal" means "retreat," they need to learn that "supervised field operations for a 40-person platoon" means serious management experience.

Remember: Even if federal hiring managers are veterans themselves, they need to see your experience in their agency's terms. And since HR specialists who screen resumes might not be veterans, clarity is crucial.

Remember this golden rule: Every piece of military experience you list should answer these questions:

- What did you do?
- How many people were involved?
- How much money or equipment were you responsible for?
- What were the results?
- Why did it matter?

So, as we dive into the details of this section, keep this in mind: You're not just listing your service - you're translating your military success story into a language civilians can understand and appreciate. You've got the experience they need; now, let's make sure they know it.

Let's break down exactly how to do this...

Military Service (Let's Break This Down Right)

Basic Military Info (The Foundation):

- Branch of Service (spell it out: "United States Marine Corps," not "USMC")
- Total years of service (active, reserve, and guard time)
- Dates of service (be specific: MM/YYYY - MM/YYYY)
- Rank/Grade at separation (and significant previous ranks if relevant)

- Type of discharge (Honorable, General, etc.)
- Service component (Active, Reserve, National Guard)

Awards and Decorations (Tell Your Story):

- Combat-related awards (these carry weight - list them first)
- Personal decorations (Achievement Medals, Commendation Medals, etc.)
- Unit awards (but only if they reflect on your performance)
- Campaign medals and service ribbons
- Badges and qualifications (especially if job-related)

Pro Tip: Don't just list awards - explain what they were for:

- Instead of: "Navy Achievement Medal"
- Try: "Navy Achievement Medal for reorganizing supply chain operations, reducing equipment downtime by 45%."

Clearance and Special Access:

- Current or previous clearance levels
- Special compartmented access
- Special program clearances
- Investigation dates and status

Deployments and Special Assignments:

- Combat deployments (locations and dates if not classified)
- Humanitarian missions
- Special duty assignments
- Joint service experiences

Breaking Down Your Military Duties (The Meat and Potatoes)

This is where the rubber meets the road - turning your military experience into something that makes civilian hiring managers sit up and take notice. Let's dive deep into how to translate your military duties into civilian powerhouse statements.

The Art of Military Translation

Think of this like you're explaining your job to your civilian aunt who always asks, "But what do you actually DO in the Army?" You need to break everything down into basic elements that anyone can understand. Let's look at some real-world translations:

Combat Arms Positions:

1. **Infantry Squad Leader**
    - Too Military: "Led infantry squad in combat operations."
    - Civilian-Friendly: "Supervised 13-person team in high-stress environments. Managed $1.5M in equipment while executing time-sensitive projects. Developed and implemented safety protocols resulting in zero workplace accidents across 200+ operations."

2. **Tank Commander**
    - Too Military: "Commanded M1A2 tank and crew."
    - Civilian-Friendly: "Led 4-person team operating and maintaining $8.5M specialized equipment. Coordinated complex technical operations with multiple teams. Achieved 95% equipment readiness rate through preventive maintenance program."

3. **Artillery Section Chief**
   - Too Military: "Served as section chief for M777 howitzer."
   - Civilian-Friendly: "Supervised 8-person technical team operating precision equipment. Managed quality control for operations with zero tolerance for error. Trained 15 new team members with a 100% certification rate."

Support Positions:

1. **Supply Sergeant**
   - Too Military: "Ran company supply room and managed property book."
   - Civilian-Friendly: "Managed inventory control and logistics operations for the 150-person organization. Maintained accountability of $3.5M in equipment with zero losses. Implemented a new tracking system reducing inventory time by 40%."

2. **Communications Specialist**
   - Too Military: "Operated and maintained tactical communications equipment."
   - Civilian-Friendly: "Managed organization's communications infrastructure, including network setup and maintenance. Provided technical support for 200+ users. Maintained 99.9% system uptime in challenging environments."

3. **Motor Pool Sergeant**
   - Too Military: "Ran battalion motor pool operations."
   - Civilian-Friendly: "Supervised 15-person maintenance facility servicing 70+ vehicles valued at $15M. Developed preventive maintenance schedule, reducing downtime by 35%. Managed parts inventory and procurement with a $500K annual budget."

Special Skills and Qualifications

Let's break down more military skills into civilian terms:

Combat Skills:

- Instead of: "Combat Lifesaver"
- Try: "Emergency Medical First Responder certified in trauma care and emergency medical procedures."

Technical Skills:

- Instead of: "COMSEC Custodian"
- Try: "Manager for classified communications security systems with Secret clearance. Maintained 100% accountability of sensitive items worth $2M+"

Leadership Courses:

- Instead of: "Graduated Warrior Leader Course"
- Try: "Completed 200-hour advanced leadership and management training program focusing on team dynamics, conflict resolution, and performance evaluation."

Quantifying Your Experience

Remember the magic formula: Numbers + Action + Result

Examples:

1. **Training Management:**
    - Weak: "Conducted training for unit"
    - Strong: "Developed and executed 52-week training program for 150 personnel, resulting in 98% qualification rate on

mission-critical skills and 25% improvement in team performance metrics"

2. **Resource Management:**
   - Weak: "Managed unit equipment"
   - Strong: "Supervised inventory control system tracking 5,000+ items valued at $10M+. Implemented new digital tracking system reducing loss rate to zero and cutting inventory time by 60%"

3. **Personnel Development:**
   - Weak: "Responsible for soldier development"
   - Strong: "Mentored and developed 30 team members resulting in 12 promotions and 15 special duty assignments. Created career development program adopted by entire organization"

Handling Combat Experience

This needs special attention. You want to emphasize leadership and management skills without focusing on the combat aspects:

- Instead of: "Led troops in combat"
- Try: "Directed 40-person team in high-pressure environments requiring split-second decision making and constant risk assessment"
- Instead of: "Conducted combat patrols"
- Try: "Led complex operations requiring coordination between multiple teams and agencies. Maintained perfect safety record across 200+ missions"

Special Programs and Additional Duties

Don't forget these often-overlooked responsibilities:

1. **Additional Duties:**
   - Equal Opportunity Representative becomes: "Diversity and Inclusion Program Manager"
   - SHARP Representative becomes: "Sexual Harassment Prevention Program Coordinator"
   - Safety Officer becomes: "Occupational Safety Program Manager"

2. **Special Programs:**
   - Master Fitness Trainer becomes: "Physical Fitness Program Developer and Implementation Specialist"
   - Unit Prevention Leader becomes: "Substance Abuse Prevention Program Coordinator"
   - MWR Representative becomes: "Quality of Life Program Coordinator"

Pro Tips for Translation

1. **Use Action Verbs:**
   - Instead of "Responsible for..." use:
     - Managed
     - Developed
     - Implemented
     - Coordinated
     - Supervised
     - Led
     - Created
     - Achieved

2. **Focus on Universal Skills:**
   - Leadership
   - Project management
   - Risk assessment
   - Team building
   - Problem-solving
   - Crisis management
   - Quality control
   - Training development

3. **Highlight Intangible Skills:**
   - Decision-making under pressure
   - Cross-functional team coordination
   - Multicultural communication
   - Change management
   - Process improvement
   - Strategic planning

Remember: Every military duty can be translated into valuable civilian experience. The key is breaking down your responsibilities into their basic elements:

- What did you manage? (People, equipment, money)
- What did you achieve? (Statistics, improvements, awards)
- What problems did you solve? (Efficiency, processes, systems)
- What was your impact? (On mission, on people, on organization)

The goal isn't to hide your military service - it's to help civilians understand just how valuable that service makes you to their organization.

Education and Training (Making Every Course Count)

This is where you show you're both a warrior and a scholar. Remember, education comes in many forms.

Formal Education:

Civilian Education:

- Degrees earned (including in-progress degrees)
- Major field of study
- Minor/concentration areas
- GPA (if it's good and recent)
- Relevant coursework
- Academic honors
- Research projects
- Leadership positions in student organizations

Military Education: Translate these into civilian terms:

- Instead of: "PLDC/WLC/BLC," Try: "Basic Leadership Development Course - 200 hours of intensive leadership and management training."
- Instead of: "Advanced Individual Training," Try: "Technical Specialty Training in [your field] - 6 months of specialized instruction."

Professional Military Education:

Service Schools:

- Break down what you learned
- Focus on transferable skills
- Highlight leadership development
- Include hours/weeks of training

Example: Instead of: "Completed ANCOC," Try: "Senior Leadership Academy: 400 hours of advanced management training including:

- Personnel management
- Resource allocation
- Strategic planning
- Crisis management
- Budget oversight
- Performance evaluation"

Technical Training and Certifications:

Military Technical Schools:

- Convert military course names to civilian equivalents
- Include length of training
- List specific skills gained
- Mention any civilian equivalent certifications

Civilian Certifications:

- Industry certifications (CompTIA, PMP, etc.)
- Safety certifications (OSHA, etc.)
- Technical certifications
- Professional licenses

Additional Professional Development:

Specialized Training:

- Computer/software training
- Safety courses
- Quality assurance programs
- Management seminars
- Leadership workshops

Continuing Education:

- Recent relevant courses
- Online certifications
- Professional workshops
- Industry conferences

Pro Tips for Education Section:

1. **Chronological Order:**
   - List most recent education first
   - Include dates for everything
   - Show progression in your field

2. **Relevance Matters:**
   - Emphasize training relevant to the job
   - Focus on transferable skills
   - Highlight leadership development

3. **Numbers Add Weight:**
   - Include course hours
   - Note class sizes if you were an instructor
   - Mention certification scores if impressive

4. **Keep It Current:**
   - Focus on recent training
   - Update certifications regularly
   - Show continuous learning

Remember: Your military service and education have given you skills that many civilian candidates don't have. The key is translating these experiences into terms that hiring managers can understand and appreciate. Don't downplay your military education - those courses were intense and valuable. Just make sure to explain them in ways that highlight their civilian applications.

And one final note: Keep copies of all your certificates, diplomas, and course completion documents.

Creating Your Own (The DIY Approach)

Want more control over how your resume looks? You can create your own and upload it. Just make sure you include all the same info as above.

Making Your Military Experience Make Sense: The Art of Military Translation

Here's the deal - most hiring managers haven't served. When you say you were a "71L" or talk about being a "BN S4 NCOIC," their eyes are going to glaze over faster than a private's during a PowerPoint safety brief. Even if they support the military, they probably don't speak our language. And let's be honest - military speak can sound like alphabet soup to the uninitiated.

Think about it this way: Imagine someone telling you they were a "Level III Integrated Solutions Deployment Facilitator." Sure, those are all English words, but strung together? Might as well be speaking Klingon. That's exactly how civilian hiring managers feel when they see military jargon on your resume.

Breaking Down the Translation Process

Let's start with some real-world examples of military positions and how to translate them:

Administrative Roles:

- Military: "42A Battalion S-1 NCOIC"
- Civilian: "Human Resources Manager overseeing personnel operations for the 800-person organization. Managed payroll, benefits, and career development programs with a 99.9% accuracy rate."

Supply and Logistics:

- Military: "92Y Company Supply Sergeant"
- Civilian: "Inventory Control Manager responsible for $4M in equipment. Implemented a new tracking system reducing loss rates to zero and cutting inventory time by 50%."

Leadership Positions:

- Military: "Platoon Sergeant, 11B Infantry"
- Civilian: "Operations Manager leading a 40-person team in high-pressure environments. Responsible for training, safety, and mission execution with zero workplace incidents over 24 months."

The Translation Formula

Here's your formula for success: Position + Scope + Impact = Civilian Understanding

Let's break it down:

1. **Position (What you did)**
    - Military: "Squad Leader"
    - Civilian: "Team Leader"
    - Better: "First-line Supervisor"

2. **Scope (Size of responsibility)**
    - Add numbers: People, dollars, equipment
    - Include geographic reach
    - Note time periods

3. **Impact (What you achieved)**
    - Quantify results
    - Show improvements
    - Highlight innovations

Real-World Examples (Before and After):

Example 1: Combat Arms

- Military Version: "11B Squad Leader, conducted combat operations in Afghanistan"
- Civilian Translation: "Team Leader directing 12-person unit in high-stress environments. Coordinated complex operations with multiple agencies. Maintained 100% personnel and equipment accountability while managing $1.5M in assets."

Example 2: Intelligence

- Military Version: "35F All-Source Intelligence Analyst, produced INTSUMs"
- Civilian Translation: "Intelligence Operations Specialist is analyzing complex data from multiple sources to produce time-sensitive reports for senior leadership. Provided crucial decision-making support affecting 2,000+ personnel."

Example 3: Communications

- Military Version: "25B Information Technology Specialist, managed SIPR/NIPR networks"
- Civilian Translation: "Information Technology Manager maintaining secure computer networks for 500+ users. Achieved 99.9% uptime while ensuring compliance with federal cybersecurity requirements."

Special Considerations

Combat Experience: Be proud of your combat experience, but translate it into relatable terms:

- Instead of: "Conducted combat patrols in hostile territory."
- Try: "Led teams in high-risk environments requiring quick decision-making and precise execution."

Security Clearances: Don't just list them - explain their value:

- Instead of: "Held TS/SCI"
- Try: "Maintained Top Secret security clearance demonstrating highest levels of trust and reliability."

Awards and Decorations: Translate their meaning:

- Instead of: "Awarded AAM."
- Try: "Received performance award for exceptional management of $3M equipment modernization project."

The "Civilian Test"

Here's a quick test for your translations - read them to someone who's never served. If they can understand:

1. What you did
2. How many people/resources have you managed
3. Why it was important

Then you've got a good translation. If they look confused, keep working on it.

Common Translation Mistakes to Avoid

1. **The Alphabet Soup**
    - Bad: "Led PMCs for BN's TWVs"
    - Good: "Supervised maintenance operations for the 50-vehicle fleet"

2. **The Undersell**
    - Bad: "Worked in supply"
    - Good: "Managed inventory control system tracking 3,000+ items valued at $5M+."

3. **The Oversell**
    - Bad: "Commanded troops in worldwide operations."

- Good: "Led 30-person team operating across three international locations."

4. **The Jargon Jumble**
    - Bad: "Maintained PMCS and 5988E forms"
    - Good: "Developed equipment maintenance tracking system improving readiness by 45%."

Pro Tips for Translation

1. **Use Action Verbs** Strong civilian-friendly verbs include:
    - Managed
    - Supervised
    - Coordinated
    - Developed
    - Implemented
    - Led
    - Trained
    - Analyzed

2. **Quantify Everything** Include numbers for:
    - People supervised
    - Budget managed
    - Equipment value
    - Improvement percentages
    - Time saved
    - Money saved

3. **Focus on Universal Skills** Emphasize:
    - Leadership
    - Project management
    - Problem-solving

- Team building
- Risk management
- Process improvement

Remember: Your military experience is incredibly valuable - it just needs to be translated so others can understand that value. Think of yourself as a translator, turning your military accomplishments into civilian success stories. Every military task, every responsibility, and every achievement can be translated into terms that will make civilian hiring managers understand just how much you can bring to their organization.

The key is to make your military experience work for you, not against you. When done right, your military background won't be a mystery to civilian hiring managers - it'll be your secret weapon.

Some Real Talk About Common Mistakes (And How to Avoid Them)

Let me save you some headaches by learning from those who've walked this path before. I've seen way too many stellar veterans get passed over because their resumes didn't do their experience justice. Let's break this down and get real about what trips people up.

1. The Modesty Problem (Or Stop Selling Yourself Short!)

Look, I get it. In the military, we're taught that "we" accomplishments matter more than "I" accomplishments. The unit gets the credit, not the individual. That's great for unit cohesion, but it's killing your federal resume. Here's what you need to know:

What Often Happens:

- "Helped with training" (When you actually developed and led the entire program)

- "Assisted in operations" (When you were the primary planner and executor)
- "Part of team that..." (When you were the team leader)

How to Fix It:

- If you led it, say you led it
- If you created it, say you created it
- If you managed it, say you managed it

Real World Examples:

Too Modest: "Participated in unit training activities"

Better: "Designed and implemented a comprehensive training program for 150 personnel, resulting in a 95% first-time qualification rate and setting new battalion standards."

Too Modest: "Helped maintain vehicles"

Better: "Supervised 10-person maintenance team responsible for 40 tactical vehicles valued at $7.5M, achieving 98% operational readiness rate."

2. The Language Barrier (Military Speak vs. Civilian Understanding)

This isn't just about acronyms - it's about entire concepts that civilians don't understand. You need to translate not just the words but the meaning.

Common Translation Fails:

- Military Terms That Need Translation:
    - "Led PT" → "Developed and conducted physical fitness training programs"
    - "NCOIC" → "Operations Manager" or "Department Supervisor"
    - "Company Operations" → "Organizational Operations"

- "Mission Planning" → "Strategic Project Planning"

Better Translations with Context: Instead of: "NCOIC of Arms Room," Try: "Manager of secure weapons facility controlling $2M in sensitive assets with 100% accountability record."

Instead of: "Ran company training room," Try: "Administered professional development programs for 150 personnel, managing certification requirements and maintaining training records with 100% compliance rate."

3. The Detail Deficit (Or: Paint the Whole Picture)

The federal government wants ALL the details. This isn't the time for bullet points - it's time for complete sentences that tell the whole story.

What Most People Write: "Managed supply room."

What They Should Write: "Managed organizational supply operations including:

- Daily oversight of $1.5M inventory
- Implementation of a new digital tracking system
- Supervision of 5 supply specialists
- Processing of 200+ monthly transactions
- Maintenance of 100% accountability
- Achievement of zero-loss record for 24 months
- Reduction of processing time by 35%."

Pro Tips from the Trenches (The Real Deal)

1. **The Save Game (Don't Lose Your Progress!)**
    - Set a timer for every 20 minutes to remind you to save
    - Keep a backup Word document with your entries
    - Use the "copy" function before hitting any submit button
    - Save after completing each position

o   Save after any major section

2. **The Multiple Resume Strategy (Your Resume Arsenal)**

Create different versions for different situations:

- Leadership-focused resume (emphasize personnel management)
- Technical-focused resume (emphasize systems and equipment)
- Project management resume (emphasize planning and execution)
- Training-focused resume (emphasize instruction and program development)

Example of Different Emphasis: Same Experience, Different Focus:

Leadership Version: "Led 30-person team in complex operations, developing five new supervisors and achieving 100% mission completion rate."

Technical Version: "Managed technical operations utilizing $4M in specialized equipment, maintaining a 99% operational readiness rate."

3. **Keyword Strategy (Playing the Game Smart)**

Don't just sprinkle keywords - integrate them naturally:

Basic Approach: "Managed projects"

Better Approach: "Applied project management principles to oversee multiple simultaneous initiatives, including:

- Project scheduling and milestone tracking
- Resource allocation and budget management
- Risk assessment and mitigation
- Stakeholder communication
- Quality control measures"

The Bottom Line (Making It All Count)

Your federal resume is telling your professional story - make it a good one. Think of it like writing an operations order - you need to include all the essential information, but it needs to be clear enough that anyone can understand it.

Keep in Mind:

- Every military experience has civilian value - you just need to explain it right
- Numbers and results matter - quantify everything you can
- Context is crucial - explain why your achievements matter
- Updates are essential - keep your resume current

Final Checks Before Submission:

1. Is everything translated into civilian terms?
2. Have you quantified your achievements?
3. Are your keywords naturally integrated?
4. Does each entry tell a complete story?
5. Would your civilian aunt understand what you did?

Remember: You're not just listing what you did - you're showing what you can do. Your military career has given you incredible skills and experience. Now it's time to make sure everyone else can see that, too.

Keep this document living and breathing. Update it when you:

- Complete a new project
- Learn a new skill
- Receive an award
- Achieve a significant result
- Take on new responsibilities

You've done the hard work in your military career. Now, it's just about telling that story in a way that gets you your next mission.

Debrief: Chapter 8 - Thriving in Your New Civilian Career

1. **Adapt to Civilian Work Expectations:**
   Embrace the differences in workplace culture, where collaboration, flexibility, and individual initiative often take precedence over hierarchical structures.

2. **Prioritize Continuous Learning:**
   Stay updated on industry trends, technologies, and best practices by attending workshops, pursuing certifications, or enrolling in training programs.

3. **Set Realistic Career Goals:**
   Focus on incremental achievements and long-term growth. Your first civilian job is a stepping stone toward more significant opportunities.

4. **Develop a Professional Brand:**
   Build a strong reputation through reliability, teamwork, and quality work. Enhance your online presence with a polished LinkedIn profile and a clear narrative of your professional strengths.

5. **Seek Feedback and Mentorship:**
   Regularly solicit constructive feedback from supervisors and colleagues. Use their insights to refine your skills and advance your career.

6. **Cultivate Work-Life Balance:**
   Learn to manage time effectively, balancing professional responsibilities with personal interests and family commitments. This balance contributes to sustained career satisfaction.

7. **Expand Your Professional Network:**
   Continue building relationships within your organization and

industry. Networking can lead to new opportunities, collaborations, and mentorships.

8. **Embrace Your Military Values:**
Apply the discipline, leadership, and mission focus you developed in service to excel in civilian roles. These qualities set you apart and make you a valuable team member.

Chapter 9: What Do You Want To Do?

After years of service, everyone's asking you, "So, what's next?" Family at gatherings, friends in conversation, and even strangers at the store. Maybe you've developed a standard answer just to end the conversation. Or maybe you're the one lying awake at 2 AM, mind racing through possibilities, wondering if you should take that contracting job, go back to school, or try something completely different.

Here's the deal: We're not talking about some temporary gig to pay bills while you figure things out, or taking a job just because your buddy from the unit works there. This is about your next mission – your actual career. The job you want to wake up for, not just drift into while planning something else. You spent years serving with purpose; your civilian career deserves the same dedication.

Yes, bills need paying. But you've got skills, experience, and discipline employers would kill for. You've got the GI Bill, maybe a security clearance. These are tools in your arsenal, not handcuffs locking you into one path.

And here's something crucial: It's okay if your dream job has nothing to do with your service. Maybe you were a great infantryman but loved designing software or worked on helicopters but dreamed of starting a business. You've earned the right to choose your path, and you've got the tools to make it happen.

So let's focus on what you want, not what you should do. What makes you come alive? What impact do you want to have? The same determination that got you through military service will help you build your civilian career. Only this time, you're defining the mission.

Start With the Basics: What Lights Your Fire?

Let's dig into what really makes you tick professionally. Not what looks good on paper, not what impresses people at parties, but what actually gets you energized and ready to roll.

Think back to your service – and I mean really think about it. Strip away the rank structure, the daily grind, and all the mandatory fun. Focus on those moments when time flew by because you were so invested in what you were doing. You know what I'm talking about – those times when you actually looked up and realized chow was over because you were so absorbed in your work.

The Hidden Gems in Your Military Experience

Maybe you:

- Loved training new recruits - not just going through the motions, but actually seeing that light bulb moment when a concept clicked for them. Remember that feeling when your trainee finally mastered that task you'd been working on? That might mean you're a natural teacher or mentor.
- Got a kick out of fixing complex systems - and not just fixing them, but figuring out why they broke in the first place. Were you the one people called when something was really FUBAR because you

actually enjoyed the challenge? That's not just mechanical aptitude – that's problem-solving gold.
- Found yourself naturally taking charge during projects - even when you weren't the highest-ranking person there. Did people just start looking to you for direction? That's leadership, pure and simple, and it's rare as hell.
- Enjoyed analyzing intelligence and solving puzzles - maybe you were the one who could spot patterns others missed, or you had a knack for connecting seemingly unrelated pieces of information. That's not just analysis – that's strategic thinking.
- Discovered you had a knack for logistics and planning - making sure all the pieces were in the right place at the right time. Remember that field exercise that went smoothly because you thought ten steps ahead? That's project management gold in the civilian world.

The Not-So-Obvious Indicators

But let's go deeper. Think about:

- The additional duties you volunteered for (yeah, those rare times you actually volunteered)
- The problems you solved just because they bugged you, not because you had to
- The topics you read about or watched videos on during your downtime
- The skills you helped others with, even when it wasn't your job
- The tasks that made you lose track of time

Real Talk: The Good, The Bad, and The "Never Again"

Here's an exercise: Grab a paper (or your phone, whatever works) and make three lists:

1. "Hell Yeah" List:
    - Tasks that got you pumped
    - Problems you loved solving
    - Responsibilities you actually looked forward to

2. "Meh" List:
    - Things you were good at but didn't love
    - Tasks that neither excited nor annoyed you
    - Skills you developed but don't really care about

3. "Hell No" List:
    - Tasks that drained your energy
    - Responsibilities that made you dread going to work
    - Things you never want to do again, even if you're good at them

Connecting the Dots

These aren't just random preferences – they're clues to what really drives you. Let's break it down:

- If you loved training others, maybe your future isn't about what you teach but the fact that you teach. The subject matter might be completely different from what you did in the military.
- If complex systems were your thing, think broader than just military equipment. Every industry has complex systems needing people who understand them.
- If leadership lit your fire, remember that civilian leadership looks

different from military leadership – but the core skills translate perfectly.

The Translation Game

Let's play a game called "Military to Civilian Translation." Take those moments that got you excited and think about how they might look in the civilian world:

- Training recruits → Corporate trainer, technical instructor, teacher, coaching consultant
- Systems repair → IT specialist, systems analyst, technology consultant, quality control manager
- Natural leadership → Project manager, team leader, startup founder, operations director
- Intelligence analysis → Data analyst, market researcher, business intelligence specialist, cybersecurity analyst
- Logistics planning → Supply chain manager, operations coordinator, event planner, production manager

Reality Check

Here's the thing: Sometimes, what you loved doing as a "side" part of your military job could become your main civilian career. What additional duty did you enjoy? It might be a full-time gig somewhere. That problem you solved because it annoyed you? Companies pay good money to people who take that kind of initiative.

Remember: You're not looking for an exact match to your military experience. You're looking for the elements that energized you, that made you feel competent and satisfied, that gave you that sense of purpose you had in the service.

Take your time with this. Grab a coffee, find a quiet spot, and really think about what parts of your service lit that fire inside you. Because of those moments? They're not just memories – they're your compass pointing toward what you should be doing next.

The key isn't just identifying what you're good at – plenty of veterans are good at lots of things they never want to do again. The key is finding that sweet spot where your skills, your interests, and your energy all line up. That's where your next mission lies.

The "No BS" Assessment

Let's cut through the noise and get down to what really matters. No corporate speak, no fluffy personality tests, just straight-up honest questions that'll help you figure out your next move. Grab something to write with – you'll want to take notes.

The Questions You Need to Answer (For Real)

1. **If money wasn't an issue, what would you do all day?**

And I mean, really think about this. Don't give me the "I'd sit on a beach" answer – we both know you'd be bored after a week. Think deeper:

- What would you do after you got tired of sleeping in?
- What projects would you start?
- What problems would you try to solve?
- What skills would you want to master?

Here's the thing: Your answer probably contains clues about your ideal career. If you'd spend time rebuilding classic cars, maybe automotive engineering or custom fabrication is your path. If you'd teach kids sports, maybe coaching or youth development is calling you.

2. **What problems do you actually enjoy solving?**

This isn't about what problems you CAN solve – we know you can solve a lot of them. This is about the ones you WANT to solve:

- Are you a person who enjoys untangling complex logistics?
- Do you get satisfaction from mediating conflicts between people?
- Do you love cracking technical challenges?
- Are you energized by finding ways to make processes more efficient?

Break it down:

- What types of problems make you lean in instead of check out?
- What issues do you find yourself thinking about even when you're off duty?
- What kinds of challenges make you say "I got this" instead of "Not this again"?

3. **What tasks make you lose track of time?**

You know those moments when you look up and realize you missed chow because you were so locked in? That's gold right there:

- What were you doing in those moments?
- What aspects of the task captured your attention?
- Why did it engage you so completely?

Think about:

- Times you voluntarily stayed late to finish something
- Projects you worked on during your free time
- Skills you practiced just because you wanted to get better

4. **What do people always come to you for help with?**

This is huge because it's not just about what you're good at – it's about what others see in you:

- Are you the go-to person for explaining complex concepts?

- Do people seek your advice on personal matters?
- Are you the one they call when technology goes haywire?
- Do they come to you for help organizing and planning?

Make two lists:

1. What people officially come to you for (your job duties)
2. What they unofficially seek you out for (your natural strengths)

The second list? That's often where the gold is.

5. **What skills did you develop in service that you genuinely enjoyed using?**

Notice I said "genuinely enjoyed," not just "were good at":

- Which qualifications or certifications did you pursue because you wanted to, not because you had to?
- What skills did you practice or improve in your free time?
- What abilities make you feel confident and capable?

Digging Deeper: The Follow-Up Questions

Now, let's take it a step further. For each answer above, ask yourself:

1. Why did I enjoy this?
2. What specific aspects appealed to me?
3. How could this translate to civilian work?

The Reality Filter

Time to run your answers through some real-world filters:

- Could you do this for 40+ hours a week?
- Would you still enjoy it if you had to do it on someone else's terms?
- Does this have realistic career potential?
- What parts could you compromise on, and what parts are non-negotiable?

Putting It All Together

Look for patterns in your answers:

- Are there common themes?
- Do certain types of work keep coming up?
- What environments seem to match your preferences?
- What values show up repeatedly?

The Hard Truth

Here's the deal: This assessment isn't about finding the perfect job. That doesn't exist. It's about identifying what matters enough to you that you're willing to put up with the inevitable BS that comes with any job. Because every job has its own kind of BS – you're just looking for the kind you can live with.

Action Steps

1. Write down your answers to all these questions. Actually, write them down – don't just think about them.
2. Look for patterns in your responses.
3. Research jobs that match these patterns.
4. Find veterans working in fields that interest you and talk to them.
5. Consider what additional training or education you might need.

Red Flags to Watch For

Your answers might be BS if:

- You're picking something just because it's what you know
- You're choosing based mainly on salary
- You're only considering jobs your buddies are doing
- You're letting your security clearance dictate your path
- You're picking something because it's "practical," but you hate it

Remember: This isn't a test you can fail. It's a tool to help you figure out your next mission. Take your time with it. Be honest with yourself. The military taught you to be methodical and thorough – apply that same approach here. Your future self will thank you.

Bottom Line

The point of this assessment isn't to magically reveal your perfect career. It's to help you identify what actually matters to you in your work life. Because when you know that, you can make better decisions about your next steps.

Take this seriously. You spent years serving your country – now it's time to figure out how to serve yourself and your future just as well.

Breaking Free from the "Should" Trap

Let's talk about the elephant in the room: all those voices telling you what you "should" do with your career. And I'm not just talking about your well-meaning family members or that guy from your unit who's already made the transition. I'm talking about that voice in your own head, too – the one that keeps pushing you toward the "safe" choice.

The "Smart" Choice Syndrome

Here's something that trips up a lot of vets: choosing a career because it seems like the "smart" choice. Let's break down these "shoulds" that might be floating around your head right now:

The Defense Contractor Pipeline

"You should get into defense contracting – that's where the money is!"

Sure, the money can be great. And yes, lots of vets do well in this field. But let's be real:

- Are you excited about the work or just the paycheck?
- Do you actually want to stay in the defense world, or are you ready for something different?
- Are you choosing this because it's familiar and comfortable or because it genuinely interests you?

The Security Clearance Golden Handcuffs

"You can't let that clearance go to waste!"

Look, your security clearance is a valuable asset – no argument there. But here's the truth:

- It's a tool in your toolkit, not your whole identity
- It opens doors, but you don't have to walk through them
- It has an expiration date anyway – so make decisions based on your long-term goals

The "Stay in Your Lane" Pressure

"With your military background, you should stick to what you know."

This one's particularly sneaky because it sounds logical. But:

- Your military experience taught you how to learn and adapt
- Your skills are more transferable than you might think
- You're allowed to want something completely different

Real Talk: The Cost of "Should"

Let's talk about what happens when you let "should" drive your career choices:

The Three-Year Itch

You take the "smart" job, and three years in, you're:

- Making good money but dreading Monday mornings
- Feeling stuck because now you have golden handcuffs
- Watching civilians with less experience doing what you actually want to do

The Delayed Dreams Effect

"I'll just do this for a few years, and then..."

- Those few years turn into a decade
- Your "real" dreams get pushed further back
- You build a lifestyle around a job you don't love

The Identity Crisis

You find yourself:

- Still introducing yourself by your military rank or job
- Feeling like you're just playing a role
- Struggling to see yourself beyond your military identity

Breaking Free: Your Permission Slip

Here's your official permission slip to:

1. Ignore the "Smart" Choice
    - Even if it pays well
    - Even if others don't understand
    - Even if it seems like "throwing away" your experience
2. Start Fresh
    - In a completely different field
    - With entry-level positions if necessary
    - Learning totally new skills

3. Take Risks
    - Start your own business
    - Change industries entirely
    - Create a unique career path

The Reality Check Questions

Before making any career decision, ask yourself:

1. Whose voice is this?
    - Is it really your desire, or someone else's expectation?
    - Are you choosing this, or is fear choosing it?
    - What would you do if no one was watching or giving advice?
2. Fast Forward Five Years
    - Will this choice align with your personal goals?
    - Can you see yourself still being passionate about this work?
    - Does this path lead to where you actually want to go?
3. The Gut Check
    - Does thinking about this career energize or drain you?
    - Are you excited to learn more about it?
    - Would you choose this if the pay was average?

Making Your Own Path

Your military experience and clearance are assets, not obligations. They're:

- Tools to use, not chains to bind you
- Stepping stones, not permanent paths
- Part of your story, not the whole book

Strategic Moves for Breaking Free

1. Research Phase
    - Look beyond the obvious veteran career paths
    - Find veterans who took unconventional routes
    - Explore industries you're curious about, not just comfortable with
2. Testing the Waters
    - Take classes in different fields
    - Shadow professionals in various industries
    - Try side projects or volunteer work
3. Building Your Bridge
    - Use your GI Bill strategically
    - Build new skills while maintaining your current job
    - Network outside the veteran community

The Liberation Plan

1. Identify Your "Shoulds"
    - Write down all the career advice you've received
    - Mark which ones are based on others' expectations
    - Cross out anything that doesn't align with your interests
2. Create Your "Want To" List
    - Dream jobs (no matter how impractical they seem)
    - Work environments that appeal to you
    - Skills you want to develop
3. Bridge the Gap
    - Find ways your military experience supports your new direction

- Identify skills you need to acquire
- Make a timeline for transition

Remember: Your military service was about serving a mission larger than yourself. Your civilian career should be about building a life that serves you. You've earned the right to choose your own path – don't let anyone's "shoulds" tell you differently.

Your military experience is a foundation to build on, not a cage to live in. Use it as a launch pad, not a landing zone.

The Great Skills vs. Interests Reality Check

Picture this: You're a Personnel Chief who can make a 200-person unit's admin work like a Swiss watch. Awards? Done. Evaluations? Perfect. Training records? Spotless. Everyone says you're a natural and that you should definitely go into HR or office management after retirement.

Just one problem: You'd rather eat your own socks than spend another day organizing paperwork.

The "Good At" versus "Want To" Battle

Let's say you were a great administrator in the military. You could organize the hell out of anything. Your Excel skills were so sharp they should've been classified as a weapon. Your files were so well-organized that even your commanding officer's kid could find anything in under two minutes.

But maybe, just maybe, you're done with that. Maybe the thought of spending the next 20 years being "the organized one" makes you want to scream into your DD-214.

And you know what? That's not just okay – it's healthy.

The Wake-Up Call

Take that Maintenance Chief who could diagnose engine problems by sound alone and had a repair success rate that made other units jealous. Everyone said automotive work or facilities maintenance was the obvious choice.

Instead? They opened a bakery.

Why? Because while they were fixing engines, they were dreaming about croissants. Those maintenance skills taught them attention to detail, process management, and quality control – all crucial in baking. But more importantly, baking made them happy in a way that turning wrenches never did.

Breaking Down What Really Matters

Skills You Have and Love Using

This is your sweet spot – the things that light you up:

- Maybe it's not the paperwork you love but the problem-solving
- Not the inventory counts, but the system optimization
- Not the training records, but helping others succeed

Skills You Have But Never Want to Use Again

Be brutally honest here. You've earned that right:

- Sure, you can field strip a radio blindfolded
- Yes, you're the best at supply requisitions
- Of course, you can write award packages in your sleep But do you want to do any of that ever again?

Skills You Want to Develop

This is where it gets exciting:

- What have you always wanted to learn?
- What catches your eye when you're scrolling through job listings?
- What makes you think, "I bet I could do that"?

The Hard Truth About Transferable Skills

Your military skills are like a Swiss Army knife – they can be used for a lot more than their original purpose:

- Leadership isn't just for leading troops
- Attention to detail works in art as well as armories
- Project management applies to building websites as much as building FOBs
- Problem-solving is universal currency

Making the Leap

That Personnel Chief who dreaded more paperwork? They took those organizational skills and became a successful event planner. Instead of organizing files, they're organizing dream weddings. They have the same skills, but completely different energy.

The Maintenance Chief who chose baking? They're using the same precision and troubleshooting skills, just with butter and flour instead of oil and gaskets.

Your Turn: The Honest Assessment

Take a moment and ask yourself:

1. What skills do you actually enjoy using?
2. Which ones are just baggage you're carrying?
3. What have you always wanted to try?

The Permission Slip

Here it is, in writing: You are allowed to:

- Leave your "good at" skills behind
- Start something completely new
- Use your skills in unexpected ways
- Change your mind about your path

The Strategy Forward

1. List your skills (all of them)
2. Circle the ones you enjoy
3. Cross out the ones you're done with
4. Add things you want to learn
5. Look for jobs that match what's circled

Remember: Being good at something is not a life sentence to do it forever. Your skills are tools in your belt, not chains around your ankles. Use them to build the life you want, not the one others expect.

Your next chapter? It's yours to write. Make it one you actually want to read.

Your Official Permission Slip

Breaking the Chains of Expectation

Let's be real for a minute. You've spent years – maybe decades – following orders, meeting standards, and fitting into the military's expectations. Every move, every decision, every role was pretty much mapped out. Now you're staring at a blank canvas of civilian life, and it's both exciting and terrifying.

Here's your official permission slip. Pin it up. Take a picture of it. Hell, get it tattooed backwards on your forehead so you can read it in the mirror every morning.

You Have Permission To:

Want Something Completely Different

- Turn in your wrench for a chef's knife
- Trade your rifle for a camera
- Swap your combat boots for running shoes
- Transform your command presence into stage presence
- Choose creativity over conformity
- Pick passion over predictability

Take Your Sweet Time Figuring It Out

- Spend six months exploring different fields
- Try out three different jobs in two years
- Take classes just to see if you like something
- Shadow professionals in various industries
- Start a side hustle while keeping your day job
- Say "I'm still exploring my options" without shame

Change Your Mind. Then Change It Again

- Realize that your first civilian job isn't for you
- Quit something that looks perfect on paper but feels wrong in reality
- Start over in a new industry
- Adjust your goals as you learn more about yourself
- Pivot when your interests evolve
- Admit when something isn't working

Choose Your Own Path (Even If It Raises Eyebrows)

- Ignore the "but you'd be perfect for contracting" comments
- Smile politely at the "Why would you waste your clearance" questions
- Thank people for their concern while doing your own thing
- Build a career that makes no sense to anyone but you
- Follow your interests, even if they surprise people
- Create a new path when the existing ones don't fit

Build On Your Military Experience Without Being Trapped By It

- Use your leadership skills to lead a creative team instead of a tactical one
- Apply your precision to crafting cocktails instead of maintaining weapons
- Transform your briefing skills into public speaking
- Turn your operational planning into event coordination
- Use your adaptability to create something new
- Leverage your discipline for entrepreneurship

The Fine Print (Because There's Always Fine Print)

You also have permission to:

- Feel uncertain and move forward anyway
- Make mistakes and learn from them
- Succeed in unexpected ways
- Define success differently than others do
- Be proud of your service without being defined by it
- Create a civilian identity that's entirely your own

Breaking It Down Further

The Timeline Is Yours

- There's no "right" speed for transition
- Your battle buddy's path isn't your path
- Success isn't measured in months
- Taking time to explore isn't wasting time

The Standards Are Yours

- You get to define what success looks like
- Your goals can change as you grow
- Excellence can look different in civilian life
- You can create your own measures of achievement

The Choice Is Yours

- Your experience is a toolkit, not a template
- Your future isn't limited by your past
- Your skills can translate in unexpected ways
- Your path doesn't need anyone else's approval

Remember:

You've already proven you can:

- Adapt to new environments
- Learn complex skills
- Overcome tough challenges
- Succeed under pressure
- Lead and follow
- Make hard decisions

Now, you get to choose how to use these abilities.

Your Action Items (Because You're Still Mission-Oriented):

1. Post this permission slip somewhere visible
2. Read it when doubts creep in
3. Share it with fellow veterans who need to hear it
4. Add to it as you discover new freedoms
5. Use it as a shield against unwanted advice
6. Refer to it when making tough decisions

The Bottom Line

You spent years serving others. You followed orders, met standards, and fulfilled expectations. Now it's your turn. Your time. Your choice.

You have permission to make this next chapter exactly what you want it to be.

Sign it. Date it. Own it.

This is your permission slip for freedom. Use it.

Getting Specific: Drilling Down to Your True Career Path

Beyond the Surface Answer

"I want to work in technology" is like saying, "I want to eat food." Okay, great – but what kind? How do you want it prepared? What flavors get you excited?

Let's drill down to what you really want because specifics matter.

Breaking Down the Big Questions

What Kind of Technology?

Instead of: "I want to work in tech," Ask yourself:

- Do you want to build things from scratch or maintain existing systems?
- Are you interested in hardware you can touch or software you can create?
- Do you want to work on:
  - Mobile apps that people use every day?
  - Complex systems that keep businesses running?
  - Security tools that protect data?
  - Networks that connect people?
  - Artificial intelligence and machine learning?
  - Virtual reality applications?

What Problems Do You Want to Solve?

Instead of: "I want to help people," Get specific:

- Do you want to:
  - Make systems more efficient?
  - Protect people from cyber threats?
  - Help businesses grow?
  - Make technology more accessible?
  - Improve communication systems?
  - Create better user experiences?

Think about:

- What problems drive you crazy?
- What inefficiencies make you want to fix them immediately?
- What challenges do you enjoy tackling?

- What type of victories make you feel accomplished?

Who Do You Want to Help?

Instead of: "I want to make a difference," Define your audience:

- Are you passionate about:
    - Helping small businesses compete?
    - Supporting fellow veterans?
    - Making life easier for everyday users?
    - Assisting medical professionals?
    - Enabling educators?
    - Empowering creative professionals?

Consider:

- Who are the end users of your work?
- Whose problems really matter to you?
- What groups do you understand best?
- Who would you be proud to serve?

What Kind of Environment Do You Want to Work In?

Instead of: "Somewhere professional," Get detailed:

- Are you looking for:
    - A fast-paced startup where you wear multiple hats?
    - An established company with clear processes?
    - A remote position with flexible hours?
    - A collaborative team environment?
    - A mix of fieldwork and desk time?
    - A creative space with room for innovation?

Think about:

- Your energy levels throughout the day

- Your preferred work schedule
- Your ideal team size
- Your perfect balance of structure and flexibility

What Does Your Ideal Day Look Like?

Instead of: "A good job with good pay" Break it down hour by hour:

- Morning:
    - Are you starting early or sleeping in?
    - Working from home or commuting?
    - Starting with meetings or diving into solo work?
- Mid-day:
    - Collaborating with team members?
    - Solving technical problems?
    - Meeting with clients?
    - Building new features?
- Afternoon:

Deep focused work?

Training others?

Testing and troubleshooting?

Planning and strategy?

Red Flags to Watch For

You're not being specific enough if you're saying:

- "Something in computers"
- "A good company"
- "Whatever pays well"
- "A normal 9-5"

- "Anything with tech"

Green Lights That Show You're on Track

You're getting specific when you can say:

- "I want to develop mobile apps for small businesses"
- "I want to work remotely with a team of 5-7 people"
- "I want to create accessibility tools for disabled veterans"
- "I want to start at 7 AM and focus on coding until lunch."

The Reality Check

After you've gotten specific, ask yourself:

1. Does this actually exist?
2. Are there jobs that match this vision?
3. What training would I need?
4. Who's already doing this?
5. How can I test this path before committing?

Next Steps

6. Research specific job titles that match your detailed vision
7. Find people already doing what you want to do
8. Look up the actual day-to-day responsibilities
9. Identify the skills and certifications needed
10. Create a concrete plan to bridge any gaps

Remember: The more specific you get, the clearer your path becomes. Don't settle for vague ideas when you can create a detailed roadmap to exactly where you want to go.

Taking Action: Making Your Career Move Real

From Planning to Doing

You've done the soul-searching. You've figured out what you want. Now it's time for the part that should feel familiar – executing the mission. But this time, you're the one calling the shots.

Your Action Plan Broken Down

1. **Research Specific Job Titles**

Don't just scratch the surface here. Dig deep:

Immediate Actions:

- Go beyond the first page of job listings
- Look at different variations of job titles
    - Example: "Project Manager" could be:
        - Technical Project Manager
        - Agile Scrum Master
        - Program Coordinator
        - Operations Lead
        - Delivery Manager

Deep Dive Steps:

- Read at least 20 job descriptions for each title
- Note the common requirements
- Track salary ranges
- Identify required certifications

- Look for emerging trends in the field

2. **Find Veterans Who've Made the Move**

Where to Look:

- LinkedIn Groups (search industry + veterans)
- Professional associations
- Company veteran resource groups
- Veteran job fairs
- Local veteran business groups

How to Approach:

- Be direct but respectful
- Keep initial contact brief
- Specific questions get better responses
- Offer value back when possible

What to Ask:

- What surprised them most about the transition?
- What training actually mattered?
- What would they do differently?
- What skills translated unexpectedly well?
- What challenges weren't they prepared for?

3. **Get the Real Picture of Daily Work**

Research Methods:

- Informational interviews
- Job shadowing
- Industry blogs and forums
- Professional social media
- Company review sites

Key Questions to Answer:

- What's a typical day really like?
- What are the common challenges?
- What tools and software are used?
- How is success measured?
- What's the work-life balance reality?

Red Flags to Watch For:

- High turnover rates
- Vague job descriptions
- Unrealistic requirements
- Poor work-life balance
- Limited growth opportunities

4. **Training and Education Gap Analysis**

Consider Multiple Paths:

- Certifications
- Degree programs
- Boot camps
- Online courses
- Apprenticeships
- On-the-job training

Evaluation Criteria:

- Time investment
- Cost vs. benefit
- Industry recognition
- Hands-on experience
- Employment rates

5. **Strategic Networking**

Building Your Network Map:

- Inner Circle: Direct contacts
- Second Ring: Their contacts
- Outer Ring: Industry connections

Networking Venues:

- Professional associations
- Industry conferences
- Online forums
- Local meetups
- LinkedIn groups
- Veteran organizations

Networking Strategy:

- Set monthly connection goals
- Track your interactions
- Follow up consistently
- Share valuable content
- Offer help before asking for it

Creating Your Action Timeline

Immediate Actions (Next 30 Days)

- Create a spreadsheet of target job titles
- Join 3 relevant professional groups
- Set up job alerts
- Update your LinkedIn profile
- Reach out to 5 veterans in your target field

Short-Term Goals (90 Days)

- Complete basic certifications
- Attend industry events
- Build a professional portfolio
- Start informational interviews
- Begin training programs

Medium-Term Goals (6 Months)

- Complete advanced certifications
- Gain practical experience
- Build industry relationships
- Start job applications
- Consider internships or volunteering

Overcoming Common Roadblocks

Time Management

- Block schedule your research
- Use lunch breaks for networking
- Study during commute time
- Set specific research hours

Financial Planning

- Budget for certifications
- Research GI Bill options
- Look for veteran scholarships
- Consider employer reimbursement
- Plan for transition period

Knowledge Gaps

- Use free online resources
- Join study groups
- Find a mentor
- Take advantage of veteran programs

Remember

- Progress over perfection
- Consistent small actions add up
- Keep updating your plan
- Stay flexible but focused
- Document everything

Your Daily Checklist

Morning:

- Review job alerts
- Check industry news
- Plan networking contacts

Evening:

- Update progress tracker
- Review next day's goals
- Follow up on connections

The Bottom Line

Taking action doesn't mean doing everything at once. It means making consistent, focused progress toward your goal. Break it down, track it, and keep moving forward.

Start with one action today. Just one. Then another tomorrow. Build momentum. You've done harder things in the military – you've got this.

Remember

This isn't about finding just any job. It's about finding YOUR job. The one that makes sense for who you are now and who you want to become. Don't rush this process. Take time to explore, ask questions, and maybe even try a few things out.

Your service gave you discipline, adaptability, and a strong work ethic. Now it's time to use those qualities to build a civilian career that actually means something to you. Not just a job you can do, but one you want to do.

What's your next mission going to be?

Debrief: Chapter 9 - Balancing Family, Career, and Personal Growth

1. **Prioritize Open Communication:**
   Keep your family involved in your transition journey. Discuss career plans, potential moves, and adjustments to ensure everyone feels included and supported.
2. **Set Family-Centric Goals:**
   Align your career aspirations with your family's needs. Consider factors like location, work-life balance, and school or healthcare requirements when making decisions.

3. **Establish Healthy Boundaries:**
   Learn to separate work from personal life. Create routines and boundaries that allow you to be fully present with your family and avoid burnout.

4. **Embrace Flexibility:**
   Transitioning into civilian life may bring unexpected challenges for you and your family. Be prepared to adapt plans as needed while maintaining focus on long-term stability.

5. **Encourage Family Resilience:**
   Support your spouse and children in finding their own paths, whether it's pursuing careers, education, or hobbies. Celebrate their growth as part of the overall transition.

6. **Access Family Support Resources:**
   Use programs like Military OneSource, veteran community organizations, and family counseling services to navigate challenges and strengthen your family's foundation.

7. **Invest in Personal Growth:**
   Balance your responsibilities by dedicating time to your own physical, emotional, and professional development. A strong sense of self contributes to a thriving family dynamic.

8. **Celebrate Wins Together:**
   Acknowledge and celebrate milestones, both big and small, during your transition. Recognizing successes fosters unity and keeps morale high for everyone.

Chapter 10: Where to Find Civilian Jobs

Let's talk about finding a civilian job. Not the interviews, not the resumes, not the networking – just straight-up where to look and how to find open positions. If you're reading this, you're probably wondering "Where are all these civilian jobs I keep hearing about?" Don't worry – they're out there, and we're going to show you exactly where to find them.

Think of this as your road map to job hunting. In the military, you knew exactly where to go for your next assignment – check the board, talk to your assignment manager, or wait for orders. The civilian world isn't that straightforward, but there are specific places and methods to find jobs. Here's the real deal on where and how to look.

First, understand that civilian jobs pop up all the time. Unlike the military where jobs open up with PCS seasons or end of contract dates, civilian companies hire whenever they need someone. That means new jobs appear daily – sometimes hourly. Your job search needs to be regular and consistent.

Here's something they don't tell you in TAP class: only about 20% of available jobs are posted on the major job boards you hear about. The other 80%? They're filled through other channels. That's why you need to know all the places to look, not just the obvious ones.

The civilian job hunt is like running multiple reconnaissance missions at once. You need to:

- Monitor multiple sources

- Track different leads
- Follow up on opportunities
- Stay organized
- Keep records of where you've looked
- Note which sources are producing the best leads

You also need to understand that civilian job titles aren't standardized like military ones. The same job might be called:

- Manager at one company
- Lead at another
- Coordinator at a third
- Director at a fourth

This means you can't just search for one title – you need to search for multiple variations of the same role. What we called a "Logistics Specialist" in the military might be:

- Supply Chain Coordinator
- Materials Manager
- Inventory Specialist
- Operations Analyst
- Logistics Coordinator
- Distribution Manager

Even location searches are different. Instead of just searching for "Camp Pendleton" or "Fort Bragg," you need to think about:

- City names
- County names
- Metropolitan areas
- Regions
- Remote opportunities
- Hybrid positions
- Travel roles

And here's something else that's different: in the civilian world, job requirements are often wish lists, not hard requirements. In the military, if a position required a specific school or qualification, that was non-negotiable. In the civilian world, job postings might list ten "requirements" but actually only need five of them. Don't let a long list of requirements scare you off.

The timing is different too. Unlike military assignments that might post months in advance, civilian jobs often need to be filled quickly. A job posted today might:

- Need someone to start next week
- Be filled before the posting comes down
- Stay open for months
- Close suddenly without warning
- Reopen after being closed

That's why you need a systematic approach to your search. You can't just check once a week or wait for jobs to come to you. You need to be actively searching, regularly checking multiple sources, and ready to apply quickly when you find something promising.

In the following sections, we'll break down exactly where to look, how to search effectively, and how to track your progress. We'll cover everything from major job boards to industry-specific sites, from company career pages to recruiter relationships. Think of it as your field manual for civilian job hunting – complete with intel on where to find the opportunities you're looking for.

The jobs are out there. You just need to know where to look and how to find them. Let's get started with the specifics.

The Basics: Job Boards

Picture this common scenario: A service member fresh from final formation sits down with an energy drink, planning to knock out their job search in an afternoon. They heard about Indeed.com at TAP class, so they figure that's the place to start. Eight hours and 200 applications later, they're confident the calls will start rolling in. Three weeks later – nothing but automated rejections and crickets.

This happens to thousands of transitioning service members yearly. They treat the job search like a direct assault when it should be more like a long-term reconnaissance mission. Job boards are tools, not magic wands. You wouldn't go into battle with just one weapon, and you shouldn't attack your job search with just one method.

Job boards are like the chow hall – everyone uses them because they're convenient and get the job done. But just like you wouldn't eat there for every meal when better options exist, don't rely solely on job boards. They're a good starting point, but that's all – a starting point. Think of them as your basic load-out. Essential gear, but how you use them matters more than simply having them.

Major Job Sites

Let's break down each of these job sites and what they're good for. Each one has its own strengths, and knowing how to use them properly can make the difference between wasting time and landing interviews.

Indeed.com - The Complete Guide

The biggest player in the game – think of it like the Fort Hood of job sites. Over 3 million companies post jobs here, with new ones popping up every 10 seconds. But size isn't everything – it's how you use it.

What Makes Indeed Different:

- Aggregates jobs from company websites and other job boards - this means if a company posts a job on their website, it usually shows up here
- Has the most up-to-date listings (many companies post here first)
- Offers salary comparisons and company reviews
- Includes a resume database employers actually use

The Indeed Game Plan

1. **Setting Up Your Profile**

Don't just throw your resume up there and hope for the best. Here's how to do it right:

- Upload multiple versions of your resume for different types of jobs
- Fill out every single section of your profile
- Add your certifications and licenses
- Include a professional-looking photo (yes, it matters)
- Write a clear, professional summary
- List your skills using civilian keywords
- Make your profile public so employers can find you

2. **Search Like a Pro**

The "Advanced Job Search" is your best friend. Here's how to master it:

Location Strategy:

- Start with a 25-mile radius, then adjust based on results
- Use the "remote" filter if you're open to work-from-home

- Try searching by city, then by state for different results
- Consider searching multiple locations if you're willing to relocate

Salary Filters:

- Always set a minimum (don't waste time on low-ball offers)
- Check salary estimates before applying
- Use the salary filter to negotiate better - if you see similar jobs paying more, you know the range
- Remember some postings don't list salaries - don't automatically skip these

Date Posted Strategy:

- Check "Last 24 hours" first thing each morning
- Use "3 days" for your main search
- Only go back further if you're in a very specialized field
- Older posts might mean the company is struggling to fill the position - this could be a red flag

Job Type Filters:

- Be specific about full-time, part-time, contract
- Consider contract-to-hire positions
- Check "temporary" if you need something while searching
- Multiple job types can be selected - use this to your advantage

3. **Advanced Search Techniques**

Keywords:

- Use both military and civilian terms
- Try abbreviations AND spelled-out terms
- Include certification names
- Use industry-specific software names
- Add skill-based keywords

Boolean Search Tips:

- Use quotation marks for exact phrases: "project manager."
- Use OR for alternatives: manager OR supervisor OR lead
- Use NOT to exclude: manager, NOT sales
- Combine them: ("project manager" OR "program manager") NOT junior

4. **Application Strategies**

The "Easy Apply" Feature:

- Good for high-volume applications
- Better when your resume closely matches the job
- Still customize your cover letter
- Follow up on the company website if possible

Direct Applications:

- Usually takes longer but often more effective
- Let you customize application materials
- Better for jobs requiring specific qualifications
- Often preferred by larger companies

5. **Following Up**

After Applying:

- Note the company name and position
- Record the date you applied
- Save the job description (they disappear after closing)
- Set a reminder to follow up in one week
- Connect with company recruiters on LinkedIn

6. **Power User Tips**

Save Time:

- Create job alert emails

- Save searches for regular checking
- Use the mobile app for quick applications
- Keep your profile updated
- Check "similar jobs" at the bottom of postings

Avoid Common Mistakes:

- Don't apply to jobs older than 30 days
- Don't ignore the company reviews
- Don't skip the salary research
- Don't apply without matching at least 60% of the requirements
- Don't forget to check the company's direct website

7. **Red Flags to Watch For:**

- Jobs reposted multiple times
- Salaries well above market rate
- Vague job descriptions
- No company information
- Too many urgent/immediate start positions
- Companies with poor reviews
- Missing or unclear location information

8. **Weekly Indeed Routine:**

Monday:

- Check weekend postings
- Update your profile
- Review saved searches

Tuesday-Thursday:

- Morning: Check new postings
- Afternoon: Follow up on applications
- Evening: Research companies

Friday:

- Final check for the week
- Plan next week's search
- Update application tracking

Remember: Indeed is a tool, not a full job search strategy. Use it as part of your larger job search mission, but don't rely on it exclusively. Combine it with other job boards, networking, and direct company applications for the best results.

LinkedIn Jobs - The Complete Guide

It's not your typical job board – it's like having your resume, network, and job applications all in one spot. A lot of veterans skip LinkedIn because it seems too "corporate," but here's why that's a mistake.

What Makes LinkedIn Different:

- Employers can see your full professional profile
- Shows you who posted the job and who you might know at the company
- Tells you how many people have applied
- Lets you see where other veterans work

The LinkedIn Battle Plan

1. **Building Your Profile (Your Digital Military Record)**

Your profile is your digital storefront. Make it count:

Profile Picture:

- Professional headshot (no uniform photos)
- Business casual or business professional attire
- Clear, well-lit, recent photo

- Smile - you want to look approachable

Background Photo:

- Professional scene or company logo
- Industry-related image
- Clean, uncluttered design
- No military photos unless working in the defense industry

Headline:

- More than just a job title
- Include key skills or certifications
- Use industry keywords
- Make it attention-grabbing

About Section:

- Write in first person
- Tell your career story
- Highlight major achievements
- Include keywords for your industry
- Keep it to 3-4 short paragraphs

Experience Section:

- Translate military roles to civilian terms
- Focus on achievements, not just duties
- Use numbers and metrics
- Include relevant military accomplishments
- List volunteer work and side projects

Skills Section:

- Add at least 30 relevant skills
- Get endorsements for top skills
- Take skill assessments

- Pin your most important skills
- Update regularly

2. **Networking Strategy**

Connect With:

- Former military colleagues
- Industry professionals
- Company recruiters
- Alumni from your school
- People in target companies

Groups to Join:

- Veteran professional groups
- Industry-specific groups
- Location-based groups
- Company alumni groups
- Professional associations

Engagement Plan:

- Like and comment on posts
- Share relevant articles
- Post industry insights
- Engage with company posts
- Support other veterans

3. **Job Search Tactics**

Setting Up Job Alerts:

- Use multiple job titles
- Set location preferences
- Include salary ranges
- Specify industry
- Add preferred companies

Using Easy Apply:

- Customize for each application
- Check application status
- Follow up with recruiters
- Save jobs for later
- Track your applications

Advanced Search Techniques:

- Use Boolean operators
- Search by Company
- Filter by experience level
- Check company connections
- Look at similar jobs

4. **Company Research**

Follow Companies:

- Target employers
- Competitors
- Industry leaders
- Growing startups
- Veteran-friendly businesses

What to Track:

- New job postings
- Company updates
- Employee posts
- Growth news
- Culture posts

5. **Recruiter Interaction**

When Recruiters View Your Profile:

- Check their company
- View their recent activity
- Send a connection request
- Follow their company
- Engage with their posts

Message Templates:

- Thank you notes
- Follow-up messages
- Connection requests
- Interview follow-ups
- Status check-ins

6. **Premium Features (Worth It?)**

LinkedIn Premium Career:

- Worth it during an active job search
- See who viewed your profile
- Compare yourself to other applicants
- Send InMail to recruiters
- Access salary insights

How Long to Keep It:

- 1-3 months during heavy search
- Cancel when job secured
- Reactivate for future searches
- Use free trial strategically

7. **Weekly LinkedIn Routine**

Monday:

- Check weekend job postings
- Update profile if needed
- Review connection requests

- Check company updates
- Engage with feed

Wednesday:

- Apply to new positions
- Follow up on applications
- Connect with new people
- Share an update or article
- Check "Jobs You May Like"

Friday:

- Final applications for the week
- Schedule next week's tasks
- Review profile views
- Engage with network
- Save interesting jobs

8. **Common Mistakes to Avoid**

Profile Mistakes:

- Incomplete sections
- Military jargon
- Poor quality photo
- No recommendations
- Outdated information

Networking Mistakes:

- Generic connection requests
- Not engaging with the network
- Ignoring messages
- Over-posting
- Being too salesy

Application Mistakes:

- Mass applying
- Not researching companies
- Skipping cover letters
- Not following up
- Ignoring company culture

9. **Power User Tips**

Stand Out:

- Get recommendations from senior connections
- Write articles on your expertise
- Share industry insights
- Create original content
- Help other veterans

Visibility Tricks:

- Update your profile regularly
- Engage daily (even briefly)
- Use relevant hashtags
- Comment thoughtfully
- Share your achievements

Remember: LinkedIn is a powerful tool that combines networking, job searching, and personal branding. Use it consistently but don't let it consume all your time. Spend 30 minutes daily maintaining your presence, and schedule focused job search time separately.

The key to LinkedIn's success is being authentic, professional, and consistent.

ZipRecruiter - The Complete Guide

Think of this as a carpet bombing run for your job search – one application hits multiple employers. But there's a strategy to using it effectively. ZipRecruiter is different from other job sites because it actively promotes your profile to employers rather than just letting you apply for jobs.

What Makes ZipRecruiter Different:

- Uses AI to match you with jobs
- Sends your profile to multiple employers at once
- Employers can reach out to you directly
- Shows you how strong a match you are for positions

The ZipRecruiter Strategy Guide

1. **Profile Setup (Your Target Package)**

Your Basic Profile:

- Professional summary (clear and focused)
- Work history (civilian terms)
- Education and training
- Certifications and clearances
- Skills (both technical and soft)
- Availability and preferences

Resume Tips:

- Upload multiple versions
- Target different industries
- Use different skill emphases
- Include keywords from job posts
- Keep file names professional

Assessment Questions:

- Answer ALL of them
- Be honest about experience
- Complete optional ones too
- Update answers periodically
- Take skill tests when offered

2. **Using the AI Matching System**

How the AI Works:

- Scans your profile and resumes
- Matches keywords and skills
- Considers experience level
- Looks at location preferences
- Evaluate your responses to assessments

Maximize Your Match Score:

- Use industry-standard terms
- Include specific skills
- List software proficiency
- Add certifications
- Update regularly

3. **Application Strategy**

"Job Fit" Scoring:

- Focus on 80%+ matches first
- Look closely at 60-80% matches
- Understand why you match
- Use feedback to improve profile
- Don't ignore lower matches entirely

Response Time:

- Set up mobile alerts
- Check messages daily
- Respond within 24 hours
- Be ready for quick interviews
- Keep your calendar updated

4. **Search Techniques**

Basic Search:

- Use multiple job titles
- Try different locations
- Set salary requirements
- Filter by job type
- Check company ratings

Advanced Filters:

- Experience level
- Industry-specific
- Company size
- Benefits offered
- Remote options

5. **Managing Employer Contact**

When Employers Reach Out:

- Research company quickly
- Check company reviews
- Prepare basic questions
- Have resume ready
- Set up phone/video capability

Response Templates:

- Interest confirmation
- Schedule interview
- Request more information
- Follow up
- Thank you messages

6. **Tracking System**

Keep Records Of:

- Applications submitted
- Employer contacts
- Interview requests
- Follow-up dates
- Job post saves

Using the Dashboard:

- Check application status
- Monitor profile views
- Track employer responses
- Save interesting jobs
- Review past applications

7. **Daily ZipRecruiter Routine**

Morning:

- Check new matches
- Respond to messages
- Review "Invited to Apply"
- Update availability
- Apply to the best matches

Afternoon:

- Research companies
- Prepare applications
- Follow up on interviews
- Update profile if needed
- Save interesting jobs

8. **Power User Tips**

Maximize Visibility:

- Log in daily
- Update profile weekly
- Apply within 48 hours
- Complete all assessments
- Engage with all employer contact

Alert Setup:

- Multiple job titles
- Various locations
- Salary ranges
- Industry specifics
- Company types

9. **Common Pitfalls to Avoid**

Profile Mistakes:

- Incomplete information
- Military-heavy language
- Missing skills
- Outdated contact info
- Poor job title matches

Application Mistakes:

- Slow response time
- Generic responses
- Not researching companies
- Ignoring assessment questions
- Missing employer messages

10. Success Metrics

Track Your Results:

- Application to response ratio
- Employer contact rate
- Interview conversion rate
- Job match quality
- Profile view frequency

Adjust Based On:

- Response patterns
- Interview results
- Job match accuracy
- Employer feedback
- Application success rate

11. Best Practices

Profile Maintenance:

- Weekly updates
- Fresh achievements
- New skills
- Updated preferences
- Current availability

Communication:

- Professional tone
- Quick responses
- Clear availability
- Follow-up protocol
- Thank you messages

Remember: ZipRecruiter works best when you're actively engaged with it. The AI system learns from your interactions, so the more you use it, the better your matches become. Don't just set it and forget it – treat it like an ongoing mission that needs regular attention and updates.

Key to Success: Balance between casting a wide net and maintaining quality in your applications. Just because you can apply to many jobs quickly doesn't mean you should apply to everything. Stay focused on your target positions and use the tools to your advantage.

Glassdoor - The Complete Intel Platform

More than just a job board – it's your intel-gathering platform. Think of Glassdoor as your S2 shop for the civilian job market. It's where you gather intelligence before entering unfamiliar territory. Here's your complete reconnaissance guide.

What Makes Glassdoor Different:

- Real salary data from employees
- Actual interview questions companies ask
- Employee reviews of companies
- Photos of offices and work environments
- Information about benefits and culture

The Glassdoor Intelligence Guide

1. **Company Research (Your Recon Mission)**

Before The Application:

- Overall company rating
- CEO approval rating
- Recommend to friend percentage
- Business outlook opinions
- Company culture indicators

Red Flags to Watch:

- High turnover mentions
- Poor work-life balance
- Declining business trends
- Negative management reviews
- Lack of career growth

Green Flags to Note:

- Veteran-friendly mentions
- Good training programs
- Clear advancement paths
- Positive leadership reviews
- Strong benefits package

2. **Salary Intelligence**

Using Salary Data:

- Compare similar job titles
- Check location differences
- Note experience requirements
- Look at bonus structures
- Review benefits value

"Know Your Worth" Tool:

- Input your experience
- Add certifications
- Include location
- Note industry specifics
- Update regularly

Compensation Package Elements:

- Base salary
- Bonuses
- Stock options
- Benefits value
- Additional perks

3. **Interview Reconnaissance**

Interview Prep:

- Common questions asked
- Interview difficulty rating
- Interview length
- Process steps
- Required preparations

Types of Interviews to Prepare For:

- Phone screenings
- Video interviews
- Technical assessments
- Panel interviews
- Culture fit discussions

4. **Review Analysis**

Reading Employee Reviews:

- Look for patterns
- Check dates
- Note department differences
- Read between the lines
- Consider company responses

Focus Areas:

- Work-life balance
- Career opportunities
- Compensation/benefits
- Senior management
- Culture and values

5. **Using the Job Search Function**

Search Strategy:

- Filter by rating
- Use salary filters
- Check experience level
- Note post date
- Review easy-apply options

Application Tracking:

- Save interesting jobs
- Note application dates
- Track follow-ups
- Record interview dates
- Save company research

6. **Benefits Analysis**

Compare Benefits:

- Health insurance
- Retirement plans

- PTO policies
- Professional development
- Work flexibility

Hidden Benefits to Look For:

- Training programs
- Tuition reimbursement
- Certification support
- Veteran programs
- Career development

7. **Company Culture Intel**

Culture Indicators:

- Communication style
- Leadership approach
- Work environment
- Team dynamics
- Growth opportunities

Office Environment:

- Physical workspace
- Remote options
- Equipment provided
- Office locations
- Facilities available

8. **Advanced Intelligence Gathering**

Company Updates:

- Recent news
- Growth plans
- Leadership changes
- New initiatives

- Industry position

Competitor Analysis:

- Similar companies
- Industry standards
- Market position
- Growth trajectory
- Employment brand

9. **Using Photos and Media**

What to Look For:

- Office Layout
- Work environment
- Dress code
- Team activities
- Facility quality

Reading Between the Lines:

- Employee engagement
- Company culture
- Professional atmosphere
- Workstyle
- Team dynamics

10. **Interview Process Intel**

Preparation Tips:

- Study reported questions
- Note interview structure
- Review required skills
- Prepare examples
- Research interviewers

Common Assessments:

- Technical tests
- Personality assessments
- Skills evaluations
- Culture fit questions
- Background checks

11. Best Practices for Intel Gathering

Daily Operations:

- Check company updates
- Monitor salary trends
- Review new reviews
- Track interview reports
- Note culture changes

Information Organization:

- Create company profiles
- Track salary data
- Save interview notes
- Document red flags
- Record green flags

12. Strategic Intelligence Use

Decision Making:

- Company Comparison
- Salary negotiations
- Interview preparation
- Offer evaluation
- Career planning

Long-term Monitoring:

- Industry trends
- Company growth
- Management changes
- Culture shifts
- Market conditions

Remember: Glassdoor is your intelligence-gathering platform. Use it before, during, and after your job search process. The more intel you gather, the better prepared you'll be for interviews, negotiations, and making informed decisions about your career moves.

Key to Success: Cross-reference information from multiple sources. Don't rely solely on Glassdoor - use it as one piece of your total intelligence-gathering operation. Compare what you find here with LinkedIn, company websites, and other sources to get the complete picture.

Monster and CareerBuilder - The Old Guard That Still Delivers

The old guard of online job searching. Think of these sites like the seasoned NCOs of the job board world - they might not have all the flashy new features, but they know their stuff and still get results. They are not as trendy as LinkedIn or Indeed, but they're still in the fight and often have opportunities you won't find elsewhere.

What Makes Them Different:

- Lots of traditional industry jobs
- Often used by government contractors
- Good for finding recruiter connections
- Many older, established companies still post here first

Making These Sites Work For You

1. **Profile Setup (The Foundation)**

Monster Profile:

- Professional Summary
- Work History
- Education details
- Technical skills
- Certifications
- Security clearances
- Availability status

CareerBuilder Profile:

- Career objectives
- Industry experience
- Preferred locations
- Salary requirements
- Work authorization
- Travel preferences
- Relocation options

2. **Resume Strategy**

Resume Versions:

- Industry-specific versions
- Skill-focused versions
- Location-based versions
- Experience-level versions
- Security clearance versions

Resume Tips:

- Use their resume builders
- Include keywords from job posts

- Update monthly
- Keep formatting simple
- Use civilian terminology

3. **Working with Recruiters**

Recruiter Interaction:

- Respond within 24 hours
- Keep communication professional
- Ask about multiple opportunities
- Request company information
- Maintain recruiter relationships

Recruiter Red Flags:

- Requesting personal information
- Asking for payment
- Pressuring for quick decisions
- Being vague about positions
- Not representing specific companies

4. **Using the Career Tools**

Monster's Tools:

- Resume assessment
- Career personality test
- Salary calculator
- Skills gap analysis
- Interview preparation

CareerBuilder's Tools:

- Resume Builder
- Job fit scorer
- Career tests
- Salary research

- Skills evaluations

5. **Search Techniques**

Basic Search:

- Use multiple job titles
- Try different locations
- Include industry keywords
- Check company names
- Filter by experience level

Advanced Search:

- Salary ranges
- Job type
- Travel requirements
- Security clearance
- Remote options

6. **Application Strategy**

Before Applying:

- Research the company
- Check salary ranges
- Review job requirements
- Look for keywords
- Note application deadlines

After Applying:

- Save the job posting
- Track the application
- Follow up after a week
- Connect with recruiters
- Research similar roles

7. **Industry Focus**

Traditional Industries:

- Manufacturing
- Healthcare
- Finance
- Government contracting
- Construction
- Transportation
- Logistics

Defense Sector:

- Contractor positions
- Security-cleared jobs
- Base support roles
- Technical positions
- Program management

8. **Weekly Routine**

Monday:

- Check new postings
- Update availability
- Review saved searches
- Respond to recruiters
- Update profile

Mid-Week:

- Apply to new positions
- Follow up on applications
- Check recruiter messages
- Research companies
- Save interesting jobs

Friday:

- Final applications
- Weekly follow-ups
- Update job alerts
- Plan next week
- Review results

9. Special Features

Monster's Unique Features:

- Military skills translator
- Virtual career fairs
- Resume visibility controls
- Company profiles
- Industry Insights

CareerBuilder's Unique Features:

- Job competition data
- Company research tools
- Mobile application options
- Skills matching
- Labor market data

10. Best Practices

Profile Maintenance:

- Monthly updates
- Fresh accomplishments
- New skills
- Current contact info
- Updated preferences

Application Tracking:

- Company names
- Position titles
- Application dates
- Recruiter contacts
- Follow-up status

10. Making the Most of Older Technology

Working with Limitations:

- Keep formatting simple
- Use standard file formats
- Double-check submissions
- Save confirmation emails
- Screenshot applications

Maximizing Results:

- Complete all fields
- Use all keyword spaces
- Fill out assessments
- Answer all questions
- Provide all requested info

11. Success Metrics

Track Your Results:

- Application responses
- Recruiter contacts
- Interview requests
- Offer rates
- Salary ranges

Adjust Based On:

- Response patterns
- Industry trends
- Location results
- Position levels
- Salary targets

Remember: These sites might seem old school, but they're still valuable tools, especially for traditional industries and defense contractors. Many companies have been using these platforms for years and trust them for their hiring needs.

Key to Success: Use these sites as part of your overall strategy, especially if you're interested in traditional industries or government contracting. Their established networks can open doors that newer platforms might miss.

ClearanceJobs.com - Your Cleared Career Gateway

Think of ClearanceJobs.com as a restricted access job site – it's the specialized platform where your security clearance is actually an advantage. This isn't your standard job board; it's a targeted platform specifically for cleared professionals.

What Makes ClearanceJobs Different:

- Requires active clearance verification
- Only cleared candidates and employers
- Direct messaging with security officers and recruiters
- Specific salary data for cleared positions
- Network of cleared professionals

The ClearanceJobs Strategy Guide

1. **Profile Setup (Your Cleared Portfolio)**

Security Information:

- Current clearance level
- Investigation date
- Polygraph status (CI/FS)
- Clearance verification
- Special accesses
- Compartments

Professional Details:

- Technical skills
- Relevant contracts
- Government agencies
- Contract vehicles
- Certifications (8570/8140)
- Program experience

2. **Clearance-Specific Elements**

Clearance Documentation:

- Investigation dates
- Reinvestigation timeline
- Clearance transfer status
- Current employer
- Clearance verification process

Special Access Programs:

- List relevant SAPs
- Note read-on status
- Include program types
- Document special skills

- Note facility clearances

3. **Working with Cleared Recruiters**

Recruiter Interaction:

- Verify their credentials
- Check company FSO info
- Discuss clearance transfer
- Ask about contract details
- Confirm facility clearances

Questions to Ask:

- Contract length
- Clearance requirements
- Investigation requirements
- Program details (if releasable)
- Site access needs

4. **Job Search Strategy**

Search Parameters:

- Clearance level required
- Polygraph requirements
- Contract vehicles
- Government agencies
- Geographic locations
- SCIF requirements

Contract Focus:

- Prime contractors
- Sub-contractors
- Direct government
- Contract length
- Contract type

5. **Location Considerations**

Facility Requirements:

- SCIF access
- Base access
- Facility clearance level
- Special compartments
- Physical location

Geographic Factors:

- Cleared facilities nearby
- Government installations
- Contractor presence
- Clearance processing centers
- Agency locations

6. **Salary Understanding**

Cleared Pay Factors:

- Clearance level premiums
- Poly bump considerations
- Program-specific rates
- Contract bill rates
- Location differentials

Benefits Package:

- Clearance maintenance
- Investigation costs
- Training requirements
- Certification support
- Special program access

7. **Daily Operations**

Regular Checks:

- New position postings
- Recruiter messages
- Clearance updates
- Contract awards
- Program changes

Application Process:

- Verify requirements
- Check investigation needs
- Confirm poly status
- Review project details
- Note clearance transfer needs

8. **Network Building**

Cleared Connections:

- FSO contacts
- Program managers
- Technical leads
- Contract officers
- Cleared colleagues

Professional Groups:

- Cleared communities
- Agency-specific groups
- Contract teams
- Technical specialties
- Program areas

9. **Interview Preparation**

Clearance Topics:

- Investigation status
- Poly experience

- Program Knowledge
- Agency familiarity
- Access history

Technical Preparation:

- Relevant projects
- Cleared experience
- Program familiarity
- Agency systems
- Contract experience

10. Common Pitfalls

Avoid These Mistakes:

- Discussing classified details
- Revealing program specifics
- Naming sensitive projects
- Posting sensitive locations
- Sharing contract details

Security Awareness:

- OPSEC considerations
- Social media presence
- Public information
- Contact methods
- Meeting locations

11. Career Progression

Clearance Value:

- Maintain investigation currency
- Keep poly current
- Document special access
- Track program experience

- Note contract experience

Growth Opportunities:

- Higher clearance levels
- Additional polytypes
- New program access
- Agency expansions
- Contract advancement

12. **Pro Tips for Success**

Maximize Visibility:

- Regular profile updates
- Active network building
- Quick response times
- Current availability
- Clear career goals

Best Practices:

- Keep FSO informed
- Track investigation dates
- Document access changes
- Maintain certifications
- Update contract experience

Remember: ClearanceJobs is a specialized platform, so treat it differently than standard job boards. Your clearance is a valuable asset; make sure your profile and activity reflect its value while maintaining proper security protocols.

Key to Success: Stay active on the platform. Cleared positions often move quickly, and having an updated, active profile can make a difference in landing premium opportunities.

Special Note: Never post specific classified program details, project names, or locations. Keep all information at the publicly releasable level.

Pro Tips for All Job Sites:

1. Don't rely on any single site
2. Set up alerts with specific criteria:
    - Job titles (and variations)
    - Location preferences
    - Salary ranges
    - Company names
    - Industry keywords
3. Organize Your Search:
    - Keep a spreadsheet of where you've applied
    - Track application dates
    - Note any responses
    - Save job descriptions (they often disappear after posting closes)
    - Record any communication with recruiters
4. Time Management:
    - Check new postings first thing in the morning
    - Apply to jobs posted within the last 48 hours when possible
    - Spend no more than 2-3 hours per day on job boards
    - Set aside time weekly to update your profiles

Remember: Job boards are tools, not magic wands. They work best when:

- You use them consistently
- You fill out profiles completely
- You apply to jobs promptly
- You track your applications
- You follow up appropriately
- You combine them with other job search strategies

The spray and pray method doesn't work – you need to be tactical about your applications. Quality over quantity wins every time.

Industry-Specific Gold Mines

Different industries post jobs in different places:

Tech Jobs

- Dice.com
- BuiltIn (for tech hubs like Austin, NYC, etc.)
- Stack Overflow Jobs
- GitHub Jobs

Manufacturing/Logistics

- Manufacturing.net
- LogisticsJobs.com
- Supply Chain 247

Healthcare

- HealtheCareers
- Hospital Career Sites
- Healthcare Job Sites

Finance

- eFinancialCareers
- Banking Job Sites
- Insurance Company Sites

Company Career Pages

Go straight to the source:

1. Make a list of companies you're interested in
2. Bookmark their career pages
3. Sign up for their talent communities
4. Set up job alerts directly from them

Pro Tip: Many companies post jobs on their own sites before job boards. Check company sites first.

The Hidden Job Market

This is where most jobs actually are:

Recruiting Firms

- Research firms specializing in your industry
- Connect with veteran-friendly recruiters
- Submit your resume to multiple firms
- Stay in regular contact

Professional Associations

- Join industry associations
- Check their job boards
- Attend their events
- Read their newsletters

LinkedIn (The Right Way)

1. Follow companies you're interested in
2. Turn on "Open to Work" (privately)
3. Follow industry leaders
4. Join industry groups

5. Check the jobs tab daily

Veteran-Specific Resources

These often have jobs that aren't posted elsewhere:

- Veteran Job Boards
- Veteran Recruiting Events
- Company Veteran Programs
- Veteran Job Fairs

Local Resources

Don't overlook what's in your backyard:

- Chamber of Commerce job boards
- Local business journals
- Regional job sites
- Local company websites

How to Search Effectively

Search Terms That Work

Instead of searching for your MOS, try:

- Industry keywords
- Skill-based terms
- Job titles (multiple variations)
- Location-based terms
- Company names

Setting Up Your Search Game

1. Create job alerts on all major sites

2. Use Boolean search terms (AND, OR, NOT)
3. Save your searches
4. Check new postings daily
5. Track where you've applied

Quick Tips for Smart Searching

- Search job titles multiple ways (Manager/Director/Lead)
- Use industry abbreviations AND spelled-out terms
- Include location variations (remote/hybrid/on-site)
- Check both large and small companies
- Look for recently posted jobs (last 24-48 hours)

Red Flags When Searching

Watch out for:

- Jobs that seem too good to be true
- Vague job descriptions
- Companies asking for payment
- Outdated postings
- Sketchy company websites

Remember: Finding a job is a job. Set aside dedicated time each day to search these different sources. Keep track of where you've looked and what you've found. And most importantly, don't get discouraged if you don't find the perfect job right away. Keep searching, keep applying, and keep refining your search methods.

In the next chapter, we'll talk about what to do once you find these jobs – but for now, focus on searching smarter, not harder.

Debrief: Chapter 10 - Charting Your Long-Term Success

1. **Define Your Vision for the Future:**
   Establish a clear picture of where you want to be in 5, 10, or 20 years. Align your career, financial, and personal goals with this vision to stay focused on long-term success.

2. **Create a Career Development Plan:**
   Set incremental goals to advance your career. Pursue certifications, degrees, or skills that align with your aspirations and keep you competitive in the job market.

3. **Invest in Lifelong Learning:**
   Stay ahead of industry trends and embrace continuous learning through professional development courses, conferences, and mentorship opportunities.

4. **Build a Strong Professional Reputation:**
   Consistently deliver quality work, maintain integrity and nurture relationships. Your reputation as a reliable and resourceful professional will open doors throughout your career.

5. **Maintain Financial Security:**
   Regularly evaluate and adjust your financial plans. Contribute to retirement accounts, build savings, and manage investments to secure your future.

6. **Foster a Balanced Life:**
   Success isn't just about your career. Dedicate time to family, hobbies, and personal growth to create a fulfilling and sustainable lifestyle.

7. **Leverage Your Network for Growth:**
   Stay engaged with professional connections and veteran communities. Networking provides opportunities for mentorship, career advancement, and collaboration.

8. **Adapt to Life's Changes:**
   Be prepared to reassess and adjust your goals as circumstances evolve. Flexibility and resilience will help you navigate new challenges and seize opportunities.

9. **Give Back to Your Community:**
   Share your knowledge and experiences by mentoring other veterans or supporting causes that matter to you. Giving back enhances personal fulfillment and strengthens your network.

10. **Stay Mission-Focused:**
    Treat your civilian career like a mission. Plan carefully, execute effectively and remain adaptable. With the right mindset and preparation, you'll thrive in the long term.

Dr. Jason Piccolo

Chapter 11: Navigating USAJOBS Like a Pro

*S*tepping into the federal job hunt can feel like landing in a foreign country without a map. One day, you're in a world where everything makes sense - you know your rank, your job, your chain of command. The next, you're staring at USAJOBS, wondering what a GS-0343-12 is and why there are 17 different "Program Analyst" positions.

Trust me, you're not alone. Every veteran who's made this transition has faced that same confusion. USAJOBS might look like a maze built by bureaucrats who never heard of user-friendly design. But beneath all that government-speak and clunky interface lies a logical system - one that values exactly what you bring: your military experience, security clearance, and ability to navigate complex organizations.

Think of this as your battle plan for conquering USAJOBS. We'll break down those confusing job series (think MOS/ratings for civilians) and help you find positions matching your skills. Because despite how it looks, the federal government wants people like you - they just have a weird way of showing it.

Breaking Down Job Series (Your New MOS/Rating)

Remember when you first joined the military and had to learn a whole new language? MOS, AFSC, Rating - whatever your branch called it, it was basically just a code that told everyone what you did. The civilian world loves to make things complicated, but federal job series are actually pretty similar to what you already know.

Think back to your first day in the military when someone told you your job code. Maybe you were an 11B in the Army, an MA in the Navy, or a 3P0X1 in the Air Force. Seemed like gibberish at first, right? Eventually, you can spot another service member's job just by their code. Federal job series works the same way - they're just the government's version of MOSs.

Here's the deal: every federal job has a four-digit code, like 0080 or 2210. Just like how all infantry MOSs started with 11 or all aviation ratings started with AW, these numbers tell you what family of jobs you're looking at. The first two digits are the real key - they tell you the overall career field. The last two digits get more specific about exactly what you'd be doing.

Let me put it in military terms:

- Think of the first two digits like your basic branch or rating (Infantry, BM, Security Forces)
- The last two digits are like your specific specialty (Mortarman, Boarding Team Member, K-9 Handler)

For example, let's say you see a job listed as 0083. The '00' tells you it's in the law enforcement family (just like how the '31' series in the Army means Military Police). The '83' specifically means it's a Police Officer position. Or if you see 2210, the '22' means it's IT-related (like a 25B in the Army or IT in the Navy), and the '10' specifies what kind of IT work it is.

This numbering system might seem random at first (honestly, who came up with these numbers?), but once you get the hang of it, you'll be scanning USAJOBS listings like you used to scan ERBs/ORBs. The best part? Unlike the military, where you usually had to stick to your MOS, in the federal government, you can apply for any series you qualify for. That 0301 series (Program Management) doesn't care if you were a Grunt, a Yeoman, or a Crew Chief - it cares about your leadership and management experience.

Security & Law Enforcement: Where Military Experience Really Shines

Let's talk about one of the most natural transitions for veterans - security and law enforcement. If you spent any time handling security clearances, guarding facilities, or investigating incidents in the military, these series might feel like home. But here's the thing many veterans miss: these jobs often go way beyond what you might expect.

0080 Series - Security Specialist (The Behind-the-Scenes Power Player)

Forget everything you think you know about security work. This isn't about standing watch or checking IDs. The 0080 series is where security policy gets made, and big-picture security programs come to life.

Remember that time you had to wait forever for your security clearance? The 0080s are the ones who make that system work. Or when you had to coordinate with contractors who needed access to classified areas? Yep, that's these folks, too.

Here's what you might actually be doing:

- Running background investigation programs for entire agencies
- Creating security policies that protect classified information
- Managing security systems for massive federal facilities
- Coordinating with intelligence agencies on clearance issues
- Overseeing contractor facility clearances

Perfect example: Let's say you were a Security Forces NCOIC or a Marine Corps Security Manager. You might think your only path is police work, but in the 0080 series, you could end up managing security programs for

NASA, making sure rocket technology doesn't fall into the wrong hands. Pretty cool upgrade from checking IDs at the gate, right?

0083 Series - Federal Police Officer (Not Your Basic Beat Cop)

This is probably what most people think of first when they hear "federal law enforcement," but it's got some interesting twists. Federal police work isn't just patrolling - it's often highly specialized and can involve protecting everything from priceless art at the Smithsonian to nuclear materials at Department of Energy facilities.

Think about it this way:

- VA Police protect our nation's largest medical system
- Defense Protective Service officers guard the Pentagon
- Federal Protective Service handles security at federal buildings nationwide
- NIH Police protect billion-dollar research facilities

If you were Military Police, Security Forces, or Master-at-Arms, this is familiar territory with a federal twist. Instead of patrolling a base, you might be protecting federal judges, securing research laboratories, or managing security for major government facilities.

1811 Series - Criminal Investigator (The Federal Agent Life)

This is the series you've seen on TV, but the real job is even more interesting. Every federal agency with investigative authority hires 1811s, and each one has its own specialty:

- EPA investigators track down environmental crimes
- FDA agents investigate pharmaceutical fraud
- IRS criminal investigators follow the money in complex financial crimes
- DOD investigators handle major crimes affecting military operations

Former military investigators (CID, OSI, NCIS) have a leg up here but don't count yourself out if you worked in intelligence, operations, or even logistics. Investigation skills come in many forms - maybe you investigated supply discrepancies or conducted accident investigations.

A Day in the Life: Imagine investigating counterfeit military parts one day and coordinating with international law enforcement the next. Or maybe you're tracking down stolen art for Homeland Security Investigations.

Beyond the Obvious: Federal Career Paths You Might Not Expect

Let's shake things up a bit. While plenty of veterans gravitate toward security work (and that's great), there's a whole world of federal careers that actually match your military skills - ones you probably haven't thought about. Ever coordinated a mission? Managed personnel? Handled complex equipment? Those skills are golden across dozens of federal job series.

0343 Series - Program Analyst (The Problem Solver)

Remember how, in the military, you had to plan operations, track resources, and make things happen despite constant challenges? That's essentially what Program Analysts do, just without the camo.

Think about it:

- Did you coordinate training exercises? Those planning skills are exactly what agencies need
- Ever manage a shop's budget? That's program analysis in military speak
- Those operational schedules you built? Same thing program analysts do for civilian agencies

Real talk: A former Operations NCO might look at "Program Analyst" and think "boring desk job," but here's what you might actually be doing:

- Managing million-dollar agency initiatives
- Coordinating disaster response programs at FEMA
- Running veteran support programs at the VA
- Analyzing space mission operations at NASA
- Developing training programs for entire agencies

1102 Series - Contract Specialist (Where Mission Meets Money)

If you've ever been a supply NCO or logistics officer or handled any kind of military purchasing, listen up. The 1102 series is where you can turn those skills into a solid career. But even if you haven't, check this out:

What you might be doing:

- Negotiating contracts for new military equipment
- Managing humanitarian aid purchases for international missions
- Coordinating emergency response supply contracts for FEMA
- Handling technology acquisitions for intelligence agencies

The best part? These jobs are everywhere, from the Department of

Agriculture to the Space Force, and they often come with sweet bonuses and rapid promotion potential.

0301 Series - Program Management (The Swiss Army Knife)

This is the series that proves the military teaches you more transferable skills than you realize. The 0301 series is like the general purpose series - it's all about getting things done, no matter the mission.

Ever:

- Led a team?
- Managed a complex project?
- Coordinated between different units?
- Created standard operating procedures?
- Handled personnel issues?

Congratulations - you've got 0301 experience. These jobs show up in every agency doing critical work like:

- Managing research programs at NIH
- Coordinating international aid programs at USAID
- Running nationwide veterans' programs at the VA
- Organizing large-scale public projects at Interior

Here's a real example: A former Army Sergeant who coordinated helicopter maintenance now manages aircraft programs for U.S. Customs and Border Protection. Same core skills - planning, coordination, leadership - just in a different context.

2210 Series - Information Technology (Not Just for IT Folks)

"But I wasn't a computer specialist!" Doesn't matter as much as you'd think. If you:

- Managed any kind of technical system
- Worked with communications equipment
- Handled classified systems
- Trained others on technical equipment

You might be a great fit. Modern IT management is more about understanding systems and processes than coding. You could end up:

- Managing IT projects (think operations management but for tech)
- Coordinating cybersecurity programs
- Running data center operations
- Managing IT training programs

0560 Series - Budget Analysis (Follow the Money)

Did you manage a unit budget? Track spending for operations? Handle supply accounts? That's budget analysis in disguise. These jobs are crucial because every federal program needs someone who can:

- Plan resource allocation
- Track spending
- Forecast future needs
- Justify budgets
- Manage financial programs

Pro Tips for Searching

- Use the "Save Search" feature - get emails when new jobs pop up
- Filter for security clearance required jobs if you have one
- Look at "Similar Jobs" at the bottom of announcements
- Check the "This Job Is Open To" section first - save yourself some time

Common Job Locations You Might Not Think Of

- Military bases (civilian positions)
- Federal law enforcement training centers
- Research laboratories
- Border stations
- Federal prisons
- VA hospitals
- Federal courthouses

Insider Tips: What Nobody Tells You About Federal Job Hunting

Let's talk about what really matters when you're scanning these announcements. After years of helping veterans land federal jobs, I've seen the same pitfalls and missed opportunities come up again and again. Here's what you need to know:

Know When to Walk Away

First, let's talk about when to save your time and energy. If you see "Must be a current federal employee" or "Internal to agency only," don't waste your time unless you fit those categories. It's like trying to get into a classified briefing without a clearance - it's just not happening.

Watch out for positions requiring certifications by EOD (Entry on Duty). Unlike the military, where they might send you to school to get qualified, most federal jobs want these certs up front. If you see "Cert required by

EOD" and you don't have it, keep moving unless they specifically state they'll train you.

"Temporary promotion" or "Detail opportunity" usually means they're moving someone around internally. These aren't your best bets as a veteran trying to get into federal service.

Location Matters More Than You Think

Here's something most people miss: when a job says "Washington, DC," it doesn't always mean you have to live there. With today's telework policies, many DC jobs are actually remote positions. Look for phrases like "Duty location negotiable after selection" or "Virtual position" - these are gold for veterans who want to work from anywhere.

Also, jobs listed with "Multiple locations" often let you pick where you want to work. It's like a dream sheet, but they actually listen to your preferences.

Timing Is Everything

Want to know when to really focus your job search? Here's the inside scoop:

- Mondays are big posting days for most agencies
- The end of the fiscal year (July through September) is the hiring season
- December is usually dead quiet - good time to prep your materials, bad time to expect many openings

Grade Levels and Military Experience

Let's match your military experience to grade levels. This isn't official guidance, but here's what typically works:

- Coming in as a junior enlisted? Look at GS-5 or GS-7 positions
- NCO experience usually translates well to GS-9 or GS-11
- Senior NCOs and officers often qualify for GS-11 through GS-13
- Field grade officers and senior enlisted leaders (E-8/9) can look at GS-13 and above

But here's the real secret: these are just guidelines. Your actual leadership experience, training, and education might qualify you for higher grades. Look for positions with "career ladder" potential - these offer automatic promotions as you gain experience.

The Series Game

Some series are easier to get into than others. The 0301 (Administration) and 0343 (Program Analysis) series are like the Swiss Army knives of federal jobs - they accept a wide range of experience. Technical series like 2210 (IT) care more about what you can do than what your title was.

The Fine Print That Really Matters

Always check the "Qualifications" section carefully. Your military experience often counts more than you think. Those schools you attended? That counts as training. Leading troops? That's supervisory experience. Running a supply room? That's logistics and property management experience.

When they say "one year of specialized experience," they're talking about experience at the next lower grade level. But here's the thing - military experience often counts as a higher-grade experience than you might think. A senior NCO managing a large unit might have GS-12 equivalent experience without knowing it.

Secret Weapons for Success

- USAJobs lets you save searches and get email alerts. Use them.
- Set up multiple resume profiles for different types of jobs
- Many agencies have veteran recruitment programs - find them
- Network with veterans already in federal service
- Consider taking a lower grade to get in if the position has promotion potential

Remember: Job titles in federal service can be misleading. An "Administrative Officer" might be running major programs while a "Program Director" might be doing paperwork. Always read the full announcement, especially the duties section, to know what you're really applying for.

Real Transitions: Success Stories and Strategies

Let's look at the actual career paths veterans have taken. These examples show how military experience translates into federal careers and the strategies that worked.

Combat Arms to Program Management Success Story

An Infantry Staff Sergeant thought "All I did was combat arms - who's going to hire me?" Here's how their experience actually translated:

- Leading combat missions → Project coordination and risk management
- Training new soldiers → Program development and implementation

- Managing platoon equipment → Property accountability systems
- Coordinating with other units → Interagency collaboration

Career Path:

- Started: GS-9 Program Support (0343 series) using VRA
- 12 months: Promoted to GS-11 Program Analyst
- 24 months: Competitive promotion to GS-12
- Current: Running major emergency response programs at FEMA

Key Strategy: Focused on translating leadership and planning skills rather than tactical experience

Supply NCO to Contracting Professional

A former Army Supply Sergeant (92Y) found their perfect fit in government contracting:

Military Background:

- Unit supply management
- Budget execution
- Property accountability
- Vendor coordination

Federal Career Progress:

- Entry: GS-7 Contract Specialist trainee
- Year 1: Completed initial DAU certifications
- Year 2: Promoted to GS-9 with Level I certification
- Year 3: Reached GS-11 with Level II certification
- Current: GS-12 Contracting Officer managing major acquisitions

Strategy Used: Applied to a developmental position that included certification training

Intelligence to Program Management

An Army Intelligence Analyst (35F) found success in an unexpected place:

Military Skills Applied:

- Intelligence analysis and reporting
- Senior leader briefings
- Information security management
- Research methodology

Career Progression:

- Started: GS-9 Management Analyst at the Department of Energy
- Used analytical background to stand out in energy security
- Promoted to GS-11 after leading key assessments
- Currently: GS-13 Program Manager overseeing critical infrastructure programs

Success Factor: Applied intelligence analysis skills to civilian sector challenges

Proven Career Entry Strategies

The "Career Ladder" Path

Example from Combat Engineer to Emergency Management:

- Entered as GS-7 Emergency Management Specialist
- Automatic promotion to GS-9 at one year

- Reached target grade GS-11 at two years
- Now leads regional response programs

The Geographic Advantage

Air Force Operations NCO's Path:

- Started: Small regional office in the Midwest (less competition)
- Position: GS-9 Program Analyst
- Built experience for 18 months
- Transferred to DC headquarters as GS-11
- Now: GS-12 leading nationwide programs

The Series Jump Technique

Navy Operations Specialist's Strategy:

1. Entered as GS-7 Program Support (0343)
2. Gained project management experience
3. Moved to Operations Research (1515) series as GS-11
4. Now: GS-12 analyzing maritime programs

Agency-Specific Success Patterns

Department of Energy

Operations Experience Path:

- Former Nuclear Operations Chief
- Entry: GS-11 Program Analyst
- Current: GS-13 Program Manager
- Success Factor: Combined technical and leadership experience

Veterans Affairs

Medical Background Transition:

- Prior Service: Hospital Corpsman
- Entry: GS-7 Program Support
- Progress: Healthcare Administration
- Current: GS-12 Managing Clinical Operations
- Key Factor: Medical experience plus leadership

FEMA

Logistics Experience Route:

- Background: Transportation Management NCO
- Started: GS-9 Logistics Specialist
- Progression: Emergency Management
- Now: GS-12 Regional Response Coordinator
- Advantage: Emergency planning experience

Time-Tested Entry Methods

1. Strategic Grade Acceptance Example: Marine Corps E-7 Path

- Accepted GS-9 Program Analyst role
- Built federal resume for 12 months
- Promoted to GS-11 through Merit Promotion
- Reached GS-12 within 3 years

2. Developmental Position Strategy Former Air Traffic Controller:

- Entered: GS-7 Management Trainee
- Completed agency development program
- Current: GS-12 Program Manager
- Timeline: 3 years from entry to target grade

Your Next Mission: Making the Federal Transition

Look, transitioning to federal service isn't just about finding a job - it's about continuing your service in a different uniform. Every skill you learned in the military, from planning missions to managing people, has a place in federal service. It's just about knowing where to look and how to translate your experience.

Think about it - in the military, you learned to adapt to new situations, master complex systems, and get things done no matter what. That's exactly what federal agencies need. Whether you were coordinating artillery fire or managing a ship's supply system, you've already proven you can handle the complex, high-stakes work federal agencies do daily.

The federal government might seem like a maze of confusing terms and bureaucratic hurdles. But remember your first days in the military? Everything seemed like alphabet soup then, too. Just like you learned military systems, you'll master this one. Job series will become as familiar as MOS codes, and GS levels will be as clear as pay grades.

What makes federal service unique is that it's a culture you already understand: the mission focus, a sense of purpose, and knowledge that your work matters beyond a paycheck. You're not leaving government service - you're continuing it in a new way.

Don't let USAJOBS complexity or unfamiliar terminology discourage you. You've mastered tougher systems and learned more challenging skills. Your military experience is invaluable: proven success serving your country and getting things done in tough situations. Now it's time to apply those skills to your next mission: finding your place in federal service.

Remember: every federal employee you'll meet was once exactly where you are now, staring at USAJOBS and trying to figure it out. Many of them are veterans themselves who've made this same transition. They made it through, and so will you.

Debrief: Chapter 11 - Navigating USAJOBS Like a Pro

1. **Understand the USAJOBS Platform:**
   USAJOBS is the primary portal for federal government job openings. Familiarize yourself with its features, including job search filters, saved searches, and application tracking.

2. **Create a Detailed Profile:**
   Build a robust USAJOBS profile with accurate personal information, employment history, and preferences. A well-crafted profile helps you tailor applications to specific federal roles.

3. **Master the Advanced Search Function:**
   Use filters like location, pay grade, and hiring path (e.g., veterans' preference) to narrow your search. Save custom searches to receive automatic notifications of new opportunities.

4. **Tailor Your Federal Resume:**
   Federal resumes differ significantly from civilian ones. They should include detailed descriptions of your duties, accomplishments, and skills, often running multiple pages. Use keywords from job descriptions to align your resume with the role.

5. **Highlight Veterans' Preference:**
   If eligible, claim your veterans' preference status to gain an edge in the hiring process. Be prepared to upload supporting documents, such as your DD Form 214 or disability rating letter.

6. **Understand Job Announcements:**
   Carefully read job postings, including the "Qualifications" and

"How You Will Be Evaluated" sections. Ensure you meet the minimum requirements before applying.

7. **Focus on Keywords:**
Use keywords from the job description in your resume to pass through automated screening systems and align with the hiring agency's needs.

8. **Be Patient with the Process:**
Federal hiring timelines can be longer than private-sector ones. Use this time to follow up on applications, network within agencies, and prepare for interviews.

9. **Prepare Supporting Documents:**
Gather required documentation, such as SF-50 forms (if applicable), transcripts, and certifications, to upload with your application. Missing documents can disqualify you.

10. **Follow Up Strategically:**
After applying, monitor your application status on USAJOBS and reach out to HR contacts listed in the job posting for updates or clarification if needed.

11. **Utilize Federal Hiring Resources:**
Explore resources like the Veterans Employment Toolkit, OPM (Office of Personnel Management) guides, and federal career counseling to maximize your chances of success.

Chapter 12
The Resume: Back To Basics

Transitioning from military to civilian life means moving from a world of clear structure and standardized evaluations into one that's more fluid. Creating a resume for this new world might feel like learning a whole new language – and it is.

If you're used to military evaluations where each acronym, rank, and qualification has a specific meaning, civilian resumes can seem foreign. While your military record speaks through detailed evaluations and medals, civilian employers typically spend just 7 seconds scanning your resume. Those seconds are your opportunity to stand out – think of it like a reconnaissance mission to make an impact and leave them wanting more.

Think of your resume as your personal marketing campaign. In the military, your reputation precedes you through your record and chain of command. In the civilian world, your resume is often your only chance to make an impression before an interview. You've got amazing skills – leading teams through high-pressure situations, managing million-dollar equipment, and making critical decisions. These are incredibly valuable, but they need to be packaged in civilian terms.

Your resume isn't just a list of jobs – it's a strategic document bridging your military experience and civilian future. Every bullet point should help tell the story of why you're the perfect candidate. Remember, this isn't about downplaying your military experience – it's about translating it into language civilians understand.

The good news? You already have all the raw material for an outstanding resume. The attention to detail, discipline, and commitment to excellence you developed in the military are exactly the qualities that will help you craft a winning resume. You have what it takes – now let's put those skills to work in a new way.

Understanding the Purpose of a Resume

Your resume has one job: to get you an interview. That's it. This requires a crucial mindset shift from military documentation. You don't need to document every training exercise or duty station. Think of it like a movie trailer rather than a documentary – show the highlights that make employers want to see more.

Unlike your military record, which needed to be comprehensive for promotions and assignments, your civilian resume should showcase your greatest hits. That time, you led 50 people or managed a million-dollar budget? Include it. Routine paperwork and mandatory training? Probably not.

Unlike rigid military documents, civilian resumes need to be flexible. Think of it like having different uniforms for different situations. You'll want to adjust your resume for each job, just like you wouldn't use the same approach for every military operation. If you're applying for logistics, emphasize supply chain experience. For leadership roles, focus on team-building and successful missions.

1. This customization shows employers three things:
2. You read their job posting
3. You understand how your experience fits their needs

You're willing to communicate effectively

Think of it like adapting field exercises for changing conditions. You're taking your core experiences – your "basic load" – and configuring them to meet each job's mission requirements. Your resume isn't just a document – it's a tool for opening doors, and like any good tool, it needs to be optimized for each specific job.

Ready to dive into exactly how to create this flexible, powerful tool? Let's break it down piece by piece in the next sections.

The Essential Sections of a Resume

Contact Information

Right at the top, you'll want to put:

- Your name (you can drop the rank unless you're applying to defense contractors)
- A phone number (quick tip: make sure your voicemail message sounds professional)
- An email address (time to retire that military email – grab a professional-looking Gmail address)
- Where you live (just city and state is fine)
- Your LinkedIn profile (if you've got one set up)

Think of your professional summary like the opening of a mission brief – you've got to grab attention and communicate the key points fast. In the military, you probably started important briefings with a clear, powerful statement of purpose. Your professional summary works the same way but for civilian employers.

This isn't the place for your life story or a detailed list of qualifications. Instead, think of it as your "elevator pitch" – that quick, compelling snapshot of who you are professionally. Imagine running into your dream employer in an elevator. You've got about 30 seconds to make them want to learn more about you. What would you say?

Let's break down what makes a strong professional summary:

The Basic Formula

Your summary should include:

- Who you are professionally (your current or desired role)
- Years of relevant experience
- Your biggest strengths
- What you're looking to do next

Here's a basic example: "I'm an operations manager with 8 years of experience leading teams through high-pressure situations. I've got a knack for making complex logistics look easy and building teams that get stuff done. Looking to bring my leadership experience to a civilian operations role."

But let's look at some variations based on different backgrounds and goals:

For a Security Specialist: "Former Military Police Leader with 10 years of experience in threat assessment and team security operations. Expert at developing comprehensive security protocols and training high-performing teams. Seeking to leverage advanced security management skills in a corporate security director role."

For an IT Professional: "Combat communications specialist transitioning to civilian IT, bringing 6 years of experience maintaining critical systems under extreme conditions. Proven track record of implementing secure networks and resolving complex technical issues in fast-paced environments. Ready to apply my technical expertise and problem-solving skills in a civilian IT management position."

For a Project Manager: "Dynamic military leader with 12 years of experience executing multi-million dollar projects and leading cross-functional teams. Successfully coordinated operations across multiple locations while managing budgets, timelines, and personnel. Eager to translate my military project management experience into a civilian construction management role."

Key Tips for Your Summary:

1. Keep It Concise

- Aim for 3-4 sentences max
- Every word should earn its place
- Cut any military jargon

2. Show Your Value

- Focus on achievements over duties
- Highlight skills that transfer well
- Use strong action words

3. Make It Relevant

- Align your summary with the job you want
- Use industry-specific keywords
- Focus on transferable skills

4. Stay Current

- Focus on recent experience
- Look forward, not backward
- Show enthusiasm for your next role

Common Mistakes to Avoid:

✘ Don't Say: "Seasoned veteran seeking to utilize military experience in a civilian role." ✓ Instead, Try: "Results-driven leader with 15 years of experience managing complex operations and diverse teams in high-stakes environments."

✘ Don't Say: "Former sergeant looking for opportunities in management." ✓ Instead Try: "Experienced team leader who developed and mentored 50+ personnel while managing operations worth $2M+ in resources."

✘ Don't Say: "Hard worker with good people skills seeking new challenges." ✓ Instead, Try: "Dynamic leader with proven success building and motivating teams of 20+ through challenging projects and tight deadlines."

Customization is Key

Remember to adjust your summary based on the job you're targeting. Just like you wouldn't use the same approach for different types of missions, your summary should shift focus depending on the role:

For a Leadership Position, Emphasize:

- Team size and scope
- Leadership achievements
- Strategic planning abilities

For a Technical Role: Highlight:

- Technical skills and certifications
- System implementations
- Problem-solving abilities

For a Project Management Role: Focus on:

- Budget management
- Timeline adherence
- Cross-functional coordination

Your professional summary is often the first thing employers read, and it sets the tone for everything that follows. Make those seconds count by giving them a clear, compelling picture of your value. Think of it as your mission statement – it should leave them wanting to know more about how you can help their organization succeed.

Remember: You've briefed high-ranking officers and led troops through complex missions. You know how to communicate clearly and effectively. Now, you're just doing it for a different audience. Take that same confidence and clarity and put it to work in your professional summary.

Remember that wall of weapons and equipment you'd check out before a mission? Each piece had its purpose, and you knew exactly when and how to use each one. Your skills section works the same way – it's your civilian arsenal, showing employers all the professional tools you've mastered during your service.

Here's something interesting I learned from working with hundreds of veterans: we often take our most valuable skills for granted. What advanced communications system do you operate daily? That's high-level technical expertise. The way you kept your team focused during intense situations? That's crisis management. The time you coordinated with multiple units to complete a mission? That's cross-functional team leadership.

Breaking Down Your Technical Skills

Let's start with the tech stuff. I recently worked with a Marine who thought he didn't have any technical skills because he "just" worked in logistics. But as we talked, it turned out he'd mastered three different inventory management systems, created Excel spreadsheets that his whole unit used, and developed a new tracking system that saved hours of work each week. That's not "just" logistics – that's sophisticated technical expertise that civilian employers are hungry for.

Think about your own experience. Did you:

- Work with any computer systems or software?
- Maintain or repair equipment?
- Use any tracking or management tools?
- Create or update any databases?
- Handle any diagnostic equipment?

Each of these is a technical skill that belongs in your toolkit. And here's the key – you need to translate these into civilian terms. Instead of saying you used "GCSS-Army," say you're "experienced with enterprise resource planning (ERP) systems for inventory and supply chain management." See how that speaks more clearly to a civilian employer?

Leadership Skills: Your Military Advantage

This is where your military background really shines. I remember working with an Army Staff Sergeant who didn't think "just leading PT" was worth mentioning. But when we broke it down, he had:

- Designed and led training programs for 40+ people

- Tracked and documented individual progress
- Modified plans based on individual needs
- Motivated team members to exceed standards
- Managed safety protocols for high-risk activities

That's not just leading PT – that's comprehensive program management and leadership. These are exactly the skills civilian employers want but struggle to find.

Your leadership experience might include:

- Planning and executing missions (project management)
- Handling personnel issues (conflict resolution)
- Training new team members (employee development)
- Managing resources (budget management)
- Evaluating performance (talent assessment)

The People Skills That Set You Apart

Here's where things get really interesting. Remember how in the military, technical skills got you in the door, but people skills made you successful? It's the same in the civilian world.

I worked with an Air Force veteran who thought her experience coordinating air traffic wasn't relevant to the business consulting role she wanted. But think about what that job actually involved:

- Maintaining calm communication during high-stress situations
- Juggling multiple priorities without dropping the ball
- Making split-second decisions with major consequences
- Collaborating with different teams to achieve goals
- Adapting to changing conditions on the fly

These "soft skills" are actually your secret weapons. They're the abilities that separate good employees from great leaders.

Putting It All Together

Think of your skills section as planning a mission. You wouldn't just dump all your equipment in a pile – you'd organize it strategically based on what you need to accomplish. The same goes for your skills:

1. Start with a brain dump. Write down everything you can do, no matter how basic it seems.
2. Organize your skills into categories that make sense:
    - Technical capabilities
    - Leadership abilities
    - People skills
    - Special qualifications
1. Translate each skill into civilian terms. Ask yourself: "How would I explain this to someone who's never served?"
2. Prioritize your skills based on the job you want. Just like you'd choose different equipment for different missions, you'll emphasize different skills for different positions.

Here's the best part: unlike civilians who might have picked up one or two of these skills in entry-level jobs, you've practiced yours in high-stakes situations where lives and missions depended on your performance. That's a level of experience that sets you apart.

Remember: Every skill you list should help tell your story and show why you're the perfect person for the job. Don't just list what you can do – show how your unique combination of skills makes you the solution to their problems.

Work Experience: Translating Your Military Story

Let me tell you about Mike, a Marine Corps Sergeant who was having a tough time with his resume. "I'm just a grunt," he told me. "All I did was lead training and run missions." Just? After we talked for a while, it turned out Mike had led a 12-person team through multiple complex operations, managed millions in equipment, developed new training programs that got adopted by other units, and solved logistics problems that had been causing headaches for years.

This is what I see all the time – veterans underselling themselves because they think what they did was "just part of the job." Here's the thing: what seems routine to you can be pure gold to civilian employers.

The Art of Job Title Translation

First, let's talk about job titles. I get it – you're proud of being a Staff Sergeant or a Petty Officer, and you should be. But civilian employers might not understand what those titles mean. Think of it like speaking another language. You need to translate, not just transpose.

I remember working with Sarah, a Navy Operations Specialist. Her first resume listed her as "OS2" – clear as day to any sailor but Greek to civilian employers. We reframed her role as "Operations Coordinator," and suddenly, her phone started ringing. Same experience, different language.

Here's how this works in practice:

- Your Platoon Sergeant becomes "Senior Operations Manager"
- That Supply Specialist role translates to "Logistics Coordinator"
- Combat Engineer? That's a "Project Manager" or "Site Operations Specialist."

Telling Your Story

Now, here's where it gets interesting. Your work experience isn't just a list of jobs – it's the story of your professional growth and achievements. Let me show you what I mean.

Take James, an Army Infantry Squad Leader. His first resume bullet point reads: "Led infantry squad in tactical operations." True? Yes. Effective? No. We dug deeper into what that actually meant:

"What did your squad do?" I asked. "Well, we conducted patrols, managed security operations, trained new team members…" "How many people? What kind of results?" "Twelve people. We had the highest readiness rates in the company, and I developed a new patrol strategy that got adopted by the whole battalion."

Now we're getting somewhere! That one boring bullet point became: "Led high-performing team of 12 personnel in complex security operations, achieving top readiness rates across six platoons and pioneering new operational procedures adopted battalion-wide."

See the difference? We're still talking about the same experience, but now we're showing the impact, not just the activity.

NUMBERS TELL STORIES

Remember how everything in the military had a number attached to it? Equipment values, personnel counts, readiness rates, training scores? Those numbers are pure gold on your resume. They prove you're not just talking – you delivered real results.

Let me share another story. Tom, an Air Force Maintenance Chief, had a resume that said "Supervised aircraft maintenance." After some discussion, we discovered he:

- Led a team of 45 technicians
- Managed maintenance for 12 aircraft worth $280 million
- Achieved a 94% readiness rate (15% above squadron average)
- Reduced maintenance delays by 30%
- Saved $100K through improved inventory management

Suddenly, "supervised aircraft maintenance" became a compelling story of leadership, efficiency, and measurable results.

The "So What?" Test

For every bullet point on your resume, ask yourself, "So what?" Keep asking until you get to the real impact of what you did.

Let's try it: "Conducted training exercises." So what? "Trained 200 personnel in combat operations." So what? "Achieved 98% certification rate, highest in the battalion." So what? "Improved unit readiness and capability while saving 20 training hours per week."

Now, that's an achievement worth highlighting!

Making It Real

Remember: Your military experience isn't just a series of jobs you held or tasks you completed. It's a rich story of leadership, problem-solving, and measurable achievements. Your challenge isn't finding impressive things to put on your resume – it's recognizing that what you did every day in the military is exactly what civilian employers are looking for.

Take pride in your service, but make sure employers can see its value. After all, you earned those achievements. Now it's time to make sure they help you land your next mission.

Education

List this stuff in reverse order (newest first):

- Your degree and major
- Where you got it
- When you finished
- Any cool courses that matter for the job
- Military training that civilians would care about

Extra Sections

You might want to add:

- Volunteer work (shows you're community-minded)
- Professional certificates (the ones civilians recognize)
- Awards (translated so they make sense outside the military)
- Professional groups you're part of

Speaking Civilian: Translating Your Military Experience

Let me tell you about Marcus, a Navy Chief who was struggling with his transition to civilian life. During one of our resume sessions, he threw his hands up in frustration. "Nobody understands what I did," he said. "I try to explain my job, and their eyes just glaze over."

I get it. After years of speaking in military shorthand – where entire operations can be summed up in a handful of acronyms – it can feel like you're learning a whole new language. But here's the thing: you don't need to teach civilians military-speak. You need to translate your incredible experience into their language.

The Translation Challenge

Think about when you first joined the military. Remember that moment when your drill instructor was rattling off acronyms and jargon, and you wondered if they were even speaking English? That's exactly how civilian employers feel when they read a resume full of military terms.

I worked with a Marine Corps logistics officer who listed "NCOIC of IV MEF G-4 ops" on his resume. Perfect military communication – and completely meaningless to most civilian employers. We translated it to "Senior Operations Manager overseeing regional logistics and supply chain operations for the 10,000-person organization." Same job, different language.

The Universal Language of Leadership

Here's something fascinating I've learned working with hundreds of veterans: military leadership experience is pure gold in the civilian world – if you can explain it right. Let me show you what I mean.

Take Sarah, an Army Staff Sergeant. Her initial resume said she "Conducted platoon-level training exercises and maintained unit readiness." Sounds good to military ears, but let's break down what she actually did:

- Developed training programs from scratch
- Led a team of 40 people
- Managed schedules and resources
- Evaluated performance
- Solved personnel conflicts
- Maintained safety standards
- Achieved measurable results

Suddenly, we're not talking about "platoon-level training" anymore. We're talking about program development, personnel management, scheduling, performance evaluation, conflict resolution, safety compliance, and measurable outcomes. Now we're speaking civilian!

Real-World Translation Examples

Let's look at some common military phrases and how to transform them:

Command and Control: Military: "Commanded and controlled battalion-level operations." Civilian: "Directed operations for a 500-person organization across multiple locations."

Mission Planning: Military: "Led pre-mission planning and tactical briefings." Civilian: "Developed comprehensive project plans and led cross-functional team meetings."

Equipment Accountability: Military: "Maintained 100% accountability of sensitive items." Civilian: "Managed inventory control for high-value equipment ($5M+) with zero losses."

The Power of Context

A Captain said he moved equipment across three countries. "It was just standard logistics," he said. But as we broke it down, here's what "standard logistics" actually meant:

- Coordinated with multiple international agencies
- Managed complex customs requirements
- Tracked 200+ pieces of equipment
- Led a team of 25 people
- Met aggressive deadlines
- Maintained perfect safety record
- Came in under budget

Each of these points speaks directly to what civilian employers value:

international experience, regulatory compliance, inventory management, leadership, deadline performance, safety consciousness, and budget management.

Speaking to Civilian Priorities

Civilian employers particularly value certain aspects of military experience. Let's break them down with real examples:

Budget Management: Instead of: "Managed platoon budget," Say: "Oversaw $2M annual operational budget with zero deficiencies."

Leadership: Instead of: "Platoon Sergeant for an infantry unit," Say: "Led, trained, and mentored a 30-person team in high-pressure environments."

Project Coordination: Instead of: "OIC for field exercise," Say: "Planned and executed complex training operation involving 200+ personnel and $5M in equipment."

Risk Management: Instead of: "Conducted risk assessments," Say: "Developed and implemented risk mitigation strategies ensuring zero safety incidents over 12 months."

Quality Assurance: Instead of: "Conducted equipment inspections," Say: "Implemented quality control processes reducing equipment failures by 40%."

The Before and After Game

Original: "NCOIC of armory operations"

Step 1 (Remove military-speak): "In charge of weapons storage facility"

Step 2 (Add scope): "Managed secure facility containing $3M worth of sensitive equipment."

Step 3 (Add responsibilities): "Managed secure facility containing $3M in sensitive equipment, maintaining inventory accuracy and compliance with federal regulations."

Step 4 (Add achievements): "Managed secure facility containing $3M in sensitive equipment, achieving 100% inventory accuracy and perfect compliance record across three federal inspections."

Pro Tips from the Trenches

1. **Numbers are Universal:** Keep track of:

- Number of people led
- Budget sizes
- Equipment values
- Success rates
- Time savings
- Cost reductions

2. **Focus on Results:** Instead of: "Responsible for vehicle maintenance," Say: "Increased vehicle readiness rate from 75% to 95% through improved maintenance procedures."

3. **Highlight Universal Skills:**

- Leadership
- Problem-solving
- Project management
- Team building
- Crisis management
- Process improvement

Remember: Your military experience isn't just impressive to other service members – it's incredibly valuable to civilian employers. The key is helping them understand that value in their terms. You're not dumbing it down; you're making it accessible.

Writing About Your Achievements

Making Your Resume Fit Each Job

You can't just send the same resume everywhere. Here's how to customize it:

1. Read That Job Post Like a Detective

- Circle the main things they want
- Spot patterns in what they're asking for
- Note any specific tech skills they need

2. Line Up Your Experience

- Put your most relevant experiences at the top
- Tweak your achievements to match what they want
- Add or remove stuff based on the job

3. Use Their Language

- Copy key terms from the job post
- Use industry terms they'll recognize
- Make it sound natural, though - don't just keyword-stuff

4. Update Your Summary

- Highlight stuff that matters for this specific job
- Show you've got what they're looking for
- Make your career goals match the position

Making It Look Good

Keep it clean and professional:

The Basics:

- Keep it to 1-2 pages max for civilians and as much as needed for federal
- Use normal fonts (Arial or Calibri work great)
- Font size should be big enough to read (10-12 points)
- Leave some white space - don't cram everything together
- Use bullet points to break things up

Pro Tips:

- Save it as a PDF (keeps everything looking right)
- Name it something simple like "John_Smith_Resume.pdf"
- Keep the file size small (under 2MB)
- Put page numbers on if it's longer than one page
- Don't go crazy with colors or graphics

Stuff to Watch Out For

Don't Trip Up On:

Content Goofs:

- Including ancient history that doesn't matter anymore
- Using military jargon nobody understands
- Just listing what you were supposed to do instead of what you actually achieved
- Forgetting to include numbers and results

Format Fails:

- Cramming too much onto the page
- Going overboard with fancy designs
- Making some parts look different from others
- Organizing things in a confusing way

Strategy Mistakes:

- Sending the exact same resume for every job
- Not showing how your military skills fit civilian jobs
- Downplaying your leadership experience
- Leaving out achievements civilians would care about

Basic Errors:

- Spelling mistakes and typos
- Wrong contact info (double-check that phone number!)
- Links that don't work
- Saving it in a format they can't open

Places to Get Help

You're not in this alone. Check out these resources:

Government Help:

- VA employment services (they've got your back)
- Transition Assistance Program (TAP) - seriously, use it
- American Job Centers (free help in your area)

Non-Profit Organizations:

- Hire Heroes USA (they're awesome at resume help)
- Veteran Job Mission (connects you with employers)
- Warriors to Work (great for networking)

Online Tools:

- Military.com's Skills Translator (super helpful)
- O*NET Military Crosswalk (matches military jobs to civilian ones)
- LinkedIn for Veterans (free premium access for a year!)

Job Search Stuff:

- Veterans Job Bank
- VA for Vets
- Veteran-friendly job boards

Keeping Your Resume Fresh

Think of your resume as a living document - it needs to grow and change just like your career. Here's how to keep it current:

Smart Moves:

- Update it every few months, even if you're not job-hunting
- Keep a master version with everything you've done
- Write down your wins as they happen (with numbers!)
- Ask civilian friends in your target field to look it over
- Stay current with what's hot in your industry

Remember This: Getting your resume right takes practice. Your first try probably won't be perfect, and that's totally fine. Keep tweaking it, learning from each application, and using all those veteran resources out there.

The Bottom Line: Your military service gave you amazing skills that civilian employers need - leadership, discipline, problem-solving, you name it. A solid resume helps you tell that story in a way they'll understand. Take it one step at a time, use the resources available, and you'll nail this transition.

You've handled tougher challenges in the military - you've got this resume thing. Just take it step by step, and don't be afraid to ask for help when you need it. Your next civilian career is waiting!

Debrief: Chapter 12 - The Resume: Back to Basics

1. **Your Resume Is Your Marketing Tool:**
   Unlike military evaluations, a civilian resume is a concise, targeted document designed to secure an interview. Focus on highlights and relevant accomplishments instead of listing every duty and station.

2. **Translate Military Experience into Civilian Language:**
   Avoid acronyms and jargon. Use terms that resonate with civilian employers, like "Team Manager" instead of "Platoon Sergeant" and "Project Coordination" instead of "Mission Planning."

3. **Tailor for Each Job:**
   Adjust your resume for each role to match the job description. Highlight specific skills and experiences that align with the employer's needs. Customization shows attention to detail and genuine interest.

4. **Focus on Results and Achievements:**
   Emphasize measurable outcomes, such as "Increased operational efficiency by 25%" or "Led a team of 12 to exceed readiness goals." Numbers and results demonstrate impact and value.

5. **Essential Resume Sections:**
   - **Contact Information:** Full name, phone number, email, and LinkedIn profile.
   - **Professional Summary:** A brief, compelling snapshot of your skills and goals tailored to the role.

- **Skills:** Highlight transferable skills such as leadership, logistics, or technical expertise.
- **Work Experience:** Focus on achievements, translating military roles into civilian-friendly terms.
- **Education and Certifications:** List degrees, certifications, and relevant training.

6. **Adapt to Civilian Hiring Priorities:**
Civilian employers scan resumes quickly—make yours stand out by using clear formatting, bulleted lists, and action-oriented language. Keep it concise and visually appealing.

7. **Common Mistakes to Avoid:**
    - Overloading with military jargon.
    - Listing duties instead of achievements.
    - Using a generic resume for all applications.
    - Neglecting to proofread for typos or errors.

8. **Resources for Veterans:**
Take advantage of services like Hire Heroes USA, TAP workshops, and LinkedIn Premium for Veterans. Tools like the Military Skills Translator and O*NET Crosswalk can help align your experience with civilian roles.

9. **Keep Your Resume Updated:**
Treat your resume as a "living document." Regularly update it with new skills, certifications, and achievements. Save a master version to streamline customization for future applications.

10. **Confidence Is Key:**
Your military experience has equipped you with invaluable skills. A well-crafted resume ensures civilian employers see your full potential. Stay persistent, refine your approach, and trust in your abilities to succeed.

Chapter 13: Federal Veteran Hiring Authorities: Your Secret Weapon for Government Jobs

*L*et's talk about federal hiring authorities – a special set of rules that are different from the veteran preferences you might already know about in the private sector. Here's the deal: while many civilian companies actively recruit veterans and have great veteran hiring programs (looking at you, Boeing, Amazon, and countless others), federal hiring authorities are a whole different ballgame with their own unique set of rules.

Why am I dedicating an entire chapter to just federal hiring authorities? Because while civilian companies may give veterans preference in hiring (especially if you're a protected veteran under VEVRAA), federal hiring authorities go beyond simple preference – they're legally mandated pathways that can give you direct access to federal employment opportunities.

Think of it this way:

- Private sector: Companies often have veteran hiring initiatives, recruitment programs, and may give priority to veteran candidates. Many are also federal contractors required to take affirmative action to hire protected veterans.
- Federal sector: You get all that PLUS specific legal authorities that can let you bypass regular competitive hiring processes or give you literal point advantages in the scoring system.

Even if you're currently focused on private sector opportunities (which are awesome and abundant), understanding federal hiring authorities is worth your time because:

- Federal jobs often offer excellent benefits and competitive salaries
- Your military time counts toward retirement
- Many agencies offer unique opportunities to continue serving your country
- You might want to mix federal service with private-sector work throughout your career
- These authorities never expire – they're benefits you've earned permanently

Plus, let's be real – the federal hiring process can be about as clear as mud without a guide. That's exactly why I'm writing this chapter. Think of it as your insider's guide to a system that, while complicated, could give you additional career options beyond the private sector.

Want to stay current on all this stuff? Bookmark www.opm.gov/fedshirevets/ right now. Seriously, do it before reading any further. It's the government's official source for veteran federal employment information, and they keep it updated with all the latest changes, job postings, and program details.

Now, with that context established, let's dive into the specific federal hiring authorities that could give you a serious edge in landing a federal job...

What Are Veteran Hiring Authorities Anyway?

Think of veteran hiring authorities as your VIP pass to federal employment. There are special rules that give veterans a leg up in the federal hiring process. It's Uncle Sam's way of saying "thanks for your service" while also bringing valuable military experience into government agencies.

The Big Three Hiring Authorities (Plus Some Extras You Should Know)

Veterans' Preference: Your Federal Job Search Boost

This isn't technically a hiring authority, but it's your starting point and it's a big deal. Veterans' preference gives you extra points on your application score for competitive federal jobs. Think of it as having a head start in a race – you're still running the same course as everyone else, but you begin a few steps ahead.

How Many Points Do You Get?

There are two levels of preference points:

10-Point Preference (The Big One) You qualify for this if you:

- Have a service-connected disability (even if it's rated at just 10%)
- Received a Purple Heart (automatic qualification – thank you for your sacrifice)
- Are you receiving disability compensation from the VA
- Are a spouse, widow/widower, or parent of a veteran who died in service or who is permanently and totally disabled
- Are a spouse or parent of service members who are/were MIA or POWs

5-Point Preference (The Standard Boost): You get this if you served:

- During a war
- During the period April 28, 1952 through July 1, 1955
- For more than 180 consecutive days, other than for training, any part of which occurred after January 31, 1955, and before October 15, 1976

- During the Gulf War from August 2, 1990, through January 2, 1992
- For more than 180 consecutive days, other than for training, any part of which occurred during the period beginning September 11, 2001, and ending on a future date prescribed by Presidential proclamation or law
- In a campaign or expedition for which a campaign medal has been authorized

How Does It Actually Work?

Here's where it gets interesting. Veterans' preference isn't just about adding points to a score. It works differently depending on the type of examination:

For Numerical Ratings:

- Your points (5 or 10) get added to your final passing score
- Example: You score an 85 on the exam, you're a disabled vet, boom – you're now at 95

For Category Rating (Most Common Today):

- Qualified candidates are placed in quality categories like "Best Qualified," "Well Qualified," and "Qualified."
- If you have a preference and you're in any of these categories, you jump ahead of non-preference eligibles in your category
- With a compensable service-connected disability of 10% or more, you jump to the top of the highest quality category (unless the position is scientific or professional at GS-9 or higher)

Pro Tips for Using Veterans' Preference:

1. **Document Everything**
   - Keep your DD-214 handy (all pages, especially the one showing character of service)
   - Have your VA disability letter ready if applicable
   - Make sure your campaign medals are properly documented

2. **Know When It Doesn't Apply** Preference doesn't apply to:
   - Internal agency promotions
   - Senior Executive Service positions
   - Certain excepted service jobs
   - When you're already a permanent federal employee

3. **Use It Wisely**
   - You can use preference every time you apply for a competitive service job
   - It applies to temporary and permanent positions differently
   - Some special hiring authorities might be better than using preference – we'll cover those next

4. **Common Gotchas to Avoid**
   - Make sure your disability rating letter is current
   - Double-check that your service dates match the qualifying periods
   - Ensure your discharge was under honorable conditions
   - Don't assume preference guarantees you a job – you still need to be qualified

Remember, Veterans' Preference is just one tool in your federal employment toolbox, but it's a powerful one when used correctly. It's also worth noting that if you believe your preference rights were violated, you have the right to appeal to the U.S. Department of Labor's Veterans' Employment and Training Service (VETS).

A quick note for you overachievers: the detailed rules about Veterans' Preference can be found in Title 5, United States Code, Section 2108. But don't worry – you don't need to memorize the law. Just remember the basics we've covered here, and keep the documentation handy to prove your eligibility.

Veterans' Recruitment Appointment (VRA): The Fast Track to Federal Employment

Think of VRA as having a FastPass at Disney World, but better – because both you AND the hiring manager get to skip the long lines. This authority is a win-win that HR and hiring managers absolutely love because it lets them bring qualified veterans on board quickly without jumping through the usual bureaucratic hoops.

Why HR and Hiring Managers Love VRA

Let's be real for a minute – federal hiring can move slower than a sloth swimming in molasses. But with VRA:

- Managers can hire you directly and quickly (we're talking days or weeks instead of months)
- There's no need to post and complete the job (massive time saver)
- They get proven performers with military experience
- The two-year trial period lets them evaluate performance before permanent placement
- They can fill critical positions faster than through traditional hiring
- It helps them meet their veteran hiring goals

Why You'll Love VRA

- You can get hired for positions up to GS-11 without competing with the general public
- After two years of successful performance, you're converted to a permanent position
- You can qualify for positions based on your military experience
- There's potential for career advancement beyond GS-11 after conversion
- You keep all your veterans' benefits and preferences
- You start earning federal benefits right away

Who's Eligible for VRA?

You qualify if you are:

- A disabled veteran; OR
- A veteran who served on active duty during a war (including campaigns or expeditions for which a campaign badge is authorized); OR
- A veteran who served in a military operation for which an Armed Forces Service Medal was awarded; OR
- A recently separated veteran (within the last 3 years)

How to Use VRA Like a Pro

Step 1: Get Your Documentation Ready

- DD-214 (the long form with the character of service)
- VA disability letter (if applicable)
- Campaign medals or Armed Forces Service Medal documentation
- Resume tailored to federal positions

Step 2: Find VRA Opportunities

- Check USAJOBS.gov for VRA-eligible positions
- Look for the "Hiring Path" icon for veterans
- Network with agency veteran employment coordinators
- Attend federal job fairs (hiring managers there often have VRA authority)

Step 3: Market Yourself

- Clearly state your VRA eligibility in your application
- Translate your military skills to match job requirements
- Highlight relevant experience and training
- Be ready to explain how your military background adds value

Pro Tips for VRA Success

1. **Be Strategic**
   - Look for agencies with high veteran employment rates
   - Target positions that match your military skills
   - Don't limit yourself to your branch's civilian agencies

2. **Understand the Process**
   - You'll still need to qualify for the position
   - The two-year period is like a trial run
   - You can be promoted during the two-year period
   - Conversion to permanent status isn't automatic (but it usually happens)

3. **Make the Most of Your Two Years**
   - Document your achievements
   - Take advantage of training opportunities
   - Network within your agency

o   Learn the federal system

Real Talk About VRA

Here's the inside scoop: HR specialists and hiring managers often prefer VRA over other hiring authorities because it's simpler for them to use and gives them a chance to evaluate you before making things permanent. It's like dating before marriage – both sides get to make sure it's a good fit.

When managers have an immediate need (and they usually do), VRA lets them:

1. Skip the lengthy competitive hiring process
2. Get you on board quickly
3. Start training you for the role immediately
4. Fill critical positions with qualified veterans
5. Meet their diversity and veteran hiring goals

For you, this means:

- Faster hiring process
- Less competition
- Direct pathway to permanent employment
- Opportunity to prove yourself on the job

The Bottom Line

VRA is one of those rare situations where everybody wins. The agency gets a qualified veteran quickly, you get your foot in the door, and both sides have time to ensure it's a good match. If you're eligible for VRA, make it a key part of your federal job search strategy. Smart hiring managers are always on the lookout for good candidates they can bring on through VRA – make sure they know you're one of them.

30% or More Disabled Veteran Authority: The Ultimate Fast Track

If you have a service-connected disability rated at 30% or more, you're holding what might be the most powerful federal hiring authority out there. This isn't just a foot in the door – it's like having a master key to the entire federal building. Let's break down why this authority is such a game-changer.

Why This Authority is Special

Unlike other hiring authorities that come with various limitations, the 30% or More Disabled Veteran authority:

- Works for any grade level (yes, even senior positions)
- Applies to any job series (technical, administrative, professional – you name it)
- Has no time limits or expiration date
- Requires only a 60-day conditional period before permanent status
- Can be used multiple times throughout your career
- Doesn't require public posting of the position

Benefits for Hiring Managers

Why do hiring managers love this authority? Let me count the ways:

1. **Speed of Hire:** They can bring you on board in days rather than months
2. **Flexibility:** Works for any position they need to fill
3. **Simplicity:** Less paperwork and red tape than competitive hiring
4. **Mission Impact:** Gets qualified veterans to contribute to the mission quickly

5. **Meeting Goals:** Helps achieve disability hiring goals and veteran employment targets
6. **Retention:** Disabled veterans often have high retention rates, reducing future hiring needs

How to Leverage This Authority

Step 1: Get Your Documentation Ready

- VA Disability Rating Letter (must clearly show 30% or higher rating)
- DD-214 (Member 4 copy showing the character of discharge)
- Updated federal resume
- Current SF-15 (Application for 10-Point Veteran Preference)

Step 2: Understand Your Rights

- You can be considered for any position you qualify for
- No public job announcement is required
- You can be appointed without competition
- After 60 days of satisfactory service, conversion to permanent status is almost automatic
- You maintain eligibility even if your disability rating changes later

Step 3: Strategic Job Search

- Network with agency Veteran Employment Program Officers
- Connect with Selective Placement Program Coordinators
- Attend federal job fairs with your documentation ready
- Join veteran employee resource groups
- Consider all agencies, not just veteran-focused ones

Making the Most of Your First 60 Days

Once hired, those first 60 days are crucial. Here's how to make them count:

1. **Document Everything**
    - Keep a work journal
    - Save emails praising your work
    - Track all accomplishments
    - Document completed training

2. **Build Relationships**
    - Get to know your teammates
    - Connect with other veterans in your agency
    - Build rapport with your supervisor
    - Find a mentor if possible

3. **Learn the Culture**
    - Understand agency procedures
    - Learn the unwritten rules
    - Adapt to federal workplace norms
    - Know your performance expectations

Accommodations and Support

This authority comes with strong accommodation support:

- You have the right to request reasonable accommodations
- Agencies must make good faith efforts to accommodate your needs
- Many agencies have dedicated disability coordinators
- Special equipment or modifications can be provided if needed
- Flexible work schedules might be available
- Telework options may be offered where appropriate

Pro Tips for Success

1. **Be Proactive**
    - Don't wait for jobs to be posted
    - Reach out to agencies directly
    - Network with hiring managers
    - Keep your documentation current

2. **Know Your Worth**
    - Don't undersell yourself
    - Apply for positions matching your qualifications
    - Negotiate your starting salary
    - Consider the entire benefits package

3. **Think Long Term**
    - Look for agencies with promotion potential
    - Consider career ladder positions
    - Plan your career progression
    - Take advantage of training opportunities

Real Talk Moment

Here's something many people don't realize: this authority isn't a "charity program" – it's a strategic hiring tool that benefits both you and the agency. Hiring managers often specifically seek out 30% or more disabled veterans because:

- You bring valuable skills and perspective
- You've proven your ability to adapt and overcome challenges
- You understand federal service and mission focus
- You've already demonstrated commitment to public service
- Your military training brings added value to the workplace

The Bottom Line

The 30% or More Disabled Veteran authority is one of the most powerful paths into federal service. Use it wisely, but don't be shy about using it. You earned this benefit through your service and sacrifice. When combined with your skills and experience, it's not just about getting a job – it's about launching a rewarding federal career.

Remember: This authority is your golden ticket, but you still need to be qualified for the position. Focus on roles where your skills and experience match the requirements, and you'll be setting yourself up for long-term success in federal service.

Other Cool Authorities You Should Know About

Schedule A Authority: A Powerful Path for Those with Disabilities

Schedule A isn't just another hiring authority – it's a game-changer for individuals with disabilities, and yes, it can be used alongside your veteran status. Here's what makes it special:

Who Qualifies?

- People with severe physical disabilities
- Those with psychiatric disabilities
- Individuals with intellectual disabilities
- Veterans with service-connected disabilities may qualify
- Documentation needed from a doctor, rehabilitation specialist, or licensed medical professional

Why It's Awesome:

- No public posting requirement

- Can be used for any grade level
- Conversion to permanent status after 2 years
- Reasonable accommodations are guaranteed
- Can be faster than traditional hiring

Pro Tips for Schedule A:

1. Get your documentation right:
   - Letter must be on letterhead
   - Must specify you're qualified for the job
   - Must state that you have a qualifying condition
   - Keep multiple copies handy

2. Connect with the right people:
   - Agency Selective Placement Program Coordinators
   - Disability Program Managers
   - EEO offices

Veterans VEOA (Veterans Employment Opportunities Act)

This is your "access all areas" pass to jobs typically reserved for current federal employees. It's like having an employee badge before you're even hired.

Eligibility Requirements:

- 3+ years of active service
- Separated under honorable conditions
- For National Guard/Reserves: must have full active-duty tours (not just training)

What VEOA Gets You:

- Apply to "Status" or "Internal" job announcements
- Compete with current federal employees
- Access to Merit Promotion positions
- No grade level limitations
- Permanent positions with full benefits

Strategic Use of VEOA:

1. **Job Search Tips:**
   - Look for "Status Candidates" announcements
   - Search "Merit Promotion" listings
   - Check "Internal to Agency" postings

2. **Application Tactics:**
   - Clearly mark VEOA eligibility
   - Include DD-214 with application
   - Highlight relevant experience
   - Use a federal resume format

3. **When to Use It:**
   - When the position isn't publicly advertised
   - For higher-graded positions
   - When seeking specific agencies
   - To access more job opportunities

Military Spouse Preference (MSP): Supporting Our Military Families

This is a fantastic program that recognizes the sacrifices military spouses make. While not technically a veteran authority, it's crucial to know if you're a veteran with a spouse or if you're married to an active duty service member.

Who's Eligible:

- Spouses of active duty service members
- Spouses of 100% disabled veterans
- Widows/widowers of service members who died on active duty
- Must be relocating with a military spouse under PCS orders

Key Benefits:

- Priority consideration for DoD positions
- Preference in the selection process
- Access to positions at new duty stations
- Can be used with PPP (Priority Placement Program)
- Valid at each new duty station

How It Works:

1. **At New Duty Station:**
    - Register in Program S (Spouse Preference Program)
    - Valid for moves within the commuting area
    - Use within 30 days of reporting to the new duty station

2. **Documentation Needed:**
    - Marriage certificate
    - PCS orders

- SF-50 (if previously employed by the federal government)
- Veterans' 100% disability rating (if applicable)
- DD-214 (if spouse is a veteran)

3. **Strategic Usage:**

- Start applying before you move
- Register with the local civilian personnel office
- Network at new location
- Consider remote work options

Pro Tips for Military Spouses:

1. **Timing Is Everything:**
   - Begin job search 6 months before PCS
   - Register for MSP immediately upon arrival
   - Don't wait for orders to start networking

2. **Maximize Your Chances:**
   - Apply to multiple positions
   - Consider career ladder positions
   - Look at multiple agencies
   - Use USA Jobs, a resume builder

3. **Know Your Rights:**
   - Preference applies to most competitive service jobs
   - Valid for NAF positions too
   - Can be used with other hiring authorities
   - Doesn't expire until you accept or decline a position

The Power of Combining Authorities

Here's a pro tip many people miss: These authorities aren't mutually exclusive. You can often combine them for maximum effect:

- Use Schedule A with Veterans' Preference
- Combine VEOA with VRA eligibility
- Stack Military Spouse Preference with Schedule A
- Mix and match based on your situation

Real Talk About These Authorities

Each of these authorities has its sweet spot:

- Schedule A: Best for rapid hiring and guaranteed accommodations
- VEOA: Perfect for accessing internal positions and career growth
- MSP: Ideal for maintaining career continuity during military moves

The key is knowing which one (or combination) to use when. Consider:

1. Type of position you're seeking
2. Grade level you're targeting
3. How quickly you need to be hired
4. Location and agency preferences
5. Your long-term career goals

The Bottom Line

These "other" authorities might seem less prominent than VRA or 30% Disabled Veteran hiring, but they're incredibly powerful when used correctly. Keep them in your back pocket – you never know when they might be exactly what you need to land that perfect federal job.

Remember to check OPM's website regularly for updates to these authorities. The government occasionally tweaks the rules and requirements, and staying informed gives you an edge in your federal job search.

Pro Tips for Using These Authorities: Your Guide to Success

1. **Be Proactive and Proud About Your Status**

Let's get something straight right off the bat – these hiring authorities aren't handouts or special favors. You earned these benefits through your service, and agencies WANT to use them. Here's how to own it:

- **In Your Resume:**
    - Clearly state your veteran status in your summary
    - List all qualifying authorities you're eligible for
    - Include your disability rating if applicable
    - Mention campaign medals and service periods
    - Add "Veteran" to your email signature

- **In Your Cover Letter:**
    - State your hiring authority eligibility upfront
    - Explain which authorities you qualify for
    - Reference any service-connected ratings
    - Connect your military experience to the job

2. **Master Your Documentation Game**

Think of your documents like your military gear – you need them ready to go at a moment's notice:

Create a "Ready to Deploy" Folder (Digital and Physical) With:

- DD-214 (all copies, especially Member 4)
- VA disability letter (most recent)
- Campaign medals documentation
- SF-15 (Application for 10-Point Veterans' Preference)
- Service records
- Training certificates
- Security clearance documentation
- Professional licenses

Pro Organization Tips:

- Scan everything (high quality)
- Create a cloud backup
- Keep documents updated
- Have both color and black/white copies
- Save in multiple formats (PDF, JPG)

3. **Learn the Federal HR Language**

Speaking the language of federal HR is like learning a new MOS. Here's your crash course:

Key Terms to Know:

- Appointing Authority
- Time-in-Grade
- KSAs (Knowledge, Skills, and Abilities)
- Certification/Certificate
- Series and Grade
- Merit Promotion
- Direct Hire Authority
- Quality Categories

Where to Learn More:

- OPM.gov glossary
- Agency HR websites
- Federal HR training resources
- Veteran service organizations

4. **Build and Maintain Your Federal HR Network**

This is CRUCIAL – your network can be more valuable than any single authority. Here's how to build it:

Essential Contacts to Make:

1. **Veteran Employment Program Officers (VEPOs)**
   - Find them at every major agency
   - Schedule introduction calls
   - Add them on LinkedIn
   - Follow up regularly

2. **Agency HR Specialists**
   - Connect at job fairs
   - Request informational interviews
   - Keep their contact information
   - Send periodic check-in emails

3. **Selective Placement Program Coordinators**
   - Especially important for Schedule A
   - Can help with accommodation needs
   - Know about upcoming positions

4. **Agency Veterans' Coordinators**
   - Often, veterans themselves
   - Know the inside track
   - Can provide mentoring
   - Understand both worlds

How to Reach Out:

- "Hi, I'm [Name], a veteran interested in working at [Agency]. Could I schedule 15 minutes to learn more about veteran opportunities?"
- "I saw your agency at a job fair but couldn't attend. Could we connect to discuss veteran hiring programs?"
- "I'm a 30% disabled veteran with experience in [Field]. I'd love to learn more about positions in your agency."

Maintaining Contact:

- Set calendar reminders for follow-ups
- Share relevant articles or news
- Update them on your job search progress
- Thank them for their time and help
- Offer to help other veterans they know

5. **Work the System (Legally and Ethically)**

Agency-Specific Research:

- Find out which agencies actively hire veterans
- Research their veteran employment rates
- Look for agencies with veteran ERGs (Employee Resource Groups)
- Check which authorities they commonly use

Direct Outreach Strategy:

1. **Find the Right Contact:**
    - Check agency websites for veteran coordinators
    - Call HR departments directly
    - Use LinkedIn to find veteran program managers
    - Ask other veterans who work there

2. **Make the Connection:**
    - Introduce yourself professionally
    - Be clear about your goals
    - Have your elevator pitch ready
    - Know what you bring to the table

3. **Follow Up:**
    - Send thank-you emails
    - Keep track of conversations
    - Note any referrals or suggestions
    - Act on their recommendations

6. **Stay Current and Connected**

Key Resources to Bookmark:

- www.opm.gov/fedshirevets/
- Agency veteran program pages
- USAJobs veteran resources
- Federal HR blogs and newsletters

Regular Check-ins:

- Set up job alerts
- Follow agencies on social media
- Join veteran employee groups
- Attend virtual job fairs

The Power of Persistence

Remember this: HR specialists and veteran coordinators WANT to help you, but they're often juggling multiple priorities. Be:

- Persistent but not pushy
- Professional but personable

- Prepared but patient
- Proactive but polite

Your follow-up strategy might look like this:

1. Initial contact
2. Thank you an email within 24 hours
3. Follow-up in one week
4. Monthly check-ins with updates
5. Special reach-outs when relevant positions open

Bottom Line

The most successful veteran job seekers aren't just qualified – they're connected. Build and maintain your network like you maintain your military equipment: regularly, carefully, and with purpose. And remember, these HR contacts aren't just helping you get a job; they're helping you launch a federal career. Treat them accordingly.

Remember: Every HR specialist or veteran coordinator you connect with is potentially a long-term career ally. Nurture these relationships, keep in touch, and always, always express gratitude for their help.

The Real Bottom Line

Let's talk straight about what really matters in federal hiring. Having these hiring authorities is a lot like having specialized equipment in the military – they're powerful tools when used correctly, but you need to know how to use them effectively.

Think about it this way: these authorities open doors that might otherwise be closed. They get your resume on the right desk and give you legitimate advantages in the hiring process. But once that door is open, it's all about you.

Here's what actually matters in this process:

1. Your hiring authority gets you in the door – it's your access badge to opportunities
2. Your qualifications get you considered – just like meeting prerequisites for military schools
3. Your preparation gets you selected – think of it like preparing for a promotion board
4. Your performance keeps you employed – bringing your A-game every day

But – and this is important – these authorities aren't magic wands. They're more like tactical advantages. You still need to:

- Know which positions match your skills
- Present your qualifications effectively
- Prepare thoroughly for interviews
- Build professional relationships within agencies
- Maintain high performance standards

The most successful federal job seekers understand this balance. They use their hiring authorities strategically, prepare thoroughly, and approach the process with both confidence and humility.

Federal veteran hiring authorities are powerful tools, but they're just that – tools. Like any tool, they work best when you know how and when to use them. Take some time to understand which ones you're eligible for and how they might fit into your federal job search strategy.

Want More Info? This chapter just scratches the surface. For the complete scoop on veteran hiring authorities, eligibility requirements, and current federal job opportunities, visit *www.opm.gov/fedshirevets/*. The site is constantly updated with new information, resources, and opportunities specifically for veterans looking to join the federal workforce.

Debrief: Chapter 13 - Federal Veteran Hiring Authorities: Your Secret Weapon for Government Jobs

1. **Understand Veteran Hiring Authorities:**
   Federal veteran hiring authorities, such as Veterans' Preference, VRA (Veterans Recruitment Appointment), and the 30% or More Disabled Veteran Hiring Authority, offer pathways to secure government jobs faster and with less competition.

2. **Leverage Veterans' Preference:**
   Veterans' Preference grants eligible veterans priority in competitive hiring. Ensure you understand the distinctions between 5-point and 10-point preferences and provide supporting documentation like your DD Form 214 or VA disability letter.

3. **Utilize Special Hiring Authorities:**
   Explore non-competitive hiring options like:

   - **Veterans Recruitment Appointment (VRA):** For positions up to GS-11, available to certain veterans.
   - **30% or More Disabled Veteran:** Allows non-competitive appointments for qualified veterans with a 30% or higher disability rating.
   - **Schedule A Hiring Authority:** For individuals with disabilities, including disabled veterans, to bypass traditional competitive hiring processes.

4. **Network with Federal HR Professionals:**
   Contact agency HR specialists to discuss hiring authorities and

how to apply them to your job search. They can guide you in tailoring applications to available positions.

5. **Search for Veteran-Specific Job Postings:**
   Use USAJOBS filters to find positions that explicitly encourage veteran applicants or fall under special hiring authorities.

6. **Prepare Comprehensive Documentation:**
   Compile essential documents, including your DD Form 214, VA disability rating letter, and any other supporting materials, to verify your eligibility for hiring authorities.

7. **Target Agencies That Value Veterans:**
   Some federal agencies, such as the Department of Veterans Affairs, Department of Defense, and Homeland Security, actively seek veteran applicants for their mission alignment and transferable skills.

8. **Seek Help from Veteran Support Resources:**
   Organizations like the VA, OPM, and veteran-focused career counselors can provide personalized guidance on navigating federal hiring authorities and maximizing their benefits.

9. **Track Application Outcomes:**
   Stay proactive by monitoring your applications through USAJOBS and contacting HR specialists to confirm whether your veteran status is being applied correctly.

10. **Be Persistent and Strategic:**
    Federal hiring can be competitive and time-consuming, but leveraging these hiring authorities gives you a significant edge. Stay patient and continue refining your approach to achieve success.

PART THREE:

EXECUTE! EXECUTE! EXECUTE! MAKE IT HAPPEN

Dr. Jason Piccolo

Chapter 14: Making Your Military Story Work for You: A Guide to Cover Letters

Picture this: It's 2300 hours, and you're sitting at your desk, staring at a blank screen. The soft glow of your monitor illuminates a stack of awards, certificates, and that treasured DD-214. After years of writing ops orders, AARs, and performance reviews, you'd think this would be easy. But this is different. This time, you're trying to translate years of military excellence into civilian speak, and somehow, "led decisive combat operations" doesn't seem quite right for that corporate project manager role.

Sound familiar?

You're part of an elite group – one of the 200,000+ service members who transition into civilian life each year. The challenge isn't your experience; you've got that in spades. The challenge is telling your story in a way that resonates across the civilian-military divide. That award for managing a forward operating base's logistics? That's supply chain expertise. The time you coordinated multi-unit training exercises? That's project management gold. Your military story isn't just impressive – it's exactly what employers are looking for. You just need to know how to tell it.

Think about it: Where else but in military service do you learn to lead diverse teams, manage millions in equipment, and make critical decisions under pressure before you're 25? What other organization routinely trusts young professionals with responsibilities that would make corporate VPs nervous? Your experience isn't just relevant – it's exceptional.

But here's where many veterans get stuck. They either downplayed their service, reducing years of leadership to "followed orders and worked as part of a team," or they went the other direction, keeping all the military jargon and hoping civilian employers would figure it out. There's a better way.

This chapter isn't just about writing cover letters – it's about bridging worlds. It's about taking the skills, leadership, and excellence you demonstrated in uniform and presenting them in a way that makes civilian employers take notice. Whether you're aiming for a federal position or a Fortune 500 company, your military experience is pure gold – you just need the right tools to help others see its value.

Remember: You've already proven yourself in one of the world's most demanding environments. Now, it's time to help civilian employers understand just how valuable that experience is.

The Federal Job Hunt: Playing Chess, Not Checkers

Think of federal job applications like planning a high-stakes tactical operation. Every move matters and reconnaissance is critical. Many veterans stumble here not because they lack qualifications but because they haven't cracked the code of federal hiring. The truth is, a federal resume and cover letter are completely different from their civilian counterparts – they're more like detailed mission briefings than traditional job applications.

Before we dive into strategy, let's get real about federal hiring. These positions often receive hundreds of applications, and your first reader might be an HR specialist who's never served in uniform. They're armed with a checklist of requirements, and their mission is simple: find candidates who clearly demonstrate they meet every single one.

This is where most veterans miss their first opportunity. They submit the same cover letter they'd send to a civilian employer – concise, general, and focused on broad leadership skills. But in federal hiring, that's like bringing a knife to a gunfight.

Your Three-Move Strategy

Picture this: Instead of writing a cover letter, you're preparing a mission brief for your next commander. But this time, you've got three carefully planned moves to make your case. Let's break it down:

First Move: The Situation Brief

Your opening needs to hit hard and fast with critical information. Start with your current status, including your exact target position, years of experience, security clearance, and veterans' preference category. Here's what it should sound like:

"I am writing regarding Supervisory IT Specialist position #24-DOD-789 at the Defense Information Systems Agency. With 12 years of experience in secure networks and systems architecture, including direct supervision of enterprise-level communications platforms, I bring the technical expertise and leadership capabilities required for this role. I maintain an active TS/SCI clearance and hold both CISSP and PMP certifications."

Second Move: The Evidence

This is where you present your proof of concept – hard evidence that you can execute the mission. Take each key requirement from the job posting and match it with your experience. For example:

When they ask for project management experience, respond with: "Directed a 25-person joint service team across three combatant commands, managing a $7M modernization project. Achieved 99.9% network uptime while reducing operational costs by 30% through innovative resource allocation and process improvements."

The key is to mirror their language while translating your military achievements into federal terms. If they want someone who can "coordinate cross-functional initiatives," tell them about how you "synchronized operations across multiple units" or "integrated diverse teams to achieve mission objectives."

Final Move: The Action Plan

Your closing needs to be decisive and forward-looking. Include your administrative details (SF-15, DD-214, transcripts, security clearance transfer status) and make it easy for them to take the next step. For example:

"I have attached my SF-15, DD-214, and required certifications for your review. My TS/SCI clearance is currently active and transferable. I am available for interviews at your convenience and can be reached at [phone] or [email]. I look forward to discussing how my experience in high-stakes IT operations and team leadership aligns with DISA's modernization objectives."

Mission-Critical Tips

Document Intelligence: Study the job announcement like you're planning an operation. Every required and desired qualification should be addressed in your letter. Note their specific terms and phrases – these are your keywords.

Tactical Communication: Use active voice always. "Led," "Directed," "Implemented" – these are your power words. Back everything up with specific metrics and achievements. If you know relevant federal regulations or standards, reference them.

Quality Control: Triple-check all form numbers and position details. Verify your veterans' preference category. Ensure security clearance information is current and accurate.

Remember: In federal hiring, thoroughness beats brevity. Your cover letter might run longer than a civilian version, and that's okay. Your mission is to leave no doubt that you meet every requirement. This isn't the time for subtlety – it's the time for clear, specific evidence that you're the right person for the job.

Real Talk About Digital Applications: From Stone Tablets to AI

Let's have an honest conversation about federal HR systems. Here's the reality: you might be applying to a cutting-edge cyber security role at the NSA, but there's a decent chance your application will first go through a system that feels like it was designed when floppy disks were high-tech.

The Digital Divide

Welcome to one of the government's best-kept secrets: federal HR systems exist on a spectrum from "Space Force modern" to "Civil War era paperwork." Some agencies are running sleek, AI-powered application systems that can parse your documents like a dream. Others... well, let's just say they might as well be using carrier pigeons.

Some agencies, like the Department of Defense and Homeland Security, have modernized their systems with sophisticated applicant tracking software that can handle complex formatting and scan for keywords efficiently. These systems can process your carefully crafted PDF with all its perfect formatting and even understand the context.

But then there are the others. Picture a computer system that might have been cutting-edge when Desert Storm was happening. These legacy systems can transform your beautifully formatted cover letter into something that looks like it went through a paper shredder and was reassembled by a blindfolded person.

Playing It Safe: The Universal Approach

Since you usually can't know which type of system you're dealing with until it's too late, here's your survival guide:

Digital Formatting Strategy: Think of your application like a radio transmission in hostile territory - you want it to get through clearly regardless of who's receiving it. This means:

Plain Text Insurance Policy: Always have two versions of your cover letter ready:

- A clean, professionally formatted PDF for modern systems
- A plain text version that could survive being transmitted by Morse code

For the formatted version:

- Stick to basic fonts that have been around since computers were invented (Times New Roman, Arial, Courier)
- Use standard margins (1 inch all around)
- Avoid text boxes, columns, or any fancy formatting
- Keep bullets simple - basic rounds only
- Use standard section headers

For the plain text version:

- No bold, italics, or underlining
- Use dashes or asterisks for bullet points
- Use ALL CAPS sparingly for section headers
- Leave extra space between paragraphs for readability

Naming Conventions: Think about the poor HR specialist who's downloading hundreds of files. Make their life easier:

LastName_Agency_Position_CoverLetter (Example: Johnson_EPA_EnvironmentalEngineer_CoverLetter)

Note:

- Final_version_2_really_final
- Cover_letter_revised_new
- Please_hire_me_letter

Keyword Strategy: Speaking Their Language

Modern federal HR systems use Applicant Tracking Systems (ATS) that scan for keywords. But even the old-school systems have humans looking for specific terms. Your mission:

Exact Match Approach:

- Copy and paste key terms directly from the job announcement
- Include the exact phrase they use, then follow with your military translation. Example: "Demonstrated experience in project management (served as Battalion Operations Officer managing 15 concurrent training operations)."

Spelling Variations: Include common variations of technical terms:

- Cybersecurity (one word)
- Cyber security (two words)
- Cyber-security (hyphenated)

Acronym Strategy: Write out acronyms and include the abbreviated version: "Department of Defense (DoD) security protocols," "Information Technology (IT) infrastructure."

The Digital Paper Trail

Here's a pro tip: most people learn the hard way: federal HR systems love to lose documents. Your defense strategy:

Document Verification:

- Always save confirmation emails
- Screenshot confirmation pages
- Note application numbers
- Keep a log of submission dates and times
- Download copies of everything you submit

When Things Go Wrong (And They Will)

Technology hiccups happen. Have a backup plan:

- Save the HR contact information from the job posting
- Know the agency's HR office phone number
- Screenshot error messages
- Document submission attempts
- Be prepared to overnight hard copies if necessary

Remember: The most sophisticated cyber warrior might be reviewing your application... after it makes it through a system that considers dial-up internet modern technology. Plan accordingly, and you'll be ready for whatever digital obstacles the federal hiring process throws your way.

Your takeaway: Prepare for the worst, hope for the best, and always, always have a plain text backup of everything.

Think of it this way: You wouldn't send a single radio transmission without backup communications planned. Apply the same principle here.

Over-prepare on the technical side, and you can focus your energy on what really matters - showing them why you're the right person for the job.

Breaking into the Civilian World: Speaking Their Language

Have you ever watched a foreign film without subtitles? That's how many civilian hiring managers feel reading a typical military cover letter. Let's talk about why your impressive military achievements might be getting lost in translation – and how to fix that.

The Translation Challenge

Imagine walking into a civilian office and reporting, "Executed daily operations resulting in mission success with zero operational deficiencies." While that might earn you a coin in the military, in the civilian world, you might as well be speaking Klingon.

Here's the reality: Your military experience is incredibly valuable, but it needs translation. Think of yourself as a cultural interpreter, bridging the gap between two very different worlds.

The Art of Storytelling

Opening Moves That Work

Instead of: "Executed missions as Infantry Squad Leader in hostile environments"

Try This: "In high-pressure situations where split-second decisions impacted the safety and success of my 12-person team, I developed leadership skills that directly translate to your fast-paced technology environment."

Or This: "Leading teams through complex operations in challenging conditions taught me how to keep people focused, motivated, and performing at their best – skills that would bring immediate value to your manufacturing team."

Bridging Military-Civilian Experience

The Secret Formula: Military Achievement → Business Impact → Company Benefit

Instead of: "Maintained accountability of sensitive items valued at $5M"

Try This: "Managed and secured inventory valued at $5M, developing tracking systems that reduced loss by 99% – experience that would help optimize your supply chain operations."

Industry-Specific Translations

Technology Sector: Military: "Maintained secure communications in hostile territory" Civilian: "Ensured 99.9% uptime for critical communications systems while managing cybersecurity protocols for a 500-person organization"

Healthcare: Military: "Combat Lifesaver certified, treated casualties in high-stress environments" Civilian: "Performed urgent care procedures under extreme pressure while managing multiple priorities – skills directly applicable to your fast-paced emergency department"

Finance: Military: "Managed unit budget and procurement" Civilian: "Oversaw $2M annual budget, implementing cost-saving measures that reduced expenses by 25% while maintaining operational excellence"

Power Phrases That Resonate

Instead of Military Terms | Use Business Language "Conducted operations" → "Led projects" "Executed missions" → "Delivered results" "Commanded troops" → "Developed teams" "Maintained operational readiness" → "Ensured business continuity" "Achieved mission success" → "Exceeded performance targets"

Quantify Everything

Transform Military Metrics:

- "Led 12-person squad" becomes "Managed 12-person team with $1.5M in resources"
- "Conducted 50 missions" becomes "Completed 50 high-priority projects"
- "Zero safety incidents" becomes "100% safety record while managing high-risk operations"

The Personal Connection

End Strong:

1. Show you've done your homework: "Your company's recent expansion into renewable energy aligns perfectly with my experience managing large-scale logistics operations."
2. Make it about their needs: "My background in rapid decision-making and team leadership would bring immediate value to your fast-growing sales organization."
3. Look forward: "I'm excited about the opportunity to bring my operational excellence and team development experience to your organization's mission of revolutionizing customer service."

Digital Age Tips

1. LinkedIn Translation:
   - Use civilian job titles in your headline
   - Write descriptions using industry keywords
   - Connect military achievements to business outcomes

2. Resume Database Optimization:
   - Include both military and civilian terms
   - Use industry-standard job titles
   - Add skills that are trending in your target industry

Common Pitfalls to Avoid

1. The Rank Trap: Don't assume civilian employers understand military rank structure. Instead of "As a Staff Sergeant," say "As a mid-level manager."

2. The Acronym Avalanche: Skip the military acronyms entirely. No NCO, NCOIC, or OIC – spell out roles and responsibilities in business terms.

3. The Humility Hurdle: Military service often teaches humility and team-first thinking. While admirable, civilian cover letters need to sell your individual contributions. Don't be afraid to take credit for your achievements.

The Bottom Line

Your military experience is a gold mine of transferable skills. The key is helping civilian employers see the value through their lens. Every mission led, every crisis managed, every team developed – these experiences have profound value in the civilian world. Your job is to help them see it.

Remember: You're not just transitioning jobs; you're translating excellence from one context to another. Take pride in your service while showing employers how that service makes you their ideal candidate.

Your mission now? Help civilian employers understand that your military experience isn't just relevant – it's a competitive advantage.

Making Your Digital Mark: From Combat Boots to Corporate Success

Picture this: Your perfectly crafted cover letter, the one you spent hours fine-tuning, lands in an employer's system. But before any human eyes see your carefully chosen words, your application meets its first challenge: Artificial Intelligence. Welcome to the modern job hunt, where your first reviewer isn't human at all.

The Digital Gatekeeper

Today's hiring process is like a modern military operation - the first line of defense is automated. Applicant Tracking Systems (ATS) are the sentries of the corporate world, scanning your documents for specific indicators of qualification. Just as you wouldn't approach a checkpoint without proper credentials, you shouldn't send your cover letter without the right digital signatures.

Digital-First Strategy

Think of your application as a reconnaissance mission. Before you make contact with human resources, you need to get past the automated defenses. Here's your tactical approach:

Document Formatting:

- Keep it clean - no fancy formatting that could jam the digital works

- Use standard section headers: "Professional Experience," "Skills," and "Education."
- Stick to conventional fonts that render well across all systems
- Maintain consistent spacing and alignment
- Create both PDF and plain text versions - like having both digital and analog communications ready

Keyword Intelligence:

- Study the job posting like it's your mission brief
- Identify and use industry-standard terms
- Include both full terms and recognized abbreviations
- Mirror the language used in the company's own materials
- Layer in relevant industry buzzwords naturally throughout your letter

The Translation Matrix

Military Experience → Civilian Value "Combat operations" → "High-pressure environments" "Mission planning" → "Strategic project development" "After-action review" → "Performance analysis and improvement" "Command post operations" → "Operations management" "Battle tracking" → "Resource coordination" "Force protection" → "Risk management" "Combat logistics" → "Supply chain management"

Building Your Digital Brand

Your cover letter isn't standing alone anymore - it's part of your digital footprint. Consider this your personal campaign for civilian success:

Professional Platforms:

- LinkedIn profile aligned with your cover letter language
- Online portfolio (if applicable) using industry terminology

- Professional email address (no more .mil addresses)
- Digital copies of certificates and credentials ready to share

The Human Touch

While navigating the digital landscape is crucial, remember that, eventually, a human will read your story. This is where your military experience offers a unique advantage - you know how to be both technical and personable.

Bridging Worlds

Think about the best leaders you served under. They could explain complex operations in simple terms, relate to anyone in the unit, and inspire confidence through clear communication. That's exactly what your cover letter needs to do.

Remember:

- Tell stories that civilians can relate to
- Focus on universal leadership principles
- Share results that matter in any environment
- Connect your military excellence to their business needs

The Reality Check

Before you hit "send," run your cover letter through this final inspection:

Digital Readiness Check:

- Remove all military acronyms and jargon
- Verify industry keywords are present
- Confirm formatting is ATS-friendly
- Test readability with civilian proof-readers
- Save in multiple formats (PDF, .docx, plain text)

The Bottom Line: Your New Mission

Your military service has given you something invaluable - not just skills and experience but the ability to adapt and overcome challenges. That time, you reorganized logistics under fire? That's change management. The mission where you coordinated with multiple units? That's stakeholder engagement. The crisis you solved with limited resources? That's innovation and resourcefulness.

Every military experience has a civilian counterpart. Your challenge isn't proving you can do the job - it's helping employers see what you already know: your military background makes you uniquely qualified to excel in their organization.

Your Action Plan

1. Translate your experience
2. Format for digital success
3. Speak their language
4. Tell your story
5. Show your value

Remember: This isn't just about getting a job - it's about continuing to serve, just in a different uniform. Your mission now is to bring your leadership, discipline, and excellence to the civilian sector. They need what you have. You just need to help them see it.

And if your first attempt doesn't hit the target? Remember what you learned in the service: adapt, overcome, and keep moving forward. Every great mission requires intelligence gathering, planning, and sometimes a few revised strategies. Your transition to civilian success is no different.

Take pride in your service and confidence in your abilities, and keep refining your approach until you find the right match. After all, you've overcome tougher challenges. This is just your next mission.

A Final Word: Understanding the Two Paths

Let's be real about how your cover letter travels in both worlds. Think of it like sending two different types of communications – one through a civilian network and another through military channels.

The Tale of Two Systems

In the civilian world, your cover letter is often your first handshake – a crucial introduction that helps you stand out from the stack. Hiring managers might even read it before your resume, using it to decide if they want to learn more about you. It's your chance to tell your story, make connections, and help them see why your military experience makes you the perfect fit for their team.

The federal route? That's a different mission entirely. Your cover letter might spend some time in administrative limbo, waiting in your application package like supplies waiting to clear customs. HR specialists are primarily focused on checking qualification boxes and veterans' preference points. They're looking at your resume, your SF-50s, and your DD-214 and making sure you meet the basic requirements.

But here's the strategic value – when your federal application package finally reaches the hiring manager or selection panel, that's when your cover letter springs into action. These decision-makers, often fellow veterans or long-time civil servants, know exactly what they're looking for. They understand military experience, and your carefully crafted cover letter helps them connect the dots between your service and their needs.

The Bottom Line

Whether you're targeting civilian opportunities or federal service, your cover letter is a tactical tool that serves different purposes in different environments. In civilian hiring, it's your advanced team making first contact and establishing your value proposition. In federal hiring, it's more like a delayed-fuse asset, waiting to make its impact when it reaches the right audience.

The key to success? Prepare for both battlefields. Craft your cover letter with the same precision you'd use to plan any military operation. Because whether it's read in the first five minutes or the final round, when the right person reads it, you want it to hit the target.

Remember: In both worlds, someone is eventually going to read your story. Make it count.

Debrief: Chapter 14 - Making Your Military Story Work for You: A Guide to Cover Letters

1. **Craft a Strong Opening:**
   Begin with a compelling introduction that connects your military background to the job. Highlight your enthusiasm for the role and the unique value you bring as a veteran.

2. **Translate Your Experience:**
   Use civilian language to describe your military roles and achievements. Focus on transferable skills like leadership, project management, and problem-solving that align with the job description.

3. **Personalize Each Cover Letter:**
   Tailor your cover letter to the specific position and organization. Show that you've researched the company and understand how your skills fit their needs.

4. **Showcase Quantifiable Achievements:**
   Provide specific examples of your accomplishments. For instance:

"Led a team of 15 personnel, improving operational efficiency by 25% during high-pressure deployments."

5. **Bridge the Gap Between Military and Civilian Work:**
   Emphasize how your military training and experience prepare you for success in civilian roles. Draw parallels between military missions and the company's objectives.

6. **Demonstrate Soft Skills:**
   Highlight qualities like adaptability, teamwork, and emotional intelligence. Use examples to show how these traits contributed to your success in the military.

7. **Focus on the Employer's Needs:**
   Align your experience with the job's requirements. Explain how your background solves their problems or meets their goals, shifting the focus from you to them.

8. **Close with Confidence:**
   End with a strong closing paragraph. Reaffirm your interest in the position, express your eagerness to contribute, and invite the employer to contact you for an interview.

9. **Edit for Clarity and Impact:**
   Keep your cover letter concise (one page) and error-free. Use a professional tone and format, ensuring your message is clear and impactful.

10. **Include Relevant Attachments:**
    Mention accompanying documents like your resume, DD Form 214, or references if applicable. Ensure these are well-organized and tailored for the role.

Chapter 15: The Network Effect

The transition from military to civilian life involves navigating a different kind of battlefield—one where your network can become your most powerful ally. Just as you relied on your unit for mission success, your professional network will become your new support system in the civilian world. Like any military operation, building and maintaining this network requires strategy, persistence, and dedication to the mission.

Think of your network as a tactical support team: some members provide intelligence about industry trends and company cultures, others offer cover as you advance toward your career objectives, and still others serve as forward observers, spotting opportunities before they become widely known. Each connection in your network, like each member of your unit, brings unique capabilities and insights to support your mission.

Networking isn't just about finding your next job; it's about building lasting relationships that can support your entire career journey. In the military, you learned that the strongest units are built on trust, mutual support, and shared experiences. The same principles apply to civilian networking. Your network becomes your new band of brothers and sisters, supporting you through career transitions, celebrating your victories, and helping you navigate challenges.

Remember: In the military, you never went into battle alone. The same principle applies to your civilian career journey. Your network will become your force multiplier, providing:

- Intelligence gathering about industries and opportunities
- Reconnaissance of company cultures and work environments

- Supply lines of information and resources
- Force protection through mentorship and guidance
- Strategic support for career advancement

Network Foundation

Understanding Civilian Networking Culture

Military service members operate in a structured environment where relationships and advancement often follow clear hierarchical paths. The civilian world, however, thrives on informal connections and organic relationship building. In civilian networking, the emphasis is less on rank and more on mutual value creation.

This shift can feel like moving from a well-mapped terrain to uncharted territory. In the military, you knew exactly who to salute, who to report to, and how to address each person you encountered. The civilian networking landscape operates differently:

The Chain of Command vs. The Web of Connections

- **Military Structure**: Clear reporting lines, defined protocols, and established channels of communication
- **Civilian Reality**: Fluid relationships that cross departments, industries, and organizational levels
- **Key Adjustment**: Learn to build relationships horizontally (peers across different companies) as well as vertically (up and down organizational structures)

Communication Styles

- **Military Approach**: Direct, mission-focused, often brief and formal

- **Civilian Style**: More nuanced, relationship-focused, with varying levels of formality
- **Making the Shift**:
    - Replace "Sir/Ma'am" with first names (when appropriate)
    - Soften direct orders into collaborative requests
    - Balance professional formality with personal warmth

Building Trust

- **Military Method**: Trust often comes from rank, position, and shared military experiences
- **Civilian Way**: Trust builds through:
    - Consistent follow-through on commitments
    - Genuine interest in others' success
    - Shared professional experiences
    - Demonstrated expertise and reliability
    - Personal connections and mutual interests

The Power Dynamic

- **Military Reality**: Clear rank structure defines interactions
- **Civilian World**: Power and influence flow through:
    - Industry expertise
    - Professional reputation
    - Network breadth and depth
    - Ability to connect and help others
    - Track record of success

Think of civilian networking as building alliances rather than following a chain of command. Your goal is to create genuine connections based on shared interests, experiences, and professional goals. This means:

1. **Be a Scout**: Gather intelligence about industries and companies through informal conversations

2. **Act as a Diplomat**: Build relationships across different 'territories' (industries, companies, departments)
3. **Serve as a Bridge**: Connect others who might benefit from knowing each other
4. **Function as a Resource**: Share your unique military experiences and perspectives

Cultural Translation Tips

- **Instead of**: "Requesting permission to speak with [Rank] [Name]"
- **Try**: "I'd love to learn more about your experience in [industry]."
- **Instead of**: "I was ordered to contact you about…"
- **Try**: "[Mutual connection] thought we might have some interesting experiences to share."
- **Instead of**: Waiting for formal introductions
- **Try** Taking the initiative to connect while respecting boundaries

Red Flags to Avoid

- Over-emphasis on your military rank or achievements
- Expecting immediate responses or results
- Using military jargon or acronyms
- Treating networking like a mission to be completed

Green Lights to Follow

- Share stories that highlight universal skills (leadership, problem-solving, adaptability)
- Express genuine curiosity about others' civilian career paths
- Offer help before asking for favors
- Build relationships before you need them

Remember: In the civilian world, your network grows organically through authentic connections and mutual support. While it may feel less structured than the military environment, it can be equally powerful when approached with strategy and sincerity.

Identifying Existing Connections

Many service members make the mistake of thinking they need to build their professional network from scratch. The reality is that you've been building your network throughout your entire military career – you just need to recognize and activate these connections. Think of it as taking inventory of your allies before starting a new mission.

Your Ready Reserve of Connections

Fellow Veterans Who Transitioned Before You These are your advance scouts – they've already navigated the territory you're about to enter. Your network includes:

- Members of your former units who have transitioned
- Veterans you've served with at different duty stations
- Senior officers and NCOs who retired before you
- Veterans from your training courses and deployments

These connections are particularly valuable because they:

- Understand both military and civilian perspectives
- Can provide honest feedback about transition challenges
- Often want to help fellow veterans succeed
- May have insights into veteran-friendly companies
- Can share what worked and didn't work in their transition

Military Contractors You've Worked With These connections are your natural bridge to the civilian sector:

- Defense contractors from past projects
- Technical representatives who supported your equipment

- Civilian consultants on military installations
- Vendors who provided services to your unit
- Project managers from joint military-civilian initiatives

These contacts are valuable because they:

- Already understand how your military skills translate to civilian roles
- Often have extensive civilian industry connections
- May know about positions perfect for transitioning service members
- Can provide insights into contractor opportunities
- Understand both military and civilian work cultures

Civilian Employees at Your Duty Stations Don't overlook these civilian professionals you've worked alongside:

- Civil service employees
- Base support staff
- Human resources professionals
- Administrative personnel
- Civilian department heads

These connections can offer:

- Insights into civilian workplace dynamics
- Knowledge of government civilian positions
- Understanding of how military experience is viewed
- Potential job leads in government agencies
- Recommendations based on direct experience working with you

Family Members and Their Professional Connections Your personal network extends beyond your military connections:

- Immediate family members in civilian careers
- Extended family in various industries

- In-laws and their professional networks
- Family friends in business
- Relatives' colleagues and associates

Remember: While it might feel uncomfortable leveraging family connections, most people are happy to help family members of trusted colleagues.

Former Classmates and Instructors Education creates lasting connections:

- High school classmates in various careers
- College classmates (if you attended before service)
- Military training instructors who have transitioned
- Professional development course colleagues
- Technical school classmates

These connections offer:

- Diverse industry perspectives
- Access to alumni networks
- Potential mentorship opportunities
- Different geographical networking hubs
- Various career path insights

Members of Religious or Community Organizations: Your community involvement has built valuable connections:

- Religious congregation members
- Volunteer organization colleagues
- Sports team members
- Community service partners
- Hobby group participants

Mapping Potential Networking Routes

Create a strategic plan for expanding your network by identifying:

- Industries aligned with your skills and interests
- Geographic areas where you plan to live
- Companies that have veteran-friendly hiring practices
- Professional groups in your target field
- Alumni networks from your military training or education

Activating Your Network

Think of activating your network like planning and executing a military operation. Just as you wouldn't launch a mission without proper intelligence, planning, and resources, you shouldn't begin your networking campaign without careful preparation and strategy.

Phase 1: Intelligence Gathering (Create Your Connection Inventory)

Before you begin reaching out to your network, you need to gather intelligence – in this case, a comprehensive inventory of your connections. Like creating a battle roster, this process requires thoroughness and attention to detail.

Start by conducting a thorough review of your military career. Think of each duty station as a deployment zone where you establish valuable connections. Creating your inventory isn't just about listing names – it's about understanding the depth and potential of each relationship. Document who they are, where they are now, and most importantly, the shared experiences that connect you. Consider how you might provide value to them before asking for their support.

Phase 2: Mission Planning (Prioritize Your Outreach)

With your intelligence gathered, it's time to develop your strategy. Like any military operation, you need to prioritize your objectives and allocate your resources effectively. Start with your strongest connections – those you've maintained contact with or who have recently transitioned themselves.

These are your immediate assets. Then, consider those in your target industry or desired location. They become your secondary objectives.

Don't try to activate every connection simultaneously. Instead, plan a systematic approach that allows you to give each relationship the attention it deserves. Remember, networking is about the quality of connections, not the quantity of contacts.

Phase 3: Tactical Planning (Prepare Your Outreach Strategy)

For each connection, develop a specific tactical approach. Like planning individual missions within a larger operation, each outreach should be carefully crafted. Before making contact, review when you last spoke, what experiences you shared, and their current professional situation. Most importantly, consider how you might provide value to them. This reciprocal mindset is crucial for building lasting professional relationships.

Phase 4: Communication Protocol (Initial Contact)

Your initial contact is like establishing communications with an allied force. It should be clear, professional, and purpose-driven while maintaining a personal touch. Begin with a genuine reference to your shared experience, acknowledge their career progression, and make a specific, reasonable request for their insights.

A simple, effective outreach might read: "Hi James, I often think about the logistics challenges we tackled together during the 2019 deployment. I've noticed you've successfully transitioned into supply chain management, and I'm hoping to learn from your experience as I prepare for my own transition. Would you be open to a brief conversation about your journey?"

Phase 5: After Action Review (Track Your Network Activation)

Just as you would maintain a mission log, create a system to track your networking operations. This isn't just about keeping records – it's about learning from each interaction and improving your approach. Track when you've communicated, what was discussed, required follow-up actions, and potential introductions offered. Use this information to refine your networking strategy and ensure no valuable connection falls through the cracks.

Remember: Just as military operations require detailed planning, precise execution, and thorough follow-up, your networking campaign demands the same level of professionalism and attention to detail. Each connection represents a potential ally in your transition journey, and like any good military operation, success comes from proper planning, respectful execution, and diligent follow-through.

Building Professional Relationships

The art of building professional relationships in the civilian world requires a fundamental shift in mindset. While your military experience has given you invaluable leadership and communication skills, the civilian professional landscape operates under different protocols. Think of it as learning to speak a new language – the core concepts remain the same, but the delivery and context change significantly.

Military-to-Civilian Relationship Translation

In the military, relationships develop through shared hardships and clear hierarchies. The civilian world builds connections through more nuanced interactions and shared professional interests. Understanding these differences is crucial for your transition.

Key Mindset Shifts:

- From "I need those reports by 0900" to "Could we work together to get these reports completed by tomorrow morning?"
- From pure mission focus to balancing goals with relationships

- From clear rank structure to flexible networks where a junior employee might be your most valuable contact
- From unified command to collaborative decision-making

Professional Networking Etiquette:

- Find Common Ground: Start with shared interests rather than military achievements
- Show Genuine Interest: Ask thoughtful follow-up questions and listen actively
- Share Your Experience: Frame military insights in transferable terms
- Respect Time: Be flexible when scheduling and respect civilian time structures
- Express Gratitude: Follow up with specific, meaningful thanks
- Build Long-Term Connections: Maintain relationships through regular check-ins and shared resources

Remember: Professional relationship building in the civilian world is more marathon than sprint. Take time to develop authentic connections and look for ways to add value before making requests. Your military precision is an asset – just apply it with civilian-world flexibility.

Following Up and Maintaining Connections

Maintain your network like you would maintain mission-critical equipment:

- Regular check-ins (quarterly or bi-annual)
- Share relevant articles or opportunities
- Celebrate others' achievements
- Keep your contact information current
- Document key details about your connections

Giving Back to Your Network

In the military, we live by the principle "leave no one behind." This same ethos should guide your approach to professional networking. The strongest networks aren't built on transactions but on a foundation of mutual support and genuine commitment to helping others succeed. Think of your network as your new unit – your success is intertwined with theirs, and supporting others ultimately strengthens the entire group.

The Power of Reciprocity

Just as you relied on battle buddies during your service, your professional network thrives on mutual support. Every person who helps you in your transition journey represents an opportunity to pay it forward. This isn't about keeping score – it's about fostering a community of support that benefits everyone involved.

Consider your unique position: as a transitioning service member, you bridge two worlds. You understand both military precision and civilian business practices. This perspective makes you a valuable asset to your network in ways you might not realize.

Sharing Your Expertise

Your military experience has given you unique skills and perspectives that can benefit others. Maybe you're an expert in logistics, leadership, or crisis management. Perhaps you've mastered the art of clear communication under pressure or know how to build high-performing teams. These skills are valuable in civilian contexts.

Don't wait to be asked – look for opportunities to share your knowledge: "I noticed you mentioned struggling with team coordination across time zones. During my deployment, we developed some effective protocols for maintaining communication across distributed teams. Would it be helpful if I shared some of these strategies?"

Making Strategic Introductions

Think of yourself as a reconnaissance specialist in the civilian world. You're uniquely positioned to spot opportunities where different members of your network could benefit from knowing each other. When making introductions, be thoughtful and specific:

"Sarah, I'd like to introduce you to Mike. He's implementing the same inventory management system you mastered last year. Mike, Sarah's insights could be incredibly valuable for your rollout. Would you both be open to connecting?"

Remember to always ask permission before making introductions, and provide context that makes the connection valuable for both parties.

Sharing Opportunities

Your network has helped you discover opportunities – now it's your turn to do the same for others. When you learn about job openings, industry events, or professional development opportunities, think about who in your network might benefit. This isn't just about job postings; it could be:

- Industry conferences that align with someone's interests
- Training programs that could enhance their skills
- Speaking opportunities that match their expertise
- Projects that could use their unique capabilities
- Resources that could help them overcome current challenges

Mentoring Fellow Veterans

As you progress in your civilian career, you gain invaluable insights about the transition process. This knowledge is precious to service members who are just beginning their transition journey. Mentoring isn't just about formal relationships – it can take many forms:

- Sharing your transition story at veteran events
- Offering to review resumes for transitioning service members
- Providing insights about civilian workplace culture
- Connecting veterans with opportunities in your company

- Being a sounding board for those considering career changes

Your experience – including your mistakes and challenges – can help others navigate their own transitions more successfully.

The Art of Providing References

When you provide a reference, you're putting your own reputation on the line. This is a powerful way to give back, but it requires careful consideration. When done right, it can significantly impact someone's career:

- Speak to specific examples of their capabilities
- Focus on relevant skills and experiences
- Share concrete results they've achieved
- Discuss their ability to adapt and learn
- Highlight their leadership and teamwork qualities

Creating Ongoing Value

Think beyond one-time assistance. Look for ways to create lasting value for your network:

- Write articles sharing your unique military-to-civilian transition insights
- Create resources that others can use in their transition
- Build bridges between military and civilian professional communities
- Organize events that bring together veterans and civilian professionals
- Share your learning experiences as you progress in your civilian career

The Compound Effect

Remember the principle of force multiplication from your military days? The same applies to networking. Every person you help becomes another potential supporter for others in your network. Your assistance to one person can create ripple effects that benefit many others.

Remember: The goal isn't to keep a ledger of favors given and received. Instead, focus on building a community of mutual support. Your military training taught you the value of unit cohesion and teamwork. Apply these same principles to your professional network, and you'll build relationships that last throughout your civilian career.

Think of giving back as force preservation – by strengthening your network through genuine support and assistance; you're ensuring its longevity and effectiveness for everyone involved

Networking Channels

Veterans' Organizations and Groups

- American Legion
- Veterans of Foreign Wars (VFW)
- Student Veterans of America
- Service-specific associations
- Veteran-focused LinkedIn groups

Professional Associations

- Industry-specific organizations
- Local chambers of commerce
- Professional certification bodies
- Alumni associations
- Trade organizations

Industry-specific Networks

- Technology user groups
- Manufacturing associations

- Healthcare alliances
- Finance professional networks
- Government contractor groups

Social Media Networking

- LinkedIn best practices
- Professional Twitter engagement
- Industry-specific online forums
- Virtual networking events
- Professional blog communities

Networking Throughout Your Job Search Journey

Think of your job search as a military campaign – reconnaissance, engagement, and consolidation. Just as no military operation succeeds without proper intelligence and support, your job search thrives on strategic networking at every phase. Let's break down how to leverage your network effectively throughout this journey.

Pre-Mission Intelligence (Before Applying)

Before launching your application offensive, gather intelligence through your network. This phase is crucial – just as you wouldn't enter a combat zone without understanding the terrain, you shouldn't apply to companies without insider knowledge.

Start with reconnaissance through your network connections. Reach out to people who work at your target companies: "I've been following [Company Name] and am impressed by their innovation in [specific area]. Could you share your experience working there?" These conversations often reveal invaluable insights about company culture that you won't find in public sources.

Build relationships with potential allies – employees who might become your advocates. When someone at your target company takes an interest in your success, they often share intelligence about upcoming positions before they're posted publicly. They might tell you, "Our team is expanding next quarter. Would you like me to let you know when positions open up?"

Understanding industry trends and challenges through your network provides tactical advantages. When you can discuss current industry challenges in interviews, you demonstrate valuable perspective. Your network contacts can tell you what keeps them up at night: "The biggest challenge we're facing is..." This intelligence helps you position yourself as someone who can help solve their problems.

Engagement Phase (During Application Process)

Once you've launched your application, your network becomes your support unit. This is when those relationships you've cultivated can provide crucial support and intelligence.

Internal referrals are like having forward observers – they can guide your application through the process and provide real-time feedback. A connection might tell you, "Let me submit your resume directly to the hiring manager. They tend to prioritize referrals from current employees."

Your network can provide intelligence about the interview process: "The final round always includes a presentation about process improvement. They're looking for specific examples of leading change." This kind of insight helps you prepare more effectively than candidates without inside information.

Understanding team dynamics through your network helps you position yourself as the right cultural fit. A contact might share, "Our team values collaborative problem-solving over individual heroics. Make sure to emphasize your team-building experience."

Post-Engagement Operations (After Application)

Whether your application results in success or not, this phase is crucial for long-term career success. Think of it as securing your position or preparing for future operations.

If you receive an offer, your network can provide valuable negotiation intelligence: "The company typically offers signing bonuses to veterans" or "They're flexible on remote work arrangements if you ask." This information strengthens your negotiating position.

If you don't get the position, maintain those connections. Send a note like: "Thank you for all your support during my application process. While this opportunity didn't work out, I learned a lot about [Company/Industry] and would love to stay in touch about future possibilities."

Use each application experience as an intelligence-gathering opportunity. Ask your network contacts for candid feedback: "What could I have done differently?" Their insights will help you refine your approach for future opportunities.

Strategic Reserve (Long-term Relationship Building)

Throughout this process, remember you're not just building a network for your current job search – you're establishing a strategic reserve for your entire civilian career. Every connection you make, whether it leads to immediate opportunities or not, becomes part of your professional support network.

Keep these relationships active through regular communication:

- Share articles relevant to their interests
- Congratulate them on their professional achievements

- Offer to help with their projects or challenges
- Keep them updated on your own professional journey

Remember: Think of networking as building your own personal coalition of allies. Just as military success depends on strong alliances, your professional success will rely on the strength and depth of your network. Each phase of your job search presents unique opportunities to strengthen these relationships, gather intelligence, and position yourself for success.

The most successful transitions often come through network connections, but they rarely happen through a single conversation. It's the culmination of consistent relationship building, genuine engagement, and mutual support over time. Your military background taught you the value of unit cohesion and mutual support – apply these same principles to your professional networking, and you'll build a powerful alliance for your civilian career.

Learning from Others' Missteps

In military operations, we often learn as much from analyzing failures as we do from studying successes. The same principle applies to networking. Let's examine some real-world cautionary tales that highlight common networking mistakes and their consequences.

The Mass Message Mistake: Spray and Pray Doesn't Work

Consider Captain James's approach. Fresh from his military intelligence role, he decided to leverage LinkedIn for his civilian transition. He crafted what he thought was a compelling message about his leadership experience and sent it to over 500 connections simultaneously. The result? A mere handful of responses, mostly pointing out the impersonal nature of his approach, and several connections actually removed him from their networks.

The mistake wasn't just the mass messaging – it was failing to recognize that civilian networking requires the same precision and personal touch that military operations do. Just as you wouldn't send the same radio transmission to every unit regardless of their mission, you shouldn't send identical networking messages to every connection.

The Better Approach: Personalize each outreach. Research your contact's background, find genuine points of connection, and craft a message that shows you value their specific experience and insights.

The One-Way Street: The Cost of Taking Without Giving

Former Sergeant Sarah's story serves as another warning. Excited about transitioning into project management, she reached out to her network frequently – asking for introductions, requesting resume reviews, and seeking job referrals. However, when those same connections needed help with veteran hiring initiatives or sought her insights about military leadership, she was too busy to respond.

Within six months, her network became increasingly unresponsive. The bridges she'd burned through one-way networking couldn't support her when she needed them most.

The Better Approach: Think of networking like maintaining supply lines – it needs to flow both ways. Offer help before asking for it, and always look for ways to add value to your connections.

The Rank Reliance: When Hierarchy Hinders Connection

Lieutenant Colonel Thompson's transition story highlights another common pitfall. With 22 years of distinguished service, he naturally led with his rank in civilian networking situations. In meetings, he'd introduce himself as "Lieutenant Colonel Thompson, retired" and frequently referenced his command experience. While his military achievements were impressive, this approach created barriers rather than bridges.

Civilian counterparts felt intimidated or disconnected, and potentially valuable relationships never developed because he maintained a hierarchy-based mindset in an environment that prioritized collaborative relationships.

The Better Approach: Let your experiences and abilities speak for themselves. Focus on sharing relevant skills and achievements rather than emphasizing rank or position.

Charting Your Course: Moving Forward

As we conclude this chapter on networking, remember that your transition from military to civilian life is not just about finding a job – it's about building a sustainable career through meaningful professional relationships. The principles you learned in the military – preparation, strategic thinking, and attention to detail – are valuable assets in networking when adapted to civilian context.

Your Next Mission: Action Items

1. Begin your network mapping operation this week. Create a detailed inventory of your existing connections across all spheres – military, civilian, professional, and personal.

2. Deploy into two professional organizations aligned with your target industry. Attend their events, join their online communities, and begin building relationships before you need them.

3. Conduct one informational interview each month. These reconnaissance missions will provide valuable intelligence about your target industry while building meaningful connections.

4. Establish your network management systems. Like maintaining mission-critical equipment, your professional relationships need regular attention and care.

5. Implement weekly giving-back initiatives. Whether it's sharing insights, making introductions, or mentoring others, make supporting your network a regular part of your routine.

Final Thoughts

Your network is your most powerful asset in the civilian world – but its strength lies not in the number of connections you have but in the depth and quality of those relationships. Just as your military success depended on the trust and capability of your unit, your civilian success will depend on the strength of your professional relationships.

Remember: In the military, your rank told others what you could do. In the civilian world, your network tells others what you can do. Build it with the same dedication, integrity, and commitment to excellence that marked your military service, and it will serve as a force multiplier throughout your civilian career.

Your mission now is to take these lessons, adapt them to your situation, and begin building the professional relationships that will support your long-term success. Stay focused, stay authentic, and most importantly, stay committed to being as valuable to your network as it is to you.

Debrief: Chapter 15 - The Network Effect

1. **Understand the Power of Networking:**
   Networking is one of the most effective ways to uncover job opportunities, gain industry insights, and build relationships that propel your career forward.

2. **Start with Your Military Network:**
   Leverage connections with fellow veterans, military mentors, and service alumni. Veterans often go out of their way to support others transitioning to civilian careers.

3. **Expand to Civilian Networks:**
   Join professional associations, industry-specific groups, and local

business organizations to grow your civilian contacts and learn about opportunities in your target field.

4. **Optimize Your LinkedIn Presence:**
   Create a polished LinkedIn profile that highlights your military accomplishments and transferable skills. Engage with posts, join groups, and connect with professionals in your desired industry.

5. **Attend Networking Events:**
   Participate in job fairs, conferences, and meetups. Prepare an elevator pitch to introduce yourself and explain your career goals succinctly.

6. **Use Informational Interviews Strategically:**
   Reach out to professionals in roles or companies you admire. Ask for advice and insights, rather than directly requesting a job, to build meaningful connections.

7. **Be Consistent and Intentional:**
   Networking isn't a one-time event. Dedicate time each week to maintaining and expanding your network by following up with contacts and staying engaged.

8. **Offer Value to Your Network:**
   Networking is a two-way street. Share resources, insights, or introductions that could benefit others. Being helpful strengthens your relationships and builds goodwill.

9. **Leverage Veteran-Specific Resources:**
   Engage with veteran-focused organizations and events, such as those hosted by VFW, American Legion, or Hire Heroes USA. Many companies actively recruit veterans through these channels.

10. **Stay Patient and Persistent:**
    Networking takes time to yield results. Approach it with a long-term mindset, and remain open to opportunities that arise unexpectedly.

Chapter 16: Crushing Your Interview: Making the Leap from Military to Civilian Life

Job interviews can make even decorated veterans break a sweat. But think about it: You've briefed high-ranking officers under pressure, made split-second decisions that mattered, and led teams through situations more stressful than any conference room meeting. A job interview? Just another mission to accomplish.

The challenge? The terrain isn't familiar. The language is different. Maybe you're trading combat boots for dress shoes or wondering if your military experience translates to federal work. (It absolutely does.)

Stop thinking, "I was just a maintenance tech" or "I only worked in supply." You weren't "just" anything. You kept millions in equipment running under impossible conditions or managed combat zone logistics with perfect accountability. You were part of the world's most elite military force.

We'll cover everything: what to wear (not your service dress), how to tell your stories in civilian terms, and how to navigate corporate versus federal interviews. Think of this as your field manual for interview success - and you already have everything you need. We're just packaging it for the civilian world.

Looking Sharp: Dressing for Success (Without Breaking the Bank)

Let's talk about interview clothes - and before you start worrying about your wallet, know this: you don't need to spend a fortune to look professional. Looking sharp is about fit and presentation more than designer labels.

The Basics for Everyone

- Clean and pressed matters more than expensive
- Everything should fit well - not too tight, not too loose
- No scuffs, stains, or wrinkles
- Conservative is better than flashy
- If you can only afford one suit, make it navy or charcoal gray - they work for everything

For the Guys

The Suit

- A basic dark suit from stores like JC Penney, Kohl's, or even Target can work great
- Focus on fit - a $150 suit that fits well looks better than a baggy $1000 one
- Watch for sales - especially around holidays
- Check outlet stores and discount retailers like Burlington
- Consider thrift stores near business districts - you'd be amazed what execs donate
- **Pro Tip**: Use your military discount at major retailers

The Shirt

- White or light blue button-down
- Should be crisp and wrinkle-free

- No need for expensive brands - store brands work fine
- Get it fitted if needed - tailoring a $20 shirt can make it look like $100

The Tie

- Solid colors or simple patterns
- Shouldn't be wider than your lapels
- Check discount stores - ties are ties
- **Money-Saving Tip**: Ask other vets if they have spare ties

The Shoes

- Clean and polished black or dark brown
- You already know how to shine shoes - use those skills
- DSW and similar stores often have great deals
- **Pro Tip**: You can make cheap shoes look expensive with a good shine

For the Ladies

The Suit

- Pants or skirt suit - both are equally professional
- Department store sales are your friend
- Consider mixing and matching pieces
- **Budget Tip**: Buy one good black blazer - it goes with everything

Professional Tops

- Simple blouses or shells
- Avoid loud patterns or low necklines
- Places like Old Navy and H&M have good basics
- **Pro Tip**: White, black, and navy are always safe choices

Shoes

- Closed-toe, conservative height if heels
- Comfort matters - you might be walking
- Many professional flats are available for under $40
- **Warning**: Break in new shoes before the interview

Accessories

- Simple stud earrings
- Minimal necklaces
- Professional watch if you have one
- Wedding rings are fine
- Skip the jangly bracelets

For Federal Interviews

- Even more conservative than corporate
- Think "congressional hearing" conservative
- Dark colors rule
- Minimal patterns
- Everything buttoned and proper

Money-Saving Strategies

1. Check out:
    - Thrift stores
    - Military exchanges
    - Outlet malls
    - Department store sales
    - Online deals

2. Build Slowly:
    - Start with one good suit
    - Add pieces as you can
    - Mix and match basics

3. Get Creative:
   - Share with similarly-sized friends
   - Rent for one-off interviews
   - Check veteran support organizations

The Details Matter

- Grooming:
  - Clean, professional haircut
  - Trimmed nails
  - Light on the cologne/perfume
  - Fresh shave or neatly trimmed facial hair

- The Night Before:
  - Iron everything
  - Shine those shoes
  - Lay it all out
  - Check for loose buttons or threads

Emergency Kit

Keep in your car or bag:

- Lint roller
- Stain removal pen
- Safety pins
- Extra tie (guys)
- Breath mints
- Small sewing kit

Remember: Being pressed and polished matters more than the price tag. A clean, well-fitted $100 outfit will serve you better than wrinkled, poorly-fitted expensive clothes. You've got this!

Pro Tip: Some veteran service organizations and career centers offer interview clothing assistance or maintain lending closets. Don't be shy about asking - that's what they're there for.

Federal Interview Panels: Appearance Matters

Think of a federal interview panel as a civilian promotion board with a twist - many panel members will have military backgrounds themselves. They know what "attention to detail" looks like, and yes, they're absolutely checking out your appearance. Your dress and demeanor matter from the moment you walk in. Keep it conservative - dark suit (black, navy, or charcoal), crisp shirt, subtle tie, and shoes polished to inspection standards. For women, a conservative suit with either pants or a knee-length skirt, closed-toe shoes, and minimal jewelry. These veteran panel members will notice your military bearing and how well you maintain those high standards in civilian attire. And here's the kicker - they're taking notes on everything, including how you carry yourself. Show them you haven't forgotten what "squared away" means.

Intel Gathering: Know Your Target

The Mission Brief

Just like you wouldn't go into an operation without intel, don't walk into an interview without thoroughly researching your target. Whether it's a Fortune 500 company or a federal agency, you need to know what you're walking into.

Agency/Company Deep Dive

Start broad, then go tactical:

For Federal Agencies

- Mission and core values
- Current leadership structure
- Recent Congressional testimony
- Budget allocations
- Major initiatives and challenges
- Recent news coverage
- Agency strategic plan
- Current administration priorities affecting the agency
- Office/division you're applying to
- Partner agencies they work with

For Companies

- Products/services (try them if possible)
- Market position
- Major competitors
- Recent news/press releases
- Stock performance in public
- Company culture and values
- Growth trajectory
- Key leaders and their backgrounds
- Recent mergers or acquisitions
- Major challenges in their industry

Position Intel

- Read the job posting until you can recite it
- Understand where this role fits in the organization
- Know the reporting structure

- Research similar positions in other organizations
- Check salary ranges on sites like GlassDoor
- Connect with current employees if possible
- Review required certifications/clearances
- Understand day-to-day responsibilities

Sources for Intel

- Official websites
- Annual reports
- Social media presence
- News articles
- Employee reviews
- Industry publications
- Congressional records (federal)
- LinkedIn profiles
- Company presentations
- Veteran employee resource groups

Why This Matters

When they ask, "Why do you want to work here?" or "What interests you about our organization?" you need specific, informed answers. Show them you've done your homework. It's the difference between:

Weak: "Your agency seems like a good place to work."

Strong: "I'm particularly interested in your agency's new cybersecurity initiative. I saw in your strategic plan that you're expanding your incident response capabilities, and my experience leading a tactical communications team would directly support that mission."

Remember: Knowledge is power. The more you know about them, the better you can position yourself as the solution to their problems. This isn't just box-checking - it's preparing for success.

Federal Agency Intel: Your Pre-Interview Mission

Agency Deep Dive

Think of this as your Agency Intel Report. Every federal agency has a specific mission and culture. Your success depends on understanding both.

Mission Critical Intel

- Study their website's "About" and "Mission" pages
- Read their strategic plan (usually a 5-year outlook)
- Review recent Congressional budget testimony
- Check USA.gov for agency updates
- Research partnerships with other agencies
- Understand their role in current administration priorities
- Know their regulatory authorities
- Review recent Inspector General reports

Job Series Specifics

- Know your series (0343, 1102, 2210, etc.) inside and out
- Understand grade requirements (GS levels)
- Research career ladder potential
- Study the qualification standards
- Know the special requirements (certifications, clearances)
- Review similar positions across agencies
- Understand the promotion potential

Current Events

- Follow their social media
- Set up Google alerts for the agency
- Review press releases
- Check GAO reports
- Monitor related Congressional hearings
- Research recent policy changes
- Know current challenges and successes

Office Structure

- Research the specific office/division
- Understand reporting chains
- Know key leadership positions
- Look up recent reorganizations
- Understand where your position fits

Remember: Federal agencies love candidates who understand their mission. When they ask why you want to work there, "It's a stable job with benefits" isn't going to cut it. Show them you understand their purpose and how you'll help achieve it.

Pro Tip: Many agencies have specific strategic goals for veteran hiring. Know these numbers and how you help them meet these goals.

Know Your Story (Because You Really Are a Big Deal)

Let me tell you something I see all the time - veterans seriously underselling themselves in interviews. We've got folks who led complex missions in combat zones, thinking their experience "probably doesn't count" in the civilian world. We've got supply sergeants who managed million-dollar inventories, saying they "just worked in logistics." We need to fix this mindset right now.

The Truth About Your Service

Every single day in the military, you were building skills that civilian employers desperately wanted. That time, you reorganized the supply room? That's process improvement and inventory management. The day you had to step up when your supervisor was out? Leadership under pressure. Those countless times you had to get creative with limited resources? That's innovation and problem-solving.

Breaking Down Your Experience

Leadership (It's More Than Rank)

You've led in ways civilians can't imagine:

- Running PT = Creating and implementing fitness programs
- Managing duty rosters = Personnel scheduling and resource allocation
- Counseling troops = Employee development and performance management
- Leading missions = Project management under extreme pressure
- Training new personnel = Staff development and mentorship

Let's translate a typical day: "This morning, I ran PT for my squad, then coordinated maintenance schedules for six vehicles, trained two new troops on equipment procedures, and resolved a conflict between team members."

Civilian version: "I implemented physical fitness programs, managed fleet maintenance logistics, developed standard operating procedures, conducted new employee training, and practiced conflict resolution - all before lunch."

Resource Management

You've handled more than you realize:

- That arms room you managed? Millions in equipment
- Supply account? Large-scale inventory management
- Training schedule? Program development and implementation
- Maintenance bay? Technical project management
- Daily operations? Team supervision and workflow optimization

Problem-Solving in Action

Remember when:

- The comms went down and you found a workaround?
- Half your team was deployed but the mission still had to happen?
- Equipment broke in the field, and you got creative?
- Training space was double-booked but you still got it done?

These aren't just war stories - they're examples of:

- Crisis management
- Resource allocation
- Technical innovation
- Conflict resolution
- Strategic planning

Documenting Your Impact

Step 1: Gather Your Proof

Pull every piece of paper that shows what you've done:

- Performance evaluations (all of them)
- Award citations (even the small ones)

- Training certificates
- Special duty assignments
- Deployment records
- Letters of appreciation
- Course completion certificates
- Qualification records

Step 2: Break It Down

For each role, list out:

1. Regular Responsibilities
   - Daily tasks
   - Weekly duties
   - Monthly requirements
   - Special assignments

2. Special Projects
   - Process improvements
   - Training programs
   - Equipment upgrades
   - Team achievements

3. Crisis Management
   - Emergency responses
   - Unexpected challenges
   - Resource shortages
   - High-pressure situations

4. Numbers That Matter
   - Team sizes
   - Budget amounts
   - Equipment values
   - Success rates
   - Time savings

- Cost reductions
- Performance metrics

Step 3: Civilian Translation Examples

Military Term	Civilian Translation	Why It Matters
Squad Leader	Team Supervisor	Led 4-12 person team in high-pressure environments
Combat Mission Planning	Strategic Project Management	Coordinated complex operations with multiple stakeholders
Weapons Qualification	Technical Training & Safety Compliance	Ensured 100% team certification on sophisticated equipment
Supply Sergeant	Inventory & Logistics Manager	Managed $2M+ in assets with 100% accountability
PT Leader	Wellness Program Coordinator	Developed and led fitness programs, improving team performance by 25%

The "Just a…" Reality Check

Let's bust some myths:

"Just a truck driver" Reality: Managed safe transport of multi-million dollar equipment through hostile territories with zero losses. Coordinated complex logistics across international boundaries. Maintained 100% accountability of sensitive items.

"Just did maintenance." Reality: Led technical troubleshooting of complex systems under extreme pressure. Implemented preventive maintenance programs, reducing downtime by 40%. Managed repair priorities for million-dollar equipment fleets.

"Just worked supply" Reality: Orchestrated logistics for 500+ personnel across multiple locations. Maintained 100% accuracy in inventory valued at over $5M. Developed new tracking systems, improving efficiency by 35%.

Remember: Every day in the military, you were solving problems that would make civilian managers sweat. You operated in conditions they can't imagine, with consequences they'll never face. You're not bragging when you explain this - you're helping them understand the incredible value you bring to their organization.

Your service matters. Every single day of it. Now, let's make sure employers understand exactly why.

Behavioral Interviews: What They Are and Why They Matter

A behavioral interview is based on the principle that past performance predicts future behavior. Instead of asking hypothetical "what if" questions, interviewers ask for specific examples from your past experience. The core idea is simple: they want proof you can handle the job by showing how you've handled similar situations before.

Why Companies Use Them

- Past performance predicts future behavior
- Gets beyond rehearsed answers
- Reveals real skills and experience
- Shows how candidates think and solve problems
- Demonstrates leadership style in action

Key Areas They Probe

1. Leadership
    - Team management
    - Decision making
    - Conflict resolution
    - Project oversight

2. Problem Solving
    - Technical challenges
    - Resource constraints
    - Crisis management
    - Process improvement

3. Communication
    - Team coordination
    - Difficult conversations
    - Cross-functional work
    - Stakeholder management

4. Adaptability
    - Change management
    - New situations
    - Learning from failure
    - Flexibility

Breaking Down Interview Styles: Traditional vs. Behavioral

Traditional Interview Questions vs. Behavioral Questions

Leadership Scenarios

Traditional: "How would you motivate an unmotivated team?" Behavioral: "Tell me about the most unmotivated team you've led. What specific steps did you take to improve their performance, and what were the results?"

Why It's Different: Instead of talking about theories, you're sharing how you turned around that maintenance team that was missing deadlines, including the specific counseling sessions, training programs, and recognition systems you implemented.

Problem-Solving

Traditional: "How do you handle equipment failures?" Behavioral: "Walk me through the most significant equipment failure you've managed. What was your troubleshooting process, and how did you resolve it?"

Why It's Different: Rather than discussing general procedures, you're detailing how you fixed that communications system in the middle of a critical mission with limited resources.

Conflict Resolution

Traditional: "How would you handle disagreements between team members?" Behavioral: "Describe a time when you had to resolve a serious conflict between two team members. What actions did you take, and how did it affect team dynamics?"

Why It's Different: Instead of hypotheticals, you're explaining how you mediated between two NCOs who couldn't agree on training methods and how your solution improved unit cohesion.

Time Management

Traditional: "How do you prioritize tasks?" Behavioral: "Tell me about a time when you had multiple urgent deadlines. How did you determine priorities and ensure everything got done?"

Why It's Different: Rather than listing prioritization methods, you're sharing how you managed simultaneous requirements for a training exercise, equipment maintenance, and personnel evaluations.

Crisis Management

Traditional: "Can you work under pressure?" Behavioral: "Describe your most stressful work situation. How did you handle it, and what was the outcome?"

Why It's Different: Instead of claiming you handle pressure well, you're detailing how you managed an emergency evacuation during a natural disaster while maintaining accountability of personnel and equipment.

Why This Matters for Veterans

Your military experience is perfect for behavioral interviews because you have:

- Real crisis management experience
- Actual leadership challenges overcome
- Concrete problem-solving examples
- True team-building successes
- Measurable results and outcomes

The key is preparing your stories ahead of time and translating them into civilian terms. When they ask for specific examples, you've got a rich library of experiences to draw from - you just need to package them right.

Remember: In behavioral interviews, "I would" becomes "I did," and your military service is full of "I did" moments that civilian employers dream about.

Interview Response Techniques: Your Communication Battle Plan

Core Response Methods

STAR Method

The gold standard for behavioral interviews:

- **Situation**: Context and background
- **Task**: Your specific challenge or objective
- **Action**: Steps you personally took
- **Result**: Measurable outcomes and lessons learned

SOAR Method

Emphasizes positive outcomes:

- **Situation**: Set the scene
- **Obstacle**: Challenge you faced
- **Action**: Your response
- **Result**: Impact and achievements

CAR Method

Simplified approach:

- **Context**: Background information
- **Action**: Your response
- **Result**: Outcome and impact

PAR Method

Focus on problem-solving:

- **Problem**: Issue you faced
- **Action**: Your solution

- **Result**: Outcomes achieved

Using STAR Effectively

Leadership Example

Question: "Tell me about managing a difficult change."

Response: **Situation**: "As Motor Pool Sergeant, our unit received new diagnostic equipment with zero notice." **Task**: "Had to train 25 mechanics and implement new procedures without disrupting operations." **Action**:

- Created an accelerated training schedule
- Developed buddy system pairing experience with new users
- Built quick-reference guides
- Established 24/7 support rotation **Result**: "Completed transition two weeks early, maintained 98% readiness, zero mission delays."

Crisis Management Example

Question: "Describe handling competing priorities."

Response: **Situation**: "During deployment, simultaneously managing vehicle maintenance and convoy support." **Task**: "Need to maintain 40 vehicles while supporting daily convoy operations." **Action**:

- Reorganized maintenance shifts
- Cross-trained personnel
- Implemented priority system
- Created flexible scheduling. **Result**: "Achieved 95% vehicle readiness while supporting 100% of convoy missions."

Advanced Tips

Preparation

1. Build Story Bank
   - 2-3 leadership examples
   - 2-3 problem-solving stories
   - 2-3 team conflict resolutions
   - 2-3 process improvements

2. Structure Each Story
   - Write out STAR components
   - Practice civilian translations
   - Include specific metrics
   - Keep under 2 minutes

Delivery

1. Stay Focused
   - Stick to relevant details
   - Keep military jargon minimal
   - Emphasize your actions
   - Include measurable results

2. Common Pitfalls
   - Too much background
   - Unclear results
   - Missing metrics
   - Excessive detail

Example Story Bank

Leadership

Situation: "Leading maintenance team during major inspection." **Task**: "Improve team performance and morale." **Action**:

- One-on-one mentoring
- Skill-based training program
- Recognition system **Result**: "Passed inspection with the highest score in the battalion, zero deficiencies."

Innovation

Situation: "Supply system causing delays." **Task**: "Reduce request processing time." **Action**:

- Digitized paper system
- Streamlined approval process
- Implemented tracking **Result**: "Cut processing time by 60%, saved $50K annually."

Team Building

Situation: "New team with communication issues." **Task**: "Build cohesion and improve coordination." **Action**:

- Daily huddles
- Cross-training program
- Team feedback sessions **Result**: "Improved efficiency by 40%, zero missed deadlines."

Remember: These techniques are frameworks, not rigid scripts. Adapt them to fit your stories while maintaining clear structure and measurable results.

The Tale of Two Interview Types: Corporate vs. Federal

Let's break down what you're walking into because these two types of interviews are as different as garrison life and field ops.

The Corporate World: Fast and Fluid

Picture this: You walk into a modern office space, maybe some exposed brick walls, people in business casual rolling around on exercise balls. Welcome to corporate America. These interviews move fast - think sprint instead of ruck march.

Corporate interviews often feel like a conversation. One minute, you're discussing your leadership style; the next, you're being asked, "How many tennis balls could fit in a submarine?" (Yes, they really ask stuff like that). Don't panic - they're testing how you think, not your tennis ball math skills.

You might start with a phone screen, then video chat with HR, followed by in-person meetings with your potential boss and teammates. Each interview could have a different vibe - some formal, others casual enough that you're chatting over coffee. Be ready to adapt.

The whole process might wrap up in a week or two. They'll ask about:

- Your actual experience (behavioral questions)
- How you handle hypothetical situations
- Your personality and work style
- Whether you'd fit their culture
- Those weird brain teasers (just roll with it)

The Federal Side: Structured and Scored

Now, flip the script. Walking into a federal interview is like reporting for a promotion board, minus the marching. Everything is structured, documented, and scored. Remember all those hurry-up-and-wait moments in service? That's federal hiring in a nutshell.

The panel usually includes 3-5 people, often with military experience themselves. They've got evaluation sheets, and they're checking boxes as you speak. No pressure, but every answer you give gets a numerical score. They're literally grading you in real-time.

These questions aren't random. They're tied directly to those Knowledge, Skills, and Abilities (KSAs) from the job announcement. Pro tip: Read that announcement until you can recite it in your sleep. Every question connects back to it.

The process? Slow and steady:

- Each question is formal and specific
- Your answers need to hit certain points
- They take detailed notes
- Everything ties back to the job requirements
- The whole process could take months

Think of it this way - corporate interviews are like a tactical exercise where you need to be quick on your feet and adapt to changing situations. Federal interviews are like a planned operation where attention to detail and following specific protocols matter most.

Here's the kicker - both types want to know if you can do the job; they just have very different ways of finding out. Corporate relies more on personality and potential, while federal focuses on proven experience and documented capabilities.

Remember: In corporate, you might have to think fast and get creative. In federal, slow down and be methodical. Both are looking for quality candidates; they just go about it differently. Your military experience has prepared you for both - you just need to know which skills to lean into for each type.

Pro Tips: Your Interview Field Manual

Military-to-Civilian Translation Guide

Translating Your Military Experience: Making Your Service Make Sense to Civilians

Let's break down how to translate your military experience into language that resonates in civilian interviews. The key is keeping the impact while dropping the jargon.

Leadership Translation Examples

When you say, "Platoon Sergeant responsible for 40 PAX during combat ops," civilians hear military jargon. Instead, try "Led and developed a 40-person team during complex, high-pressure operations." This emphasizes your leadership and high-stakes management experience without requiring military knowledge to understand.

Think about your operations experience. "As Platoon Sergeant, I oversaw daily operations, training, and personnel management." That becomes, "As a senior team leader, I managed daily operations, professional development, and personnel performance for a high-performing team."

Let's look at more examples:

"Company Training NCO coordinating multiple training events" becomes "Training and Development Manager organizing multiple professional certification programs and team-building initiatives."

"First Sergeant managing 120 soldiers' discipline, training, and welfare" translates to "Senior Operations Manager overseeing personnel development, performance management, and team wellbeing for 120+ employees."

Technical Skills and Specialties

Technical roles need careful translation to highlight transferable skills:

"BN Commo Chief" might sound impressive to military ears, but "Communications Systems Manager overseeing network operations for 500+ users" speaks to civilian experience.

"Bradley Fighting Vehicle maintainer" becomes "Heavy equipment technician performing diagnostic testing and repair of complex mechanical and electronic systems valued at $4M+."

Consider "Supply Sergeant accountable for sensitive items" versus "Inventory Control Manager maintaining 100% accuracy for high-value equipment exceeding $10M."

Adding Context and Impact

Don't just translate - add context and results:

Instead of "Conducted AARs,": "Implemented regular performance review processes that improved team efficiency by 35% and reduced operational errors by 50%."

Rather than "Managed arms room,": "Directed secure storage facility maintaining perfect accountability of sensitive equipment valued over $5M through multiple federal inspections."

The key is highlighting universal skills like:

- Leadership
- Resource management
- Problem-solving
- Team development
- Project coordination
- Risk management

- Process improvement

Remember: Your military experience is incredibly valuable - it just needs the right translation to help civilians understand its worth.

Strategic Questions to Ask

Leadership & Development

- "What development opportunities exist for this role?"
- "How does your mentorship program work?"
- "What's your approach to promoting from within?"
- "How do you measure and reward performance?"

Team & Culture

- "Can you describe the team's biggest victory this year?"
- "What makes someone successful in this role?"
- "How would you describe the leadership style here?"
- "What's the most challenging aspect of the team's mission?"

Operations & Challenges

- "What are the first 90 days' priorities?"
- "What's the most pressing challenge facing the department?"
- "How does this role contribute to organizational goals?"
- "What metrics define success in this position?"

Future & Growth

- "Where do you see the department in two years?"
- "What opportunities for advancement exist?"
- "How is the organization adapting to industry changes?"
- "What new initiatives are planned?"

Pre-Mission Checklist

24 Hours Before

- Review company/agency mission statement
- Study recent news/press releases
- Research interview panel members
- Prepare your STAR stories
- Print documents (5 copies minimum):
  - Resume
  - Certificates
  - References
  - Performance evaluations
  - Awards

Night Before

- Iron and lay out clothes
- Shine shoes
- Pack portfolio/briefcase
- Charge phone
- Print directions
- Set multiple alarms
- Review the job description
- Practice STAR responses
- Pack emergency kit:
  - Stain remover
  - Backup tie
  - Breath mints
  - Business cards
  - Pen and notepad

Morning Of

- Leave early (plan for traffic)
- Check traffic and weather
- Eat something light
- Bring water
- Arrive 15-20 minutes early
- Review notes in the car
- Deep breathing exercises
- Last mirror check

Practice Makes Perfect

Mock Interview Strategies

1. Record yourself answering questions
2. Practice with non-military friends
3. Time your responses (2 minutes max)
4. Get feedback on:
    - Body language
    - Military jargon
    - Story clarity
    - Answer structure

Common Areas to Practice

- Introduction/elevator pitch
- Biggest accomplishments
- Leadership Philosophy
- Problem-solving examples
- Conflict resolution stories
- Process improvement examples
- Technical expertise demonstrations

Remember: You've planned missions, led teams, and solved complex problems under intense pressure. This interview? It's just another mission. Your preparation and experience have already set you up for success. Stay focused, trust your training, and execute your plan.

The only difference between this and your military experience? The stakes are actually lower. No one's life depends on this interview. You're just having a conversation about how your impressive skills can help your organization succeed.

Deep breath. Shoulders back. You're ready.

Debrief: Chapter 16 - Crushing Your Interview: Making the Leap from Military to Civilian Life

1. **Prepare Thoroughly:**
   Research the company, role, and industry. Understand the organization's mission and values, and prepare to explain how your background aligns with their goals.

2. **Practice Civilian-Friendly Responses:**
   Translate military accomplishments into civilian terms. Avoid military jargon, focusing instead on transferable skills like leadership, problem-solving, and adaptability.

3. **Anticipate Common Questions:**
   Be ready to answer behavioral questions like "Tell me about a time you led a team through a challenge." Use the STAR method (Situation, Task, Action, Result) to structure your responses.

4. **Tell Your Story:**
   Highlight how your military experiences prepared you for civilian

success. Share specific examples of achievements, emphasizing measurable outcomes and the impact you made.

5. **Address Perceived Gaps:**
   If asked about gaps between military and civilian roles, confidently explain how your skills and training make you uniquely qualified for the position.

6. **Showcase Soft Skills:**
   Emphasize qualities like teamwork, communication, and resilience. Demonstrate how these attributes helped you succeed in the military and how they'll benefit the company.

7. **Ask Thoughtful Questions:**
   Prepare questions about the company's culture, team dynamics, and expectations. This shows genuine interest and helps you determine if the role is a good fit.

8. **Present a Professional Appearance:**
   Dress appropriately for the role and organization. A clean, well-fitted suit or professional attire helps you make a strong first impression.

9. **Practice Confidence and Composure:**
   Use your military bearing to exude confidence and professionalism. Maintain eye contact, use a firm handshake, and avoid filler words like "um" or "uh."

10. **Follow Up After the Interview:**
    Send a thank-you email or note within 24 hours, reiterating your interest in the role and highlighting a key point from the interview discussion.

11. **Leverage Mock Interviews:**
    Practice with a mentor, career counselor, or trusted peer. Mock interviews help refine your responses and boost your confidence.

12. **Be Ready for Curveballs:**
    Some interviews include unexpected questions or scenarios. Stay

calm, think critically, and relate your answer back to your skills and experiences.

Chapter 17: What Happens After the Interview: The Next Steps

You crushed that interview - nice work! Now those post-interview jitters are setting in. Did they like you? Should you have told that deployment story? Did you thank everyone? Take a deep breath - you've faced tougher situations.

The transition from military to civilian life means switching from "Roger that" to "absolutely" from BDUs to business casual. But you've done the hardest part: showing up and translating your military experience into civilian terms.

Remember your first military evaluation? This isn't so different. That attention to detail, adaptability, and mission-focused mindset you developed in service? Those are exactly what employers want.

Think of this next phase as your new mission. Like any operation, it requires patience, strategy, and clear communication. You've been trained to handle uncertainty under pressure - perfect skills for this waiting period.

We'll break down exactly what to do next, from the crucial first 24 hours to handling different responses and negotiating offers. You didn't earn your stripes by giving up when things got challenging. Let's make your transition count.

The Waiting Game

I recently sat with a former Navy SEAL at a veterans' meetup. He'd just interviewed for a project manager position at a major tech company, and the waiting was eating at him. "In the teams, you always knew where you stood," he said, nursing his coffee. "This civilian stuff... it's different."

He's right. The post-interview waiting period can feel like being in a holding pattern with no radio contact. At least in the military, you had your daily routine, your unit, and a clear chain of command. In the civilian job search, the silence can be deafening.

The First 24 Hours and Beyond: Navigate Your Post-Interview Mission

Immediate Action Report

In the military, after-action reports document mission outcomes and lessons learned. Apply this same disciplined approach to your interview follow-up. Break down key discussion points, address concerns raised, and outline your value proposition based on military experience. Structure your response like a mission report - clear, concise, and focused on objectives achieved and next steps.

The Waiting Period: Operating in Uncertain Territory

The civilian sector operates on different timelines than military operations. While military missions have clear timelines and communication protocols, civilian hiring moves at its own pace. Create a tracking system like you would for mission planning:

Mission Tracking System

- Interview details and key points discussed
- Company personnel contacted
- Follow-up deadlines
- Required documentation
- Additional research needed
- Industry developments
- Company news and updates
- Network connections made
- Skills gaps identified

Staying Mission-Ready

Treat this waiting period like pre-deployment preparation. Focus on:

Intelligence Gathering

- Study company culture and operations
- Research industry trends
- Monitor company news
- Track market developments
- Understand the competitor landscape

Skills Enhancement

- Shadow industry professionals
- Attend professional workshops
- Complete relevant certifications
- Study industry terminology
- Practice civilian communication styles
- Develop technical skills
- Build a professional network

Managing the Emotional Terrain

The transition from military unit cohesion to civilian independence requires adaptation.

Building Your New Support Network

1. Physical Readiness

- Develop a personal fitness routine
- Set a regular workout schedule
- Maintain health standards
- Practice stress management
- Establish sleep discipline

2. Professional Development

- Join veteran organizations
- Attend industry events
- Participate in professional groups
- Connect with mentors
- Build civilian relationships

3. Knowledge Base

- Read industry publications
- Follow professional blogs
- Listen to sector podcasts
- Study market trends
- Learn company histories

The Follow-Up: Tactical Communication

Approach civilian follow-up with military precision. Establish a communication battle rhythm:

Communication Timeline

1. 24-Hour Response
   - Acknowledge interview
   - Highlight key points
   - Address any concerns
   - Reinforce qualifications
   - Express continued interest

2. Week One Check
   - Provide relevant updates
   - Share additional qualifications
   - Maintain professional contact
   - Request timeline information
   - Demonstrate continued interest

3. Week Two Position
   - Brief status inquiry
   - Share industry insights
   - Maintain visibility
   - Demonstrate value
   - Request update

4. Week Three Final
   - Professional closure
   - Leave the door open
   - Express appreciation
   - Maintain network connection

- Document lessons learned

Strategic Objectives

- Maintain a professional presence
- Demonstrate continued interest
- Provide additional value
- Gather timeline intelligence
- Build long-term relationships
- Document all communications
- Track response patterns
- Analyze feedback received
- Adjust approach as needed

Success in civilian transition requires adapting military skills to new environments while maintaining the core values of discipline, professionalism, and mission focus.

When the Wait Drags On

The Long and Short Goodbye: Understanding Federal vs Private Sector Rejections

The clock ticks differently in federal versus private sector hiring. Picture this: you've interviewed for two positions - one with a major tech company, the other a GS-12 position with the Department of Defense.

The Private Sector Timeline

Within days of your private sector interview, you might receive a LinkedIn message, email, or phone call. The hiring manager explains they've chosen another candidate but appreciate your time. They might even offer feedback about your interview performance or encourage you to apply for future positions.

Sometimes, you can read the signs even earlier. The recruiter's tone changes, responses slow down, or your follow-up emails receive polite but non-committal replies. This quick closure, while disappointing, allows you to pivot rapidly to other opportunities. You know where you stand and can adjust your job search strategy accordingly.

The Federal Waiting Game

Meanwhile, that federal position… Your USAJobs status still shows "Referred to Hiring Manager." Weeks pass. Then months. The position might close without any notification. Your carefully crafted federal resume and supporting documentation sit in digital limbo.

The status updates, if they come at all, remain cryptic:

- Referred
- Under Review
- In Progress
- Not Selected
- No longer under consideration

Sometimes, you discover the position was canceled only when you see it reposted months later. Or perhaps it vanishes entirely, leaving you to wonder if it was filled or if budget priorities shifted.

Strategic Planning

This stark difference in timelines requires dual strategies:

Private Sector Approach

Expect a resolution within weeks. Keep your network warm, but focus energy on new opportunities once you detect the subtle signs of a "no." Use the quick feedback loop to improve your interview skills and application materials.

Federal Approach

Think of it like a long-range patrol. Prepare for extended radio silence. Keep your equipment (certifications, clearances, documentation) current. Continue your mission (job search) while monitoring communication channels (USAJobs, agency websites). Don't wait for closure - maintain forward momentum with other applications.

Moving Forward

Remember: a private sector "no" lets you adapt quickly. A federal "maybe" requires patience and parallel planning. Keep both options open, understanding that each path operates on its own timeline. Your military experience taught you to adapt to different operational tempos - apply that same flexibility to your job search strategy.

The key is maintaining mission readiness while adjusting your expectations for each sector. Then, when the right opportunity comes - whether it's a swift private sector offer or a long-awaited federal position - you're prepared to move forward.

Understanding Civilian Timelines

The civilian hiring process often moves at a different pace than military operations. Waiting periods can stretch from weeks to months due to:

Common Delay Factors

- Budget cycles and fiscal year planning
- Multiple decision-makers across departments
- HR processing backlogs
- Reference and background verification
- Security clearance transfers or new investigations
- Competing candidates still in the interview process

- Internal reorganizations or priority shifts
- Contract negotiations with other departments

Productive Ways to Handle the Extended Wait

Professional Development

- Pursue relevant certifications in your field
- Take online courses related to the position
- Study industry-specific software or tools
- Practice technical skills mentioned in the interview
- Learn about the company's competitors and market position

Stay Connected to the Veteran Community

- Mentor other transitioning service members
- Volunteer with veteran service organizations
- Participate in veteran job fairs as both candidate and advisor
- Join veteran employee resource groups at target companies
- Attend veteran networking events

Keep Your Options Open

- Continue applying for other positions
- Maintain relationships with recruiters
- Attend industry conferences and meetups
- Build your civilian professional network
- Update your skills matrix based on interview feedback

Reading the Signals

Good Signs During a Long Wait

- Regular communication from the hiring manager
- Requests for additional information

- Questions about start date availability
- References being contacted
- Discussion of security clearance transfers
- Details about internal processes being shared

When to Consider Moving On

- Complete silence for over two months
- Vague responses to follow-up inquiries
- No clarity on the timeline after multiple requests
- Learning about filled positions through other channels
- Your experience growing stale or outdated

Maintaining Military Discipline in a Civilian World

Apply your military training to the waiting period:

- Set daily objectives for your job search
- Maintain a structured routine
- Keep detailed records of all communications
- Have contingency plans ready
- Stay physically and mentally fit
- Keep your support network informed

The Long Game Strategy

Your military training equipped you to:

- Adapt to changing situations
- Maintain focus under uncertainty
- Keep equipment (skills) ready for deployment
- Support your fellow service members
- Complete the mission, regardless of timeline

The civilian sector might move slower than a military operation, but the principles of success remain the same: stay prepared, maintain discipline, and keep moving forward.

The Follow-Up: The Art of Strategic Communication

In the military, communication flows through established channels with clear protocols. The civilian sector operates differently - it's more nuanced, less structured, and often requires reading between the lines. Think of your follow-up strategy as a carefully planned operation, where timing and approach can make the difference between success and missed opportunities.

Understanding Civilian Communication Culture

The Timing Challenge

Unlike military operations, where timelines are explicit, civilian hiring moves at varying speeds. Large corporations might take weeks to process decisions through multiple departments, while startups could move within days. Government contractors often have the longest timelines, especially when security clearances are involved.

Reading Between the Lines

Civilian communication tends to be less direct than military correspondence. A delayed response doesn't always indicate lack of interest - budget approvals, organizational changes, or competing priorities could be factors. Your mission is to maintain contact while gathering intelligence about your standing.

Strategic Follow-Up Operations

First Contact (Week One)

Think of your first follow-up as a reconnaissance mission. Your goal is to:

- Gather intelligence about the hiring timeline
- Reinforce your position as a strong candidate
- Demonstrate your continued interest
- Maintain professional visibility

Second Contact (Week Two)

Your second communication is like a strategic reinforcement:

- Provide updates on new qualifications or training
- Share relevant industry insights
- Demonstrate ongoing professional development
- Maintain presence without applying pressure

Final Contact (Week Three)

Consider this your extraction strategy:

- Seek closure while maintaining professionalism
- Request feedback for future operations
- Keep the door open for future opportunities
- Preserve relationships and connections

Advanced Communication Tactics

Digital Communications Strategy

- Maintain detailed records of all correspondence
- Track response patterns and timing
- Monitor company social media for relevant updates
- Engage professionally with company content
- Build connections with other team members

Professional Network Operations

- Activate veteran networks within the target company

- Engage with industry-specific groups
- Share relevant professional content
- Build relationships with key personnel
- Maintain visibility in professional communities

Intelligence Gathering

- Monitor company news and announcements
- Track industry trends and developments
- Note any organizational changes
- Watch for new position postings
- Follow quarterly business cycles

Contingency Planning

Parallel Operations

- Maintain active job search campaigns
- Develop multiple opportunity pipelines
- Build relationships with multiple organizations
- Create backup communication channels
- Prepare alternative career paths

Professional Development Operations

- Pursue relevant certifications
- Enhance industry-specific skills
- Build civilian sector expertise
- Strengthen professional network
- Develop new competencies

Communication Security

Protecting Your Professional Image

- Maintain strict professionalism in all communications
- Archive all correspondence
- Keep detailed interaction logs
- Protect confidential information
- Maintain operational security

Digital Footprint Management

- Audit your online presence regularly
- Update professional profiles strategically
- Manage privacy settings effectively
- Monitor professional mentions
- Maintain a consistent professional image

Strategic Withdrawal

Recognizing When to Move On

- Analyze response patterns
- Evaluate communication quality
- Consider market opportunities
- Assess professional growth potential
- Review alternative options

Professional Closure

- Document lessons learned
- Archive relevant communications
- Maintain professional connections
- Preserve future opportunities

- Update your tracking systems

Remember, your follow-up strategy is not just about maintaining contact - it's about positioning yourself as a valuable asset while gathering intelligence about your opportunities. Like any military operation, success depends on careful planning, precise execution, and the ability to adapt to changing circumstances.

Your military training has equipped you with unique skills - attention to detail, strategic thinking, and disciplined communication. Apply these strengths to your civilian sector follow-up strategy, but remember to translate them into civilian terms. The mission remains the same: secure the position and advance your career objectives.

The Response Scenarios: Navigating Different Outcomes

The "Yes!" - Mission Accomplished, But Stay Sharp

Getting that "yes" feels like a successful mission completion, but like any military operation, the job isn't done until all paperwork is processed and you're properly in position.

Initial Response Protocol

Before accepting, take a tactical pause. Your military training taught you to assess situations thoroughly - apply that same discipline here. Your immediate action items:

1. Acknowledgment Response
   - Confirm receipt professionally
   - Express appreciation
   - Request time to review (24-48 hours is standard)
   - Get the full offer package

2. Documentation Review

- Scrutinize base salary figures
- Map out bonus structures
- Evaluate stock options or equity grants
- Chart out benefits timeline
- Verify vacation and leave policies
- Understand healthcare coverage transition
- Review retirement contribution structures
- Examine relocation assistance details
- Confirm veteran benefit policies

3. Pre-Employment Requirements

- Security clearance transfer procedures
- Background check requirements
- Drug screening protocols
- Physical examination needs
- Required certifications
- Start date flexibility
- Equipment or uniform requirements
- Training period expectations

The "No" - Strategic Reassessment

Like any military operation, not every mission goes as planned. A "no" isn't a defeat - it's intelligence gathering for your next opportunity.

Tactical Response

1. Professional Acknowledgment

- Maintain military bearing
- Express gratitude for consideration
- Keep doors open for future opportunities

- Request performance feedback

2. Intelligence Gathering

- What qualifications were they seeking?
- Which areas need strengthening?
- How could your interview responses improve?
- What civilian sector knowledge gaps exist?

3. Network Maintenance

- Keep professional connections active
- Update your contact database
- Monitor company developments
- Stay engaged in industry discussions

4. After Action Review

- Document interview questions
- Record successful responses
- Note areas for improvement
- Update your approach strategy

The "Maybe" - Extended Operations

The "maybe" scenario requires the patience and discipline that military service instilled. You're now operating in a holding pattern requiring strategic patience and tactical flexibility.

Sustained Operations

1. Position Maintenance

- Keep communication lines open
- Provide relevant updates
- Monitor company developments
- Maintain professional presence

2. Parallel Operations
- Continue active job search
- Pursue additional interviews
- Maintain skills development
- Build industry knowledge

3. Intelligence Updates
- Track company news
- Monitor industry changes
- Note organizational shifts
- Watch for similar positions

4. Strategic Flexibility
- Prepare for quick response
- Maintain documentation readiness
- Keep references informed
- Update qualifications regularly

Remember, in civilian job hunting, like in military operations, adaptability and resilience are key. Each response scenario provides valuable intelligence for your overall career campaign. Maintain your bearing, keep your objectives clear, and stay mission-focused regardless of the outcome.

Your military service taught you that not every operation goes according to plan, but every experience provides lessons for future success. Apply that same mindset to your civilian job search campaign.

Federal vs Private Sector: Navigating Two Different Worlds

Consider two veterans, both transitioning from military service. One accepts a GS-12 position with the Department of Defense, while the other pursues a project management role in the tech industry. Their experiences with compensation highlight the stark differences between federal and private sector employment.

The Federal Path: Clear Waters

In federal service, the compensation path is crystal clear - like following a well-marked military convoy route. When you receive a federal offer, you'll know exactly where you stand:

Understanding Your Grade

- GS (General Schedule)
- GL (Law Enforcement)
- FP (Foreign Service)
- WG (Wage Grade)

Each position comes with:

- Specific grade level (GS-7 through GS-15)
- Step increase timeline
- Locality pay adjustments
- Clear overtime rules
- Standard benefits package
- Leave accrual rates
- Holiday schedules

Your military service directly impacts your federal position through:

- Veterans' preference points
- Military buy-back options
- Leave accrual rates
- Retirement calculations
- Security clearance transfer

The Private Sector: Negotiating Uncharted Territory

Private sector compensation is like entering unfamiliar terrain - you need reconnaissance, intelligence, and a solid strategy.

The Base Salary Dance

Unlike the federal GS scale where you know a GS-12 Step 1 in Denver earns exactly $89,834 (plus locality), private sector requires research and negotiation.

Total Compensation Package

Private sector offers often include:

1. Base Salary
   - Industry-dependent
   - Location-variable
   - Experience-based
   - Market-driven

2. Variable Compensation
   - Annual bonuses (10-30% of base)
   - Stock options
   - Profit sharing
   - Performance incentives
   - Sign-on bonuses

3. Benefits
   - Health insurance (multiple plans)
   - Dental/Vision options
   - Life insurance choices
   - Disability coverage
   - Retirement plans (401k with varying match)

- Paid time off (negotiable)
- Professional development funds

Negotiation Strategy

The private sector requires:

- Market research
- Industry benchmarking
- Skill valuation
- Benefit analysis
- Counter-offer preparation
- Value proposition development

Making Your Choice

Consider:

1. Career Goals

- Federal: Clear progression
- Private: Varied opportunities

2. Stability vs Potential

- Federal: Consistent, predictable
- Private: Higher ceiling, more risk

3. Work-Life Balance

- Federal: Standard hours, set holidays
- Private: Variable, often more demanding

4. Long-term Benefits

- Federal: Pension, lifetime healthcare
- Private: Often higher immediate compensation

5. Geographic Flexibility

- Federal: Nationwide opportunities

- Private: Often location-dependent

Remember: Neither path is universally "better" - it's about aligning with your goals, family needs, and long-term career aspirations.

Pro Tips for Both Paths

Federal

- Research GS grades before applying
- Understand locality pay
- Calculate military buy-back benefits
- Know your veterans' preference rights
- Review step-increase timelines

Private

- Never accept first offer
- Research total compensation packages
- Understand equity compensation
- Know market rates
- Prepare negotiation strategy
- Document everything in writing

Whether you choose federal service or private sector, remember: your military experience has value. The key is understanding how to translate that value into either system.

The Final Word: Acceptance or Rejection

When You Get the Job

Getting that job offer marks the end of one mission and the start of another. Whether it's a federal position with its clear GS grade and step increases or a negotiated private sector package, your next challenge begins.

Review your offer carefully:

- Start date and location
- Compensation package
- Benefits details
- Security requirements
- Required documentation
- Training periods
- Performance expectations

Accept the position professionally, maintain relationships with your new network, and begin planning your transition. Remember, your first day in civilian clothes is like your first day in uniform - stay sharp, observe, and learn the new culture.

When It's Not the Right Fit

A rejection isn't a mission failure - it's intelligence gathering for your next operation. Whether it comes quickly from the private sector or through months of federal silence, use this experience to strengthen your approach:

- Review interview performance
- Assess skill gaps
- Strengthen qualifications
- Expand your network
- Refine your target positions

- Maintain professional connections

Your military career taught you resilience. Each "no" brings you closer to the right "yes." Keep moving forward, maintain your bearing, and remember that the skills that made you successful in the military will serve you well in finding your next mission.

Whether celebrating an acceptance or regrouping after a rejection, remember - you've handled tougher transitions before. This is just your next deployment, and you're well-equipped for the mission ahead.

Debrief: Chapter 17 - What Happens After the Interview: The Next Steps

1. **Follow Up Promptly:**
   Send a personalized thank-you email within 24 hours of the interview. Express gratitude for the opportunity, reinforce your enthusiasm for the role, and mention a specific topic discussed during the interview.

2. **Monitor Your Application Status:**
   Keep an eye on the company's communication or application portal. If you haven't heard back within the stated timeline, reach out politely to inquire about the status.

3. **Evaluate the Fit:**
   Reflect on your impressions of the company, role, and team. Consider whether the position aligns with your career goals, values, and lifestyle preferences.

4. **Negotiate the Offer (if Applicable):**
   If you receive an offer, review the salary, benefits, and job details carefully. Be prepared to negotiate, especially if you bring unique skills or certifications to the table.

5. **Prepare for Rejection:**
   Not every interview results in a job offer. Use rejection as a learning opportunity—request feedback, if possible, and apply those insights to future interviews.

6. **Maintain Professionalism:**
   If you decline an offer, do so respectfully and express appreciation for the opportunity. Professionalism keeps doors open for future opportunities with the same organization.

7. **Continue Networking:**
   Regardless of the outcome, stay connected with people you met during the interview process. Networking can lead to other opportunities down the line.

8. **Be Patient with Federal Hiring:**
   If applying for a federal role, be prepared for a longer hiring process. Stay proactive by following up with HR contacts and continuing your job search in the meantime.

9. **Assess Multiple Offers Thoughtfully:**
   If you receive multiple offers, weigh factors like salary, benefits, growth potential, and work-life balance. Choose the role that best aligns with your goals and priorities.

10. **Celebrate Small Wins:**
    Landing interviews is an achievement in itself. Acknowledge your progress and keep building momentum toward your ultimate career goals.

Chapter 18: Post-Mission Analysis: You're Hired or Back to Base

Mission Success: You Got the Job

First 90 Days (Your Initial Operating Plan)

Learn the Company's SOP

- Request access to company policies, handbooks, and procedures
- Study internal communication protocols (email etiquette, meeting structures)
- Understand work hours, time off requests, and attendance policies
- Learn security protocols and badge access procedures
- Familiarize yourself with IT systems and required software
- Review safety procedures and emergency protocols
- Study dress code requirements and workplace culture norms

Map Out Command Structure

- Identify your direct supervisor and their expectations
- Learn your team members' roles and responsibilities
- Document key stakeholders in other departments
- Understand reporting structures and approval chains
- Know who to contact for HR, IT, and facility issues
- Identify project leaders and subject matter experts
- Learn the organizational hierarchy beyond your immediate team

Document Role-Specific Systems

- Create detailed notes on login credentials and access points
- Map your daily/weekly/monthly responsibilities
- Track deadlines and recurring deliverables
- Document standard workflows and processes
- Keep records of training received
- Note key performance metrics for your role
- Maintain a list of required reports and their frequency

Build Your Support Network

- Connect with immediate team members individually
- Join relevant employee resource groups
- Attend company social events when offered
- Participate in team meetings actively
- Find other veterans in the organization
- Join industry-specific groups within the company
- Build relationships with cross-functional teams

Secure a Battle Buddy (Mentor)

- Identify potential mentors in your field
- Look for someone with both company and industry experience
- Establish regular check-in meetings
- Ask about unwritten rules and company culture
- Learn from their career progression
- Seek feedback on your transition
- Use their network to expand your connections

Establish Your Battle Rhythm

- Create a structured daily routine
- Set up regular check-ins with your supervisor
- Block time for learning and documentation
- Schedule networking meetings

- Plan skill development activities
- Establish work-life boundaries
- Create professional development goals

Track Your Progress

- Keep a daily log of accomplishments
- Document new skills acquired
- Note challenges overcome
- Record positive feedback received
- Monitor progress against job requirements
- Track projects completed
- Identify areas for improvement

Cultural Integration

- Observe team dynamics
- Learn office politics without engaging negatively
- Understand decision-making processes
- Note communication preferences
- Recognize informal power structures
- Adapt military directness to corporate style
- Learn industry-specific terminology

Think of these first 90 days as establishing a new FOB. You're setting up your infrastructure, understanding the terrain, establishing supply lines (relationships), and preparing for sustained operations. Just like in the military, a solid foundation here sets you up for long-term success in your civilian career.

Remember: You're no longer in a military hierarchy. Civilian workplaces often have more fluid structures and informal channels of communication. Stay observant, be adaptable, and maintain your military attention to detail while learning these new systems.

Common Pitfalls to Avoid in Your New Civilian Role

The "Fix Everything" Syndrome

When transitioning to civilian work, many veterans see inefficiencies everywhere. The urge to implement military-style solutions is overwhelming - streamlining processes, establishing clear hierarchies, and implementing strict accountability measures. However, civilian organizations have their own rhythm and reasons for doing things.

The military taught us to identify problems and fix them immediately. In the civilian world, change requires buy-in, relationship-building, and an understanding of complex organizational dynamics that aren't immediately apparent.

Better Approach:

- Observe existing processes for at least 30 days
- Ask questions about why things are done in certain ways
- Suggest small improvements once you understand the culture
- Build consensus before proposing changes
- Focus on learning before leading
- Document potential improvements for future consideration
- Build relationships before suggesting major changes

The Language Barrier

Military jargon isn't just about specific terms – it's an entire communication style that can create barriers in civilian workplaces. The military speaks in direct, concise terms with specific meanings. Civilian communication often requires more context and softer delivery.

Common language adjustments needed:

- Avoid military time references

- Minimize the use of acronyms
- Soften command-style directives
- Reduce military metaphors
- Stop referencing ranks or military positions
- Transform orders into requests
- Use inclusive language rather than directive speech
- Practice active listening rather than immediate response
- Allow for discussion and debate rather than immediate execution

The "Back in the Military" Syndrome

Constantly comparing civilian workplace situations to military experiences can alienate colleagues and prevent adaptation to the new environment. While military experience provides valuable lessons, excessive reference to military solutions can make civilian coworkers feel their experience is being devalued.

How to Share Military Experience Effectively:

- Focus on relevant skills and lessons learned
- Share stories only when directly applicable
- Emphasize universal principles over military specifics
- Acknowledge different contexts require different solutions
- Use military examples sparingly and strategically
- Translate military experiences into civilian contexts
- Focus on the present challenge rather than past solutions
- Build on others' ideas instead of replacing them
- Recognize civilian expertise in their domain

The Isolation Trap

Veterans often gravitate toward other veterans – it's natural to seek out those who share your experiences. However, limiting yourself to veteran circles can stunt professional growth and network development. The civilian workplace offers diverse perspectives and opportunities that require broader relationship-building.

Building Broader Networks:

- Join company-wide initiatives beyond veteran groups
- Participate in cross-functional projects
- Attend industry events and conferences
- Engage in company social activities
- Seek mentorship from non-veteran leaders
- Join professional associations in your field
- Volunteer for diverse team assignments
- Build relationships across departments
- Learn from colleagues with different backgrounds

Team Member vs. Commander Mindset

The military instills strong leadership instincts, but civilian teams often operate with more collaborative, consensus-driven approaches. Understanding when to lead and when to follow is crucial for success.

Adapting Your Leadership Style:

- Observe team dynamics before asserting influence
- Practice collaborative decision-making
- Share credit for successes
- Admit when you don't know something
- Ask for help when needed
- Support others' leadership moments
- Contribute ideas without demanding their implementation
- Learn from civilian colleagues' expertise
- Balance assertiveness with inclusivity
- Recognize informal leadership structures
- Understand that influence often matters more than authority

- Practice patience with less structured environments

Remember: Your military experience is incredibly valuable, but it's just one chapter in your professional story. Success in the civilian workplace requires writing new chapters with different rules, relationships, and ways of achieving objectives. The skills that made you successful in the military – adaptability, discipline, teamwork, and problem-solving – will serve you well if you apply them thoughtfully to your new environment.

Building Your Civilian Career Foundation

Documentation: Your New Mission Log

In the military, every operation had its paper trail. Your civilian career needs the same attention to detail. Unlike the military's structured evaluation systems, civilian career progression often relies on your ability to showcase your impact.

Create a career journal that tracks:

- Major projects completed and their outcomes
- Cost savings achieved
- Process improvements implemented
- Team successes you contributed to
- Client/customer feedback
- Training completed
- Awards and recognition
- Leadership opportunities taken
- Innovation initiatives
- Crisis management situations
- Cross-functional collaborations
- Revenue generation activities

Strategic Networking

Think of networking like maintaining supply lines - without it, your career advancement stalls. Develop your network across three fronts:

Internal Networks

- Build relationships with departments you frequently work with
- Join cross-functional project teams
- Participate in company social events
- Connect with senior leadership when appropriate
- Build rapport with support staff
- Engage with other divisions or locations
- Develop mentoring relationships

Industry Networks

- Join professional associations
- Attend industry conferences
- Participate in webinars and online forums
- Connect with vendors and clients
- Follow industry leaders on professional platforms
- Contribute to industry publications
- Join relevant committees or working groups

Veteran Networks

- Participate in company veteran resource groups
- Connect with veteran professional organizations
- Mentor transitioning service members
- Engage with veteran hiring initiatives
- Maintain military connections
- Support veteran-owned businesses
- Share transition experiences

Professional Development Battle Plan

Treat skill development like mission training - continuous and purposeful:

Technical Skills

- Identify critical industry certifications
- Master relevant software and tools
- Learn industry-specific processes
- Stay current with technology trends
- Complete advanced training in your field
- Develop specialized expertise
- Build project management capabilities

Soft Skills

- Enhance business communication
- Develop negotiation abilities
- Practice civilian leadership techniques
- Improve presentation skills
- Learn conflict resolution methods
- Develop emotional intelligence
- Master meeting facilitation

Security Clearance Maintenance

A security clearance is like having an extra weapon in your arsenal:

- Report significant life changes
- Maintain financial responsibility
- Keep foreign contacts documented
- Update your security officer regularly
- Track clearance renewal dates
- Maintain eligibility requirements
- Consider positions requiring clearance

- Stay aware of clearance levels needed for advancement

Civilian Credentials

Keep building your civilian credentials like you'd maintain mission-essential equipment:

Education

- Consider advanced degrees
- Take relevant coursework
- Attend workshops and seminars
- Complete online learning programs
- Get industry certifications
- Maintain professional licenses
- Learn new languages if relevant

Experience Building

- Volunteer for challenging projects
- Seek stretch assignments
- Take temporary leadership roles
- Lead special initiatives
- Gain public speaking experience
- Write for industry publications
- Develop subject matter expertise

Career Progression Planning

Approach your career progression like planning a long-term campaign:

- Set clear career milestones
- Identify potential advancement paths
- Research required qualifications
- Build necessary skill sets

- Develop leadership capabilities
- Create a timeline for goals
- Review and adjust plans regularly
- Build relationships with decision-makers
- Understand promotion requirements
- Track industry trends affecting career paths

Remember: Your civilian career is a marathon, not a sprint. Like any military operation, success requires planning, preparation, and persistent execution. Keep building your foundation stone by stone, skill by skill, relationship by relationship. The discipline and dedication you learned in the military will serve you well - just apply it strategically to your new civilian battlefield.

RTB (Return to Base): Didn't Get the Job

Conducting Your Personal AAR

Not getting selected feels like missing an objective, but remember - even unsuccessful missions provide valuable intelligence. Let's break down your AAR process military-style.

Information Collection Phase

Think of this like gathering intel after an operation. Document everything while it's fresh:

Interview Intelligence

- Write down every question you remember
- Note which answers felt strong or weak
- Document any non-verbal feedback
- Record technical questions that challenged you
- List company-specific terms or concepts mentioned

- Note the interview dynamics and structure
- Document your comfort level throughout
- Record follow-up questions you asked or should have asked

Preparation Assessment

- Evaluate your research depth on the company
- Review your pre-interview practice effectiveness
- Assess your route planning and arrival timing
- Analyze your document preparation
- Review your attire choices
- Evaluate your stress management
- Rate your industry knowledge demonstration

Deep Analysis Phase

This is where we really dig into the data, like reviewing mission footage:

Qualification Match

- Compare your skills to job requirements
- Evaluate experience level match
- Review technical qualification alignment
- Assess cultural fit indicators
- Analyze leadership experience relevance
- Review required certifications
- Evaluate industry knowledge requirements

Communication Effectiveness

- Assess military-to-civilian translation success
- Review explanation clarity
- Evaluate technical term usage
- Analyze storytelling effectiveness

- Review question response structure
- Assess active listening demonstration
- Evaluate rapport-building success

Research Depth

- Company knowledge demonstration
- Industry trend awareness
- Competition awareness
- Product/service understanding
- Company culture comprehension
- Role impact understanding
- Future growth knowledge

Tactical Adjustments

Like adjusting your approach after contact with the enemy:

Resume Enhancement

- Update with newly identified keywords
- Add relevant accomplishments
- Refine military experience translations
- Strengthen civilian impact statements
- Add quantifiable results
- Update technical skills section
- Enhance leadership descriptions

Skill Development

- Identify critical skill gaps
- Research certification requirements
- Find training opportunities
- Consider education options

- Look for volunteer experiences
- Seek mentorship opportunities
- Build practical experience

Network Expansion

- Connect with interview contacts
- Expand LinkedIn presence
- Join industry groups
- Attend professional events
- Connect with veteran organizations
- Build company-specific networks
- Engage with industry leaders

Keep Moving Forward

Like regrouping after a mission - assess, adjust, advance:

Strategic Reassessment

- Review target industry fit
- Evaluate position level appropriateness
- Assess geographical constraints
- Review salary expectations
- Analyze work environment preferences
- Consider company size preferences
- Evaluate work-life balance needs

Training Operations

- Research industry certifications
- Identify quick-win credentials
- Find veteran training programs
- Consider academic options

- Look for hands-on experiences
- Seek mentorship programs
- Explore internship opportunities

Support Network Engagement

- Connect with veteran service organizations
- Engage with military transition programs
- Join veteran job seeker groups
- Find industry-specific veteran groups
- Maintain military network connections
- Build civilian professional relationships
- Connect with successfully transitioned veterans

Remember: In the military, we never left anyone behind. The civilian job market might feel like unfamiliar terrain, but you have an entire network of veterans and supporters ready to help. Use every "no" as intelligence for your next approach. Each interview is a recon mission providing valuable data for your ultimate objective - landing the right position.

Keep pushing forward with the same determination that got you through military challenges. Adapt your tactics, maintain your discipline, and stay focused on the mission. Your next opportunity is out there, and now you're better prepared to secure it.

Your Resume: The Living Fighting Position - A Tactical Guide

Understanding the Fighting Position Concept

Just as a fighting position provides security, visibility, and tactical advantage in combat, your resume serves as your professional strong point. In the military, we learned that a hasty fighting position was just the beginning - it required constant improvement to become a hardened position capable of withstanding any challenge. Your resume demands the same dedication to continuous improvement.

Daily Position Maintenance

Morning Stand-To

- Review recent accomplishments
- Document new responsibilities
- Update project statuses
- Record any wins from the previous day
- Note team contributions
- Track customer interactions
- Document problem resolutions
- Record any recognition received

Ongoing Observation

- Monitor industry trends
- Track company developments
- Note market changes
- Document competitive intelligence
- Record technological advances
- Track regulatory changes
- Monitor skill requirements
- Note emerging opportunities

Weekly Position Enhancement

Perimeter Improvements

- Update professional summaries
- Enhance skills descriptions
- Strengthen accomplishment metrics

- Refine technical terminology
- Update project outcomes
- Add team leadership examples
- Document process improvements
- Record efficiency gains

Support Structure Development

- Build supporting documentation
- Gather performance metrics
- Collect testimonials
- Document training completion
- Record certifications progress
- Update portfolio materials
- Gather project outcomes
- Record team feedback

Monthly Position Hardening

Structural Assessment

- Review position alignment with goals
- Analyze keyword effectiveness
- Evaluate format effectiveness
- Check industry relevance
- Assess qualification matches
- Review accomplishment impact
- Evaluate skill presentation
- Check certification currency

Intelligence Integration

- Incorporate market feedback
- Update industry terminology

- Add emerging skills
- Enhance technical descriptions
- Update achievement metrics
- Refine professional brand
- Strengthen value proposition
- Update digital presence

Quarterly Force Multiplication

Strategic Enhancement

- Conduct comprehensive review
- Update career objectives
- Revise professional summary
- Enhance core competencies
- Update key achievements
- Strengthen position focus
- Refine target alignment
- Update long-term goals

Position Fortification

- Add new certifications
- Update training completed
- Document major projects
- Record leadership roles
- Add speaking engagements
- Note publications
- Update industry contributions
- Record community involvement

Supply Line Management

Credential Maintenance

- Track certification status
- Monitor clearance requirements
- Update licenses
- Record continuing education
- Document professional memberships
- Track required training
- Monitor compliance requirements
- Update security credentials

Network Support

- Update LinkedIn profile
- Inform key contacts of changes
- Share major achievements
- Maintain professional connections
- Engage with industry groups
- Contribute to professional forums
- Build mentor relationships
- Strengthen peer networks

Combat Multipliers

Impact Documentation

- Calculate ROI of initiatives
- Measure efficiency gains
- Track cost savings
- Document revenue impact
- Record quality improvements
- Measure productivity gains

- Track safety enhancements
- Document innovation impacts

Professional Arsenal

- Maintain achievement portfolio
- Update project documentation
- Keep performance reviews
- Record recognition received
- Document team contributions
- Track leadership moments
- Keep success stories
- Maintain reference list

Field Manual for Resume Maintenance

Daily Tasks

- Document achievements immediately
- Update project status
- Record new responsibilities
- Note problem resolutions
- Track team contributions
- Record customer feedback
- Document process improvements
- Note training completion

Weekly Tasks

- Review and update skills
- Enhance accomplishment metrics
- Update project outcomes
- Record leadership moments

- Document team success
- Update technical proficiencies
- Record professional development
- Note industry contributions

Monthly Tasks

- Conduct format review
- Update professional summary
- Enhance keyword optimization
- Review qualification alignment
- Update digital profiles
- Check certification status
- Review industry trends
- Assess position effectiveness

Remember: Like a fighting position, your resume provides:

- Protection against market challenges
- Clear fields of fire (targeted opportunities)
- Strong defensive position (competitive advantage)
- Support for advancement (career growth)
- Tactical advantage (professional positioning)
- Strategic depth (career progression)
- Operational flexibility (career adaptability)
- Combat effectiveness (market readiness)

Your resume, like your fighting position, is never complete - it must evolve with the changing battlefield of your industry. Keep building, keep improving, keep strengthening. This is your professional strong point in the civilian sector.

The Long Game: Mission Success in the Civilian World

Your Military Experience is Your Foundation

Your military service provided more than just technical skills and leadership experience - it gave you a mindset of excellence, adaptability, and perseverance. The key isn't abandoning these qualities but translating them effectively:

Strategic Translation

- Mission focus becomes goal orientation
- Unit cohesion translates to team collaboration
- Command presence becomes executive presence
- Battle rhythm converts to project management
- Tactical planning shifts to strategic thinking
- After action, reviews become a continuous improvement
- Combat leadership transforms into business leadership

Understanding the New Battlefield

The civilian sector operates with different rules of engagement. Success requires understanding these differences:

- Decisions often require consensus rather than command
- Progress may be measured in quarters rather than days
- Multiple approaches can be equally valid
- Networks matter as much as performance
- Influence often outweighs authority
- Change is constant and expected
- Innovation comes from all levels

Building Your Arsenal

Continuous skill development is your ammunition in the civilian world:

Professional Development

- Industry certifications
- Advanced Education
- Technical training
- Leadership development
- Communication skills
- Business acumen
- Digital literacy
- Industry expertise

Network Development

- Professional associations
- Industry groups
- Veteran organizations
- Alumni networks
- Mentorship relationships
- Cross-functional teams
- Community involvement
- Social media presence

Maintaining Both Fronts

Stay connected to both your military roots and civilian future:

Veteran Community

- Mentor transitioning service members
- Support veteran initiatives
- Participate in veteran organizations
- Share transition lessons
- Maintain military friendships
- Honor service traditions
- Support military families
- Advocate for veteran causes

Civilian Integration

- Embrace new workplace cultures
- Learn industry practices
- Build diverse relationships
- Adopt civilian perspectives
- Participate in company culture
- Engage in community events
- Develop civilian partnerships
- Create professional networks

Final Orders: Remember Your Training

As you advance in your civilian career, remember:

Proven Principles

- Mission first, people always
- Attention to detail
- Lead by example
- Take initiative
- Support the team
- Maintain standards
- Drive results
- Show resilience

Adapted for Civilian Success

- Customer satisfaction is the mission
- Details matter in different ways
- Leadership through influence
- Strategic initiative
- Team collaboration
- Professional excellence
- Business results
- Corporate resilience

Mission Success Parameters

Your success in the civilian sector will be measured by:

- Professional growth
- Value creation
- Relationship building
- Problem-solving
- Innovation contribution
- Team development
- Business impact
- Personal fulfillment

Debrief: Chapter 18 - Post-Mission Analysis: You're Hired or Back to Base

1. **Analyze the Outcome:**
   Whether you're hired or not, take time to reflect on the process. Identify what worked well and what could be improved, from your resume to your interview performance.

2. **Celebrate Your Success:**
   If you landed the job, congratulate yourself! Acknowledge the effort and persistence it took to reach this milestone and prepare for the next phase of your career.

3. **Plan Your Onboarding Strategy:**
   Start strong in your new role by familiarizing yourself with the company culture, building relationships with your team, and setting clear goals for your first 90 days.

4. **Use Rejection as a Learning Tool:**
   If you weren't hired, request constructive feedback when possible.

Use this information to refine your job search strategy, improve your skills, and enhance your approach to future opportunities.

5. **Review Your Job Search Strategy:**
   Take stock of your application process. Are you targeting the right roles? Is your resume effectively tailored? Adjust your tactics based on the results and feedback.

6. **Reassess Your Goals:**
   Reflect on whether your career goals or priorities have shifted during the process. Revisit your self-assessment to ensure your efforts are aligned with your ultimate objectives.

7. **Stay Mission-Focused:**
   Whether moving forward in your new job or continuing the search, remain disciplined and persistent. Remember, every step brings you closer to long-term success.

8. **Expand Your Network:**
   Use this experience to build relationships, whether with your new colleagues or through contacts made during the job search. Networking remains a vital tool for career growth.

9. **Continue Learning:**
   Treat each phase of the job search as an opportunity to learn. Hone your interview skills, refine your resume, or gain new certifications to improve your prospects.

10. **Maintain Resilience:**
    The transition process can be challenging, but perseverance is key. Remember the discipline and adaptability you honed in the military and apply those strengths to your civilian journey.

Remember: You've been trained to adapt and overcome. You've led teams under pressure, made decisions with limited information, and accomplished complex missions in challenging conditions. The civilian sector presents different challenges, but you're well-equipped to handle them.

Your military service has given you a unique perspective and valuable skills.

The key to success is not trying to recreate the military environment but applying those strengths to your new mission. Stay focused, keep advancing, and remember - you're not starting over; you're starting differently.

The mission continues. Your objective now is professional growth and success in the civilian sector. You have the training, the discipline, and the determination. Now execute your mission with the same dedication that marked your military service.

Mission success in the civilian world isn't about perfection - it's about progress, adaptation, and resilience. You've got this, soldier. Time to move out and draw fire.

End of Mission Brief.

Dr. Jason Piccolo

About The Author:

About the Author: Dr. Jason Piccolo is a U.S. Army Veteran, having served active duty and reserve components both domestically and overseas (Iraq). Dr. Piccolo "pivoted" from service in 2006 as an Infantry Captain.

Dr. Piccolo served over 23 years as a federal agent. He brings unique insights into the challenges and opportunities facing transitioning service members and those seeking federal employment.

As a former federal hiring manager and hiring panel member, Dr. Piccolo has firsthand experience in what agencies look for in candidates. His expertise is further enhanced by his Lean Six Sigma Green Belt & Champion certification, which he leverages to help streamline the transition process for veterans.

A dedicated mentor for veterans, service members, and federal employees, Dr. Piccolo continues to serve the community through one-on-one guidance and career development support. He regularly contributes to national media outlets discussing border security and national security issues, and hosts 'The Protectors® Podcast.' He is also the author of 'Unwavering: A Border Agent's Journey.'

Dr. Piccolo holds a Doctorate in Strategic Security and combines his academic knowledge, federal service experience, and hiring expertise to provide practical, actionable guidance for those seeking to build meaningful careers after military service.